# ON LOVING GOD

by

Bernard of Clairvaux

CISTERCIAN FATHERS SERIES: NUMBER THIRTEEN B

# ON LOVING GOD

*by*

*Bernard of Clairvaux*

*with*

# AN ANALYTICAL COMMENTARY

*by*

*Emero Stiegman*

Cistercian Publications Inc.
Kalamazoo Michigan

The translation here presented has been made from the critical latin edition prepared by Jean Leclercq, OSB and Henri Rochais under the sponsorship of the Order of Cistercians and published by Editiones Cistercienses, Piazza Tempio di Diana 14, I–00153 Rome, Italy.

*Liber de diligendo deo*, SBOp 3:119–154

*The work of Cistercian Publications is made possible in part through support from Western Michigan University to The Institute of Cistercian Studies*

# TABLE OF CONTENTS

# ON LOVING GOD

by

Bernard of Clairvaux

# ON LOVING GOD

*why did he write?*

YOU WISH ME TO TELL YOU why and how God should be loved. My answer is that God himself is the reason why he is to be loved.[1] As for how he is to be loved, there is to be no limit to that love. Is this sufficient answer? Perhaps, but only for a wise man. As I am indebted, however, to the unwise also,[2] it is customary to add something for them after saying enough for the wise.[3] Therefore for the sake of those who are slow to grasp ideas I do not find it burdensome to treat of the same ideas more extensively if not more profoundly. Hence I insist that there are two reasons why God should be loved for his own sake: no one can be loved more righteously and no one can be loved with greater benefit. Indeed, when it is asked why God should be loved, there are two meanings possible to the question. For it can be questioned which is rather the question: whether for what merit of his or for what advantage to us is God to be loved. My answer to both questions is assuredly the same, for I can see no other reason for loving him than himself. So let us see first how he deserves our love.

---

1. Cf. William of St Thierry: "Love is due to God only, and for no other reason than God himself."—*The Nature and Dignity of Love*, 3; PL 184-382; tr. G. Webb and A. Walker (London: Mowbray, 1956), p. 14.

2. Rom 1:14.

3. Bernard employs here a dictum common among Classical authors: . . . *sat est dictum sapienti.* See Plautus, *Persa* 4:7 (19); Terence, *Phormio*, 3:3 (8).

### HOW GOD IS TO BE LOVED FOR HIS OWN SAKE

God certainly deserves a lot from us since he gave himself[4] to us when we deserved it least. Besides, what could he have given us better than himself? Hence when seeking why God should be loved, if one asks what right he has to be loved, the answer is that the main reason for loving him is "He loved us first."[5] Surely he is worthy of being loved in return when one thinks of who loves, whom he loves, how much he loves. Is it not he whom every spirit acknowledges,[6] saying: "You are my God, for you do not need my possessions."[7] This divine love is sincere, for it is the love of one who does not seek his own advantage.[8] To whom is such love[9] shown? It is written: "While we were still his enemies, he reconciled us to himself."[10] Thus God loved freely, and even enemies. How much did he love? St John answers that: "God so loved the world that he gave his only-begotten Son."[11] St Paul adds: "He did not spare his only Son, but delivered him up for us."[12] The Son also said of himself: "No one has greater love than he who lays down his life for his friends."[13] Thus the righteous one deserved to be loved by the wicked, the highest and omnipotent by the weak. Now someone says: "This is true for man but it does not hold for the angels." That is true because it was not necessary for the angels, for he who came to man's help in time of need, kept the angels from such a need,[14] and he who did not leave man in such a state because he loved him, out of an equal love gave the angels the grace not to fall into that state.

---

4. Gal. 1:4.
5. 1 Jan 4:9-10.
6. 1 Jn 4:2.
7. Ps 15:2 (Psalms are cited according to the Vulgate enumeration.).
8. 1 Cor 13:5.
9. The Latin text has *puritas* but, as W. Williams indicates, it means *caritas*: unmixed love. *Select Treatises of S. Bernard of Clairvaux*: De Diligendo Deo *and* De Gradibus Humilitatis (Cambridge: University Press, 1926), p. 10, n. 12.
10. Rom 5:10.
11. Jn 3:16.
12. Rom 8:32.
13. Jn 15:13.
14. Cf. Gra 29; OB 3:187; CF 19.

**II.** 2. I think that they to whom this is clear see why God ought to be loved, that is, why he merits to be loved. If the infidels conceal these facts, God is always able to confound their ingratitude by his innumerable gifts which he manifestly places at man's disposal. For, who else gives food to all who eat, sight to all who see, and air to all who breathe? It would be foolish to want to enumerate; what I have just said cannot be counted. It suffices to point out the chief ones: bread, sun and air. I call them the chief gifts, not because they are better but because the body cannot live without them. Man's nobler gifts—dignity, knowledge, and virtue—are found in the higher part of his being, in his soul.[15] Man's dignity is his free will by which he is superior to the beasts and even dominates them.[16] His knowledge is that by which he acknowledges that this dignity is in him but that it is not of his own making. Virtue is that by which man seeks continuously and eagerly for his Maker and when he finds him, adheres to him with all his might.

3. Each of these three gifts has two aspects. Dignity is not only a natural privilege, it is also a power of domination, for the fear of man hangs over all the animals on earth.[17] Knowledge is also twofold, since we understand this dignity and other natural qualities are in us, yet we do not create them ourselves.[18] Finally, virtue is seen to be twofold, for by it we seek our Maker and once we find him, we adhere to him so closely we become inseparable from him.[19] As a result, dignity without knowledge is unprofitable, without virtue it can be an obstacle.[20] The following reasoning explains both these facts. What glory is there in having something you do not know you have? Then, to know what you have but to be ignorant

15. Bernard defines what he understands by the soul in Conv 11: ". . . the whole of the soul is nothing other than reason, memory and will."—OB 4:84; CF 43.

16. Cf. Gen 1:26.

17. Gen 9:2.

18. In SC 37:5 (OB 2:11-12; CF 7) Bernard offers a moral evaluation of knowledge.

19. In SC 85:4 (OB 2:310; CF 40) Bernard defines virtue: *Est quippe vigor animi cedere nescius pro tuenda ratione; aut, si magis probas, vigor animi immobiliter stantis cum ratione vel pro ratione; vel sic: vigor animi, quod in se est, omnia ad rationem cogens vel dirigens.*

20. Cf. Bernard, Ep 372; PL 182:577; LSB, Letter 417, p. 485.

of the fact that you do not have it of yourself, for glory here, but not before God.[21] The Apostle says to him who glorifies himself: "What have you that you have not received? And if you have received it, how can you boast of it as if you had not received it?"[22] He does not say simply: "How can you boast of it," but adds: "as if you had not received it," to show the guilt lies not in boasting of something but in treating it as if it was not a gift received. This is rightly called vainglory, for it lacks the solid base of truth. St Paul marks the difference between true and vain glory: "He who boasts, let him boast in the Lord,"[23] that is, in the truth, for the Lord is truth.[24]

4. There are two facts you should know: first, what you are; secondly, that you are not that by your own power, lest you fail to boast at all or do so in vain. Finally, if you do not know yourself, do as is written: "Go follow the flocks of your companions."[25] This is really what happens. When a man, promoted to a high dignity, does not appreciate the favor received, because of his ignorance he is rightly compared to the animals with whom he shares his present state of corruption and mortality.[26] It also happens when a man, not appreciating the gift of reason, starts mingling with the herds of dumb beasts to the extent that, ignoring his own interior glory,[27] he models his conduct on the object of his senses. Led on by curiosity,[28] he becomes like any other animal since he does not see he has received more than they. We should, therefore, fear that ignorance which gives us a too low opinion of ourselves. But we should fear no less, but rather more, that which makes us think ourselves better than we are. This is what happens when we deceive ourselves thinking some good is in us of ourselves. But indeed you should detest and avoid even

21. Rom 4:2.
22. 1 Cor 4:7.
23. 1 Cor 1:31; 2 Cor 10:17. Cf. Jer 9:23-24.
24. Jn 14:6.
25. Song 1:6-7. Cf. SC 32:10; OB 1:233; CF 7.
26. Ps 48:13.
27. Cf. Ps 44:14.
28. For Bernard curiosity is the first step of pride: Hum 28, OB 3:38; see above, p. 57. Cf. also, Div 14:2; OB 6-1:135; CF 46.

more than these two forms of ignorance that presumption[29] by which you, knowingly and on purpose, seek your glory in goods that are not your own and that you are certain are not in you by your own power. In this you are not ashamed to steal the glory of another. Indeed, the first kind of ignorance has no glory; the second kind has, but not in God's sight.[30] But the third evil, which is committed full knowingly, is a usurpation of divine rights. This arrogance[31] is worse and more dangerous than the second kind of ignorance, in which God is ignored, because it makes us despise him. If ignorance makes beasts of us, arrogance makes us like demons. It is pride, the greatest of sins, to use gifts as if they were one's by natural right and while receiving benefits to usurp the benefactor's glory.

5. For this reason, virtue is as necessary as dignity and knowledge, being the fruit of both. By virtue the Maker and Giver of all is sought and adhered to, and rightly glorified in all good things. On the other hand, the man who knows what is good yet does not do it will receive many strokes of the lash.[32] Why? Because, "He did not want to understand to do well;"[33] worse again, "While in bed he plotted evil."[34] He strives like a wicked servant to lay hold of and even to steal his good Lord's glory for qualities which the gift of knowledge tells him most certainly are not from himself. Hence it follows that dignity without knowledge is quite useless and that knowledge without virtue is damnable. But the virtuous man, for whom knowledge is not harmful or dignity unfruitful, lifts up his voice to God and frankly confesses: "Not to us, O Lord, not to us, but to your name give glory;"[35] meaning, "O Lord, we attribute no part of our dignity or knowledge to ourselves: we ascribe it all to your name whence all good comes."

29. Likewise, presumption finds a place in Bernard's steps of pride as the seventh: Hum 44; OB 3:50; see above, pp. 72. Cf. also QH 11:4; OB 4:451; CF 43.

30. Rom 4:2.

31. Arrogance is Bernard's sixth step of pride: Hum 43; OB 3:49-50; see above, p. 71.

32. Lk 12:47.

33. Ps 35:4.

34. Ps 35:5.

35. Ps 113:9 (Vulgate: 113:1bis).

6. But see now, in trying to show that they who do not know Christ are sufficiently informed by natural law,[36] seen in the perfection of man's mind and body, to be obliged to love God for his own sake, we have lost sight of our subject. To state briefly what has been said, we repeat: is there an infidel who does not know that he has received the necessities for bodily life, by which he exists, sees, and breathes, from him who gives food to all flesh,[37] who makes his sun rise on the good and the bad, and his rain fall on the just and the unjust?[38] Who, again, can be wicked enough to think the author of his human dignity, which shines in his soul, is any other than he who says in the book of Genesis: "Let us make man to our own image and likeness?"[39] Who can think that the giver of knowledge is somebody different from him who teaches man knowledge?[40] Or again, who believes he has received or hopes to receive the gift of virtue from any other source than the hand of the Lord of virtue? Hence God deserves to be loved for his own sake even by the infidel who, although he is ignorant of Christ yet knows himself. Everyone, therefore, even the infidel, is inexcusable if he fails to love the Lord his God with all his heart, all his soul, all his might.[41] For an innate justice, not unknown to reason, cries interiorly to him that he ought to love with his whole being the one to whom he owes all that he is. Yet it is difficult, impossible for a man, by his own power of free will, once he has received all things from God, to turn wholly to the will of God and not rather to his own will[42] and keep these gifts for himself as his own, as it is written: "All seek what is their own,"[43] and further: ". . . man's feelings and thoughts are inclined to evil."[44]

III.    7. The faithful, on the contrary, know how totally they need Jesus and him crucified.[45] While they admire and embrace in him that charity which surpasses all knowledge,[46] they

---

36. Cf Rom 1:19ff; 2:14-15.
37. Ps 135:25.
38. Mt 5:45.
39. Gen 1:26.
40. Ps 93:10.
41. Mk 12:30.

42. See Gra 23; OB 3:103; CF 19.
43. Phil 2:21.
44. Gen 8:21.
45. 1 Cor 2:2.
46. Eph 3:19. Cf. Csi 5:28; OB 3:491; CF 37.

are ashamed at failing to give what little they have in return for so great a love and honor. Easily they love more who realize they are loved more: "He loves less to whom less is given."[47] Indeed, the Jew and Pagan are not spurred on by such a wound of love as the Church experiences, who says: "I am wounded by love,"[48] and again: "Cushion me about with flowers, pile up apples around me, for I languish with love."[49] The Church sees King Solomon with the diadem his mother had placed on his head.[50] She sees the Father's only Son carrying his cross,[51] the Lord of majesty,[52] slapped and covered with spittle; she sees the Author of life[53] and glory pierced by nails, wounded by a lance,[54] saturated with abuse,[55] and finally laying down his precious life for his friends.[56] As she beholds this, the sword of love transfixes all the more her soul,[57] making her repeat: "Cushion me about with flowers, pile up apples around me, for I languish with love."[58]

### WHENCE THE POMEGRANATES

These fruits are certainly the pomegranates[59] the bride introduced into her Beloved's garden. Picked from the tree of life,[60] they had changed their natural taste for that of the heavenly bread, their color for that of Christ's blood. At last she sees death dead[61] and the defeat of death's author.[62] She beholds captivity led captive[63] from hell to earth and from

47. Lk 7:43, 47; cf. 12:48.
48. Song 2:5 (Old Latin); cf. Song 4:9.
49. Song 2:5.
50. Song 3:11. Cf. Div 50:1; OB 6-1:270-271; CF 46.
51. Jn 19:17.
52. 1 Cor 2:8 (Old Latin).
53. Acts 3:15.
54. Jn 19:34.
55. Lam 3:30.
56. Jer 12:7; Jn 15:13.
57. Cf. Lk 2:35.
58. Song 2:5.
59. Song 6:10.
60. Gen 2:9.
61. Hos 13:14; cf. 1 Cor 15:54.
62. Heb 2:14.
63. Eph 4:8.

earth to heaven so that in the name of Jesus every knee must bend in heaven, on earth and in hell.[64] She beholds the earth which produced thorns and thistles under the ancient curse[65] blooming again by the grace of a new blessing. And in all this she thinks of the psalm which says: "And my flesh flourished again; with all my will I shall praise him."[66] She wishes to add to the fruits of the Passion which she had picked from the tree of the Cross some of the fruits of the Resurrection whose fragrance will induce the Bridegroom to visit her more often.

8. Then she says: "You are fair my Beloved, and handsome; our couch is strewn with flowers."[67] By the couch she reveals clearly enough what she desires and by declaring that it is strewn with flowers, she indicates clearly whence she hopes to obtain what she wants; not by her own merits,[68] but with flowers picked in the field the Lord has blessed.[69] Christ loved flowers; he willed to be conceived and raised in Nazareth.[70] The heavenly Bridegroom enjoys so much those perfumes that he enters willingly and often the chamber of the heart he finds decked with these flowers and fruits. Where he sees a mind occupied with the grace of his Passion and the glory of his Resurrection, he is willingly and zealously present there. Understand that the tokens of the Passion are like last year's fruit, that is, of all the past ages spent under the domination of sin and death,[71] until they appear in the fullness of time.[72] But notice that the signs of the Resurrection are like this year's flowers, blossoming in a new summer under the power of grace. Their fruit will come forth in the end at the future general resurrection and it will last forever.[73] As it is said:

64. Phil 2:10.
65. Gen 3:18; Heb 6:8.
66. Ps 27:7.
67. Song 1:15.
68. For Bernard's doctrine on merits, see SC 68:6; OB 2:200; CF 31.
69. Gen 27:27.
70. Bernard is alluding to the mystical or allegorical interpretation given to the name, Nazareth. See Miss 1:3; OB 4:16; CF 43; Tpl 13: OB 3:225; CF 19.
71. Cf. Rom 5:21.
72. Gal 4:4.
73. In regard to the fruits of the Passion and Resurrection, see Ann 1:4; OB 5:15; CF 22.

"Winter is over, the rain is past and gone. Flowers appear in our land,"[74] showing summer has come back with him who changed death's coldness into the spring of a new life, saying: "Behold I make all things new."[75] His flesh was sown in death and rose again in the resurrection.[76] By his fragrance the dry grass turns green again in the fields of the valley; what was cold grows warm again and what was dead comes back to life.

9. By the freshness of these flowers and fruits and the beauty of the field giving off the sweetest of scents the Father himself is indeed delighted in the Son who is renewing all things, so that he might say: "Behold the odor of my son is as that of a rich field which the Lord has blessed."[77] Yes, a full field, of whose fullness we have all received.[78] But the spouse enjoys greater familiarity by the fact that when she feels inclined, she may gather flowers and fruit in this field and strew them over the depths of her conscience so that the couch of her heart will give off a sweet odor for the Spouse as he enters. If we wish to have Christ for a guest often, we must keep our hearts fortified by the testimony of our faith[79] in the mercy of him who died for us and in the power of him who rose from the dead, as David said: "These two things I have heard: power belongs to God and mercy to you, O Lord."[80] The testimonies of both these are ever so believable.[81] Christ died for our sins and rose again from the dead for our justification.[82] He ascended to heaven for our protection,[83] sent the Spirit for our consolation,[84] and will some day return for our fulfillment.[85] He certainly showed his mercy in dying, his power in rising again, and both of these in the rest.

10. These are the apples, these the flowers, with which the bride, feeling how easily the strength of her love can dwindle and weaken if it is not fortified by those stimulants, asks to be nourished and strengthened until she is introduced into

---

74. Song 2:11-12.
75. Rev 21:5.
76. 1 Cor 15:42.
77. Gen 27:27.
78. Jn 1:16.
79. Eph 3:17.

80. Ps 61:12-13.
81. Ps 92:5.
82. Rom 4:25.
83. Cf. Mk 16:19.
84. Cf. Jn 16:7; Acts 9:31.
85. Cf. Acts 1:11.

the Bridegroom's chamber.[86] There she will receive the long desired caresses[87] and say: "His left hand is under my head and his right hand has embraced me."[88] Then she will feel and esteem all the signs of love she had received during her lover's first visit,[89] as coming from his left hand, altogether inferior and of little value in comparison with the infinite delights of his right hand's embrace.[90] She will experience what she had heard: "The flesh is of no use; it is the spirit that gives life,"[91] realizing what she had read: "My spirit is sweeter than honey, and my inheritance than honey and the comb."[92] What indeed follows: "My remembrance will last for ages to come,"[93] means as long as the present era lasts, in which a generation arrives as the previous one passes away,[94] the elect will not be deprived of memory's consolation until they can indulge in the feast of God's presence. Thus it is written: "They will publish the memory of your sweetness,"[95] no doubt meaning those of whom it is said just before: "Generation after generation will praise your works."[96] Therefore, memory is for the continuing ages, presence is for the kingdom of heaven, where the elect are already glorified while remembrance consoles the present generation during its pilgrimage.

**IV.**  11. It is important to point out which generation finds consolation in remembering God. Surely it is not the stubborn and defiant generation[97] to whom it is said: "Woe to you who are rich, you have your consolation,"[98] rather it is to the generation which is able to say: "My soul refused to be consoled."[99]

---

86. Song 2:5; 3:4. For Bernard's interpretation of the Bridegroom's chamber see SC 23:3, 8-9; OB 1:140, 143-145; CF 7.
87. Prov 7:18.
88. Song 2:6. See below, no. 12, p. 40.
89. Cf. Adv 4:9; OB 4:182; CF 10.
90. Ps 30:20.
91. Jn 6:64.
92. Sir 24:27.
93. Sir 24:28.
94. Eccles 1:4.
95. Ps 144:7.
96. Ps 144:4.
97. Ps 77:8.
98. Lk 6:24.
99. Ps 76:3.

And we can accept the affirmation if one adds: "I was mind-ful of the Lord and delighted."[100] It is indeed right that they who do not find pleasure in the joys of this life may think of those to come and they who refused to be consoled by the abundance of changing things, may delight in thoughts of eternity. This is the generation of those who seek the Lord, who do not seek for their own advantage[101] but for the face of the God of Jacob.[102] In the meanwhile, memory is a plea-sure for those who seek and long for God's presence, not that they are completely satisfied but that they may long all the more for him that they might be filled.[103] Thus he testifies that he himself is food: "Who eats me, will hunger for more."[104] Whoever is nourished by him says: "I shall be satisfied when your glory appears."[105] Blessed are they who go hungry now and thirst for justice, for they alone will be satisfied some day.[106] Woe to you, false and corrupt generation! Woe to you, foolish, stupid people,[107] who scorn his memory yet dread his presence! Not even now do you want to be freed from the hunter's net, since they who want to make money in this life, fall into the devil's net.[108] Even then, you cannot avoid the harsh words.[109] O the harsh and cruel sentence: "Depart ac-cursed into everlasting fire."[110] Less harsh and less awful are the words brought to our mind each day in the memorial of the Passion: "He who eats my flesh and drinks my blood has life everlasting."[111] That is, he who meditates on my death and, following my example, mortifies his members which be-long to this earth,[112] has eternal life;[113] meaning, if you share in my sufferings, you will partake of my glory.[114] Many shrink

100. Ps 76:4.
101. 1 Cor 13:5.
102. Ps 23:6.
103. Cf. Mt 5:6. See Conv 26; OB 4:100-101; CF 43.
104. Sir 24:29.
105. Ps 16:15.
106. Mt 5:6.
107. Jer 4:22; 5:21.
108. Ps 90:3; 123:7; 1 Tim 6:9. Cf. Conv 14; OB 4:88-89; CF 43.
109. Cf. Jn 6:61.
110. Mt 25:41.
111. Jn 6:55. The reference is undoubtedly to the daily celebration of the Mass.
112. Col 3:5.
113. Jn 3:36.
114. Rom 8:17.

back at these words and abandon him,[115] saying by their re-
actions: "This expression is too hard, who can listen to it?"[116]
The generation which did not regulate its heart, whose spirit
is not in good faith with God[117] speaks this way and, setting
its hopes on futile riches,[118] feels oppressed by the message of
the Cross,[119] and judges the memory of the Passion a burden.
How will it ever bear the weight of these words in his presence:
"Depart accursed into the everlasting fire which was prepared
for the devil and his angels?"[120] This stone will crush him on
whom it falls.[121] However, the righteous generation[122] will be
blessed, for as with the Apostle, either present or absent,[123] it
seeks to please God. They will hear: "Come you blessed of
my Father, possess the kingdom prepared for you since the
beginning of the world."[124]

Then the generation which did not regulate its heart[125] will
learn too late how easy was Christ's yoke in comparison with
this sorrow and light was his burden[126] from which they with-
drew their stiff necks[127] as if it were a rough and heavy load. O
wretched slaves of Mammon,[128] you cannot glory in the Cross
of our Lord Jesus Christ[129] and at the same time trust in hoards
of money or chase after gold[130] and taste how sweet is the
Lord.[131] As a result, you will no doubt find him severe when
present, since you failed to remember him when absent.

12. On the other hand, the faithful soul sighs deeply for
his presence, rests peacefully when thinking of him, and must

115. Jn 6:67; 18:6.
116. Jn 6:61.
117. Ps 77:8.
118. 1 Tim 6:17.
119. 1 Cor 1:18.
120. Mt 25:41.
121. Mt 21:44.
122. Ps 111:2.
123. 2 Cor 5:9.
124. Mt 25:34
125. Ps 77:8.
126. Mt 11:30.
127. Deut 9:13; 31:27.
128. Mt 6:24.
129. Gal 6:14.
130. 1 Tim 6:17.
131. Ps 33:9.

glory in the degradation of the Cross[132] until it is capable
of contemplating the glory of God's revealed face.[133] Thus
Christ's bride and dove[134] pauses for a little and rests amidst
her inheritance after receiving by lot,[135] from the memory of
your abundant sweetness,[136] Lord Jesus, silver-tinted wings,[137]
the candor of innocence and purity, and she hopes to be filled
with gladness at the sight of your face,[138] where even her back
will glitter like gold[139] when she is introduced with joy into the
splendor of the saints.[140] There she will be enlightened by rays
of wisdom. Now she may glory and say: "His left hand is
under my head and his right hand embraces me."[141] His left
hand is symbolic of his unsurpassable charity which made him
lay down his life for his friends,[142] while his right hand por-
trays the beatific vision which he promised them and the joy
of his majestic presence. The vision of God which makes us
resemble him, and its incalculable delight are rightly figured
by the right hand, as the Psalmist joyfully sings: "In your
right hand are everlasting joys."[143] In the left hand is well
placed that admirable, memorable, and always to be remembered love, because the bride reclines on it and rests until
evil is past.[144]

13. In this way the Bridegroom's left hand is rightly under
the bride's head, so that, as she leans back, her head is supported on it, meaning the intention of her mind, lest bending
down it should be enticed by carnal and worldly desires.[145]
Because "the corruptible body weighs down the soul and
the earthly dwelling preoccupies the mind busy with many

132. Gal 6:14.
133. 2 Cor 3:18. Cf. OS 4:3; OB 5:357; CF 37.
134. Song 5:1-2.
135. Ps 67:14.
136. Ps 144:7.
137. Ps 67:14.
138. Ps 15:11.
139. Ps 67:14.
140. Ps 109:3.
141. Song 2:6.
142. Jn 15:13.
143. Ps 15:11.
144. Ps 56:2.
145. Gal 5:16; Tit 2:12.

thoughts."[146] What else is achieved by meditating on such
great and so undeserved mercy, such gratuitous and so proved
a love, such unexpected condescension, undaunted mildness,
and astonishing kindness? What else, I insist, will all these
carefully considered qualities achieve if they do not, in a
wonderful way, captivate the mind of him who, completely
freed from all unworthy love, considers them and attract it
deeply so that it despises in comparison whatever cannot be
desired without despising them? Then the bride surely runs
more eagerly in the odor of their perfumes.[147] She loves ar-
dently, yet even when she finds herself completely in love, she
thinks she loves too little because she is loved so much. Nor is
she wrong. What can requite so deep a love by so great a lover?
It is as if a tiny grain of dust[148] were to gather all its strength
to render an equal love to the Divine Majesty who anticipates
its affection and is seen entirely bent on saving it. Finally,
"God so loved the world that he gave his only begotten Son"[149]
was no doubt spoken of the Father; and the words "He gave
himself up"[150] were undoubtedly meant of the Son. It is said
of the Holy Spirit: "But the Paraclete, the Holy Spirit, whom
the Father will send in my name, will teach you all things and
will make you remember all I have said to you."[151] God therefore loves, and loves with all his being, for it is the whole
Trinity that loves, if the word *whole* can be said of the infinite,
the incomprehensible, or indeed of a simple being.

V.   14. Whoever meditates on this is, I believe, sufficiently
aware why man ought to love God, that is, whence God deserves to be loved. On the other hand, the infidel has neither
the Father nor the Holy Spirit because he has not the Son.[152]
"He who honors not the Son, honors not the Father who sent

146. Wis 9:15. This is a favorite quotation of Bernard, see Gra 37, 41 (OB
3:192-193, 196; CF 19); Conv 30 (OB 4:106; CF 43); Pre 59 (OB 3:292; CF
1:148); etc.
147. Song 1:3.
148. Is 40:15.
149. Jn 3:16.
150. Is 53:12.
151. Jn 14:26.
152. 1 Jn 5:12; cf. 2 Jn 9.

him,"[153] nor does he honor the Holy Spirit whom the Son sent.[154] Hence it is no wonder that he loves less him whom he knows less.[155] Nevertheless, even he is aware he owes him all whom he knows is the maker of all his being. What then should he be for me who hold my God to be not only the generous giver, the liberal administrator, the kindest consoler and the watchful governor of my life, but above and beyond that, the richest redeemer, the eternal defender who enriches and glorifies, as it is written: "With him is plentiful redemption;"[156] and also, "He entered the sanctuary once and for all, after winning eternal salvation."[157] The Psalmist says about our conversion: "He will not forsake his saints: they will be kept safe forever."[158] The Gospel says of enriching: ". . . good measure, pressed down, shaken up, and overflowing they will pour into your bosom;"[159] and again: "The eye has not seen, the ear has not heard, nor has the heart of man conceived what God has prepared for those who love him."[160] St Paul says of our glorification: "We are waiting for our Savior and Lord Jesus Christ, who will reform the body of our lowness, molding it into a likeness of his glorified body."[161] And again, "The sufferings of this life are not to be compared with the future glory to be revealed in us."[162] Better still: ". . . that which is but a passing, light tribulation in this life, produces in us a degree of glory beyond measure for the life to come, as we contemplate the things that are unseen, not those that are seen."[163]

15. What shall I render to the Lord for all these gifts? [164] Reason and natural justice urge the infidel to surrender his

153. Jn 5:23.
154. Jn 15:26; 16:7.
155. Cf. Lk 7:47.
156. Ps 129:7.
157. Heb 9:12.
158. Ps 36:28.
159. Lk 6:38.
160. 1 Cor 2:9.
161. Phil 3:20-21.
162. Rom 8:18.
163. 2 Cor 4:17-18.
164. Ps 115:12. Cf. Gra 48; OB 3:201; CF 19. This text was used at the Mass in reference to receiving the Eucharist.

whole being to him from whom he received it and to love him
with all his might. Faith certainly bids me love him all the
more whom I regard as that much greater than I, for he not
only gives me myself, he also gives me himself. The age of
faith had not yet come, God had not yet appeared in flesh,
died on the Cross, risen from the grave, or returned to the
Father. He had not yet commended his great charity in us[165]
about which I have said so much. Man had not yet been
ordered to love his Lord God with all his heart, all his soul,
and all his strength,[166] that is, with all he is, knows and can
do. Yet God is not unjust when he claims for himself his
works and gifts.[167] Why would not an artifact love its artist, if
it is able to do so? Why would it not love him all it can, since
it can do nothing except by his gift? In addition, the fact that
man was made out of nothing, gratuitously and in this dignity,
renders the debt of love clearer and proves the divine exaction
more just. Besides, how much did the benefit increase when
God, multiplying his mercy, saved men and beasts?[168] I am
speaking of us who exchanged our glory for the likeness of a
calf that eats grass,[169] who have become by sin like irrational
beasts.[170] If I owe all for having been created, what can I add
for being remade, and being remade in this way? It was less
easy to remake me than to make me. It is written not only
about me but of every created being; "He spoke and they were
made."[171] But he who made me by a single word, in remaking
me had to speak many words, work miracles, suffer hardships,
and not only hardships but even unjust treatment. "What
shall I render to the Lord for all that he has given me?"[172] In
his first work he gave me myself; in his second work he gave
me himself; when he gave me himself, he gave me back myself.
Given, and regiven, I owe myself twice over. What can I give
God in return for himself? Even if I could give him myself a
thousand times, what am I to God?[173]

165. Rom 5:8.
166. Deut 6:5; Mk 12:30 and parallel places.
167. Heb 6:10.
168. Ps 35:7-8.
169. Ps 105:20.
170. Ps 48:13, 21.
171. Ps 148:5.
172. Ps 115:12.
173. Cf. Job 9:3.

### HOW GOD SHOULD BE LOVED

**VI.** 16. Briefly repeating what has been said so far, consider first how God merits to be loved, that there is to be no limit to that love, for he loved us first.[174] Such a one loved us so much and so freely, insignificant as we are and such as we are, that, as you recall I said in the beginning, we must love God without any limit. Finally, as love offered to God has for object the one who is immeasurable and infinite—for God is both infinite and immeasurable—what, I ask, should be the aim or degree of our love? What about the fact that our love is not given gratuitously but in payment of a debt? Thus the Immeasurable loves, the Eternal loves, that Charity which surpasses knowledge loves;[175] God, whose greatness knows no end,[176] to whose wisdom there is no limit,[177] whose peace exceeds all understanding, loves[178]—and we think we can requite him with some measure of love? "I shall love you, O Lord, my fortress, my strength, my refuge, my deliverer,"[179] and whatever can be held desirable and lovable for me. My God, my help, I shall love you as much as I am able for your gift. My love is less than is your due, yet not less than I am able, for even if I cannot love you as much as I should, still I cannot love you more than I can. I shall only be able to love you more when you give me more, although you can never find my love worthy of you. For, "Your eyes have seen my imperfections, and all shall be written down in your book,"[180] all who do what they can, even if they cannot do all they should. As far as I can see, it is clear enough to what extent God ought to be loved and that by his own merit. By his own merit, I say, but to whom is the degree of this merit really clear? Who can say? Who can understand it?

**VII.** 17. Let us see now how he is to be loved for our advantage. How far from the reality is our knowledge of it? Never-

---

174. 1 Jn 4:10.
175. Eph 3:19.
176. Ps 144:3.
177. Ps 146:5.
178. Phil 4:7.
179. Ps 17:2-3.
180. Ps 138:16.

theless, it is not right to keep silent about what has been seen, even if it falls short of the truth. When asking above why and how God is to be loved, I said the question may be understood in two ways: it may mean by what merit of his God deserves our love or what benefit do we acquire in loving him. Both questions it seems may be asked. After speaking of God's merit in a way no doubt unworthy of him, but according to the gift I have received, it remains for me, to speak of the reward in so far as it also will be given to me.

## GOD IS NOT LOVED WITHOUT A REWARD

God is not loved without a reward, although he should be loved without regard for one. True charity cannot be worthless, still, as "it does not seek its own advantage,"[181] it cannot be termed mercenary.[182] Love pertains to the will, it is not a transaction; it cannot acquire or be acquired by a pact. Moving us freely, it makes us spontaneous. True love is content with itself; it has its reward, the object of its love. Whatever you seem to love because of something else, you do not really love; you really love the end pursued and not that by which it is pursued. Paul does not evangelize in order to eat; he eats in order to evangelize; he loves the Gospel and not the food.[183] True love merits its reward, it does not seek it. A reward is offered him who does not yet love; it is due him who loves; it is given to him who perseveres. When we have to persuade people in lesser affairs we cajole the unwilling with promises and rewards, not those who are willing. Who would dream of offering a man a reward for doing something he wants to do? No one, for example, pays a hungry man to eat, a thirsty man to drink, or a mother to feed the child of her womb.[184] Who would think of using prayers or prizes to remind a man to fence in his vine, to dig around his tree, or to build his own home? How much more the soul that loves God seeks

181. 1 Cor 13:5.
182. Bernard distinguishes mercenary love from that of the son, and also that of the slave. See below, no. 36, p. 127.
183. 1 Cor 9:18.
184. Is 49:15.

no other reward than that God whom it loves. Were the soul to demand anything else, then it would certainly love that other thing and not God.

18. Every rational being naturally desires always what satisfies more its mind and will. It is never satisfied with something which lacks the qualities it thinks it should have. A man with a beautiful wife, for example, looks at a more attractive woman with a wanton eye or heart; a well dressed man wants more costly clothes; and a man of great wealth envies anyone richer than he. You can see men who already own many farms and possessions, still busy, day after day, adding one field to another,[185] driven by an excessive passion to extend their holdings.[186] You can see men living in homes worthy of a king and in sumptuous dwellings, none the less daily adding house to house,[187] through restless curiosity building up, then tearing down, changing squares into circles.[188] What about men promoted to high honors? Do we not see them striving more and more in an insatiable ambition to go higher still? There is no end to all this, because no single one of these riches can be held to be the highest or the best. Why wonder if man cannot be content with what is lower or worse, since he cannot find peace this side of what is highest or best? It is stupidity and madness to want always that which can neither satisfy nor even diminish your desire. While enjoying those riches, you strive for what is missing and are dissatisfied, longing for what you lack. Thus the restless mind, running to and fro among the pleasures of this life, is tired out but never satisfied; like the starving man who thinks whatever he stuffs down his throat is not enough, for his eyes see what remains to be eaten. Thus man craves continually for what is missing with no less fear than he possesses with joy what is in front of him. Who can have everything? A man clings to the fruits of his work (however small they may be), never knowing when he will have the sorrow of losing them, yet he is certain to lose them some day.[189] In like manner a

---

185. Is 5:8.
186. Ex 34:24; Amos 1:13.
187. Is 5:8.

188. Horace, Ep 1:1 (100).
189. Cf. I Tim 6:7; Job 1:21.

perverted will contends for what is best, and hastens in a straight line toward what will afford it the most satisfaction. Rather vanity makes sport of it in those tortuous ways, and evil deceives itself.[190] If you wish to accomplish in this way what you desire, to gain hold of that which leaves nothing further to be desired, why bother about the rest? You are running on crooked roads and will die long before you reach the end you are seeking.

19. The wicked, therefore, walk round in circles,[191] naturally wanting whatever will satisfy their desires, yet foolishly rejecting that which would lead them to their true end, which is not in consumption but in consummation. Hence they exhaust themselves in vain instead of perfecting their lives by a blessed end. They take more pleasure in the appearance of things than in their Creator,[192] examining all and wanting to test them one by one before trying to reach the Lord of the universe. They might even succeed in doing so if they could ever gain hold of what they wish for; that is, if any one man could take possession of all things without him who is their Principle. By the very law of man's desire which makes him want what he lacks in place of what he has and grow weary of what he has in preference to what he lacks, once he has obtained and despised all in heaven and on earth,[193] he will hasten toward the only one who is missing, the God of all. There he will rest, for just as there is no rest this side of eternity, so there will be no restlessness to bother him on the other side. Then he will say for sure: "It is good for me to adhere to God."[194] He will even add to that: "What is there for me in heaven and what have I desired on earth, if you?"[195] And, also: "God of my heart, God, my lot forever."[196] Therefore, as I said, whoever desires the greatest good can succeed in reaching it, if he can first gain possession of all he desires short of that good itself.

20. This is altogether impossible because life is too short,

---

190. Ps 26:12.
191. Ps 11:9.
192. Rom 1:25.
193. Eph 1:10.

194. Ps 72:28.
195. Ps 72:25.
196. Ps 72:26.

strength too weak, competition too keen, men too fatigued by the long road and vain efforts; wishing to attain all they desire, yet unable to reach the end of all their wants. If they could only be content with reaching all in thought and not in deed. They could easily do so and it would not be in vain, for man's mind is more comprehensive and subtle than his senses. It even anticipates the senses in all things and they dare not contact an object unless the mind approves its utility beforehand. I think this is what is alluded to in the text: "Test all and hold on to what is good."[197] The mind looks ahead for the senses and these must not pursue their desires unless the mind gives its consent. Otherwise, you do not ascend the Lord's mountain or stand in his holy place,[198] because you have received your soul in vain, that is, your rational soul; while you follow your senses like a dumb beast, your sleepy reason offers no resistance. Those who do not think ahead run alongside the road,[199] they do not follow the Apostle's counsel: " . . . run, then to win . . . . "[200] When will they reach him whom they do not want to reach until they have tested all the rest? The desire to experience all things first is like a vicious circle, it goes on forever.

21. The just man is not like that. Hearing about the evil conduct of those who remain inside the circle[201] (for many follow the wide road which leads to death),[202] he prefers the royal road which turns neither to the right nor to the left.[203] Finally the Prophet confirms: "The path of the just is straight, and straight forward for walking."[204] These are the ones who take a salutary short-cut and avoid the dangerous, fruitless round-about way, choosing the shortened and shortening word,[205] not desiring everything they see, but rather selling all they have and giving it to the poor.[206] It is clear that "Blessed are the poor, for theirs is the kingdom of heaven."[207] All run, indeed,[208] but one must distinguish between runners. At length,

197. 1 Thess 5:21.
198. Ps 23:3-4.
199. Cf. Is 59:8.
200. 1 Cor 9:24.
201. Ps 30:14.
202. Mt 7:13.

203. Num 20:17;21:22.
204. Is 26:7.
205. Rom 9:28.
206. Mt 19:21 and parallels.
207. Mt 5:3.
208. 1 Cor 9:24.

"The Lord knows the way of the just, the way of the wicked will
perish."[209] As a result, "Better is a little to the just than all
the wealth of the wicked."[210] As Wisdom says and folly learns,
money never satisfies those who love it.[211] Rather, ". . . they
that hunger and thirst for justice will have their fill."[212]
Justice is the vital, natural food of the rational soul; money
can no more lessen the mind's hunger than air can that of the
body. If you see a hungry man open wide his mouth to the
wind and puff up his cheeks with air to satisfy his hunger, will
you not think he is out of his mind? It is no less folly to think
a rational soul will be satisfied rather than merely puffed up
by any kind of material goods. What do material things mean
to the mind? The body cannot live on ideas or the mind subsist on meat. "Bless the Lord, my soul, he satisfies your desires with good things."[213] He satisfies with good things, he
incites to good, maintains in goodness, anticipates, sustains,
fulfills. He makes you desire, he is what you desire.

22. I said above that God is the reason for loving God. That
is right, for he is the efficient and final cause of our love. He
offers the opportunity, creates the affection, and consummates
the desire. He makes, or rather is made himself lovable. He
hopes to be so happily loved that he will not be loved in vain.
His love prepares and rewards ours.[214] Obligingly he leads the
way; reasonably he requites us; he is our sweet hope. Rich for
all who call on him,[215] although he can give us nothing better
than himself. He gave himself to merit for us; he keeps himself
to be our reward; he serves himself as food for holy souls;[216]
he sold himself in ransom for captive souls.[217] O Lord, you are

209. Ps 1:6.
210. Ps 36:16.
211. Cf Eccles 5:9.
212. Mt 5:6.
213. Ps 102:1, 5.
214. Cf. 1 Jn 4:19.
215. Rom 10:12.
216. Wis 3:13.
217. For a fuller understanding of Bernard's doctrine on the Redemption by
Christ, see Abael 14-15; PL 182:1064-1065. Vacandard sees in the previous phrase
used here, "He gave himself to merit for us. . . ." (*se dedit in meritum*) the
whole essence of Bernard's doctrine on the Redemption. See E. Vacandard, *Vie
de saint Bernard, Abbé de Clairvaux*, 2 vols. (Paris:Lecoffre, 1895), 2:74. See
also, W. Williams, "Introduction" in *Select Treatises*, pp. 4-5.

so good to the soul who seeks you,[218] what must you be to the one who finds you? More wonderful still, no one can seek you unless he has already found you. You wish to be found that you may be sought for, and sought for to be found. You may be sought and found, but nobody can forestall you. Even when we say: "In the morning my prayer will come before you,"[219] we must remember that, without our first receiving divine inspiration, all prayer becomes lukewarm. Let us now see where our love begins, for it has been shown where it ends.

VIII. 23. Love is one of the four natural passions.[220] There is no need to name them, for they are well known. It would be right, however, for that which is natural to be first of all at the author of nature's service. That is why the first and greatest commandment is: "You shall love the Lord, your God. . . ."[221]

### THE FIRST DEGREE OF LOVE: MAN LOVES HIMSELF FOR HIS OWN SAKE

Since nature has become more fragile and weak, necessity obliges man to serve it first. This is carnal love by which a man loves himself above all for his own sake. He is only aware of himself; as St Paul says: "What was animal came first, then what was spiritual."[222] Love is not imposed by a precept; it is planted in nature. Who is there who hates his own flesh?[223] Yet should love, as it happens, grow immoderate, and, like a savage current, burst the banks of necessity, flooding the fields of delight, the overflow is immediately stopped by the commandment which says: "You shall love your neighbor as yourself."[224] It is just indeed that he who shares the same nature should not be deprived of the same benefits, especially that

218. Lam 3:25.
219. Ps 87:14.
220. Bernard frequently treats of the four basic passions; see, eg, SC 85:5; OB 2:310; CF 40; QH 14:9; OB 4:474; CF 43; Div 50:2; OB 6-1:271; CF 46; Quad 2:3; OB 4:361; CF 22. These are Classical; see, eg, Juvenal, *Satires* 1:85-86.
221. Mt 22:37.
222. 1 Cor 15:46.
223. Eph 5:29.
224. Mt 22:39.

benefit which is grafted in that nature. Should a man feel over-
burdened at satisfying not only his brethren's just needs but
also their pleasures, let him restrain his own if he does not
want to be a transgressor. He can be as indulgent as he likes
for himself providing he remembers his neighbor has the same
rights. O man, the law of life and order[225] imposes on you the
restraint of temperance, lest you follow after your wanton
desires[226] and perish, lest you use nature's gifts to serve through
wantonness the enemy of the soul. Would it not be more just
and honorable to share them with your neighbor, your fellow
man, than with your enemy? If, faithful to the Wiseman's
counsel, you turn away from sensual delights[227] and content
yourself with the Apostle's teaching on food and clothing,[228]
you will soon be able to guard your love against "carnal desires which war against the soul"[229] and I think you will not
find it a burden to share with those of your nature that which
you have withheld from the enemy of your soul. Then your
love will be sober and just if you do not refuse your brother
that which he needs of what you have denied yourself in
pleasure. Thus carnal love becomes social when it is extended
to others.

24. What would you do if, while helping out your neighbor,
you find yourself lacking what is necessary for your life? What
else can you do than to pray with all confidence to him[230]
"who gives abundantly and bears no grudges,[231] who opens
his hand and fills with blessings every living being?"[232] There
is no doubt that he will assist us willingly in time of need, since
he helps us so often in time of plenty. It is written: "Seek
first the kingdom of God and his justice, and the rest will be
added thereto."[233] Without being asked he promises to give
what is necessary to him who withholds from himself what he
does not need and loves his neighbor. This is to seek the kingdom of God and implore his aid against the tyrany of sin, to
prefer the yoke of chastity and sobriety rather than let sin
reign in your mortal flesh.[234] And again, it is only right to

225. Sir 45:6.
226. Sir 18:30.
227. *Ibid.*
228. 1 Tim 6:8.
229. 1 Pet 2:11.

230. Acts 4:29; 28:31.
231. Jas 1:5.
232. Ps 144:16.
233. Mt 6:33; Lk 12:31.
234. Rom 6:12.

share nature's gifts with him who shares that nature with you.

25. Nevertheless, in order to love one's neighbor with perfect justice,[235] one must have regard to God. In other words, how can one love one's neighbor with purity, if one does not love him in God? But it is impossible to love in God unless one loves God. It is necessary, therefore, to love God first; then one can love one's neighbor in God.[236] Thus God makes himself lovable and creates whatever else is good. He does it this way. He who made nature protects it, for nature was created in a way that it must have its creator for protector. The world could not subsist without him to whom it owes its very existence. That no rational creature may ignore this fact concerning itself or dare lay claim through pride to benefits due the creator, by a deep and salutary counsel, the same creator wills that man be disciplined by tribulations so that when man fails and God comes to his help, man, saved by God, will render God the honor due him. It is written: "Call to me in the day of sorrow; I will deliver you, and you shall honor me."[237] In this way, man who is animal and carnal,[238] and knows how to love only himself, yet starts loving God for his own benefit, because he learns from frequent experience that he can do everything that is good for him in God[239] and that without God he can do nothing good.[240]

THE SECOND DEGREE OF LOVE: MAN LOVES GOD FOR HIS
OWN BENEFIT

**IX.** 26. Man, therefore, loves God, but for his own advantage and not yet for God's sake. Nevertheless, it is a matter of prudence to know what you can do by yourself and what you can do with God's help to keep from offending him who keeps you free from sin. If man's tribulations, however, grow in frequency and as a result he frequently turns to God and is frequently freed by God, must he not end, even though he had a heart of stone[241] in a breast of iron, by realizing that it is

235. Mk 12:30-31.
236. Mk 12:30.
237. Ps 49:15.
238. 1 Cor 2:14.
239. Phil 4:13.
240. Jn 15:5.
241. Ezek 11:19; 36:26.

God's grace which frees him and come to love God not for his own advantage but for the sake of God?

### THE THIRD DEGREE OF LOVE: MAN LOVES GOD FOR GOD'S SAKE

Man's frequent needs oblige him to invoke God more often and approach him more frequently. This intimacy moves man to taste and discover how sweet the Lord is.[242] Tasting God's sweetness entices us more to pure love than does the urgency of our own needs. Hence the example of the Samaritans who said to the woman who had told them the Lord was present: "We believe now not on account of what you said; for we have heard him and we know he is truly the Savior of the world."[243] We walk in their footsteps when we say to our flesh, "Now we love God, not because of your needs; for we have tasted and know how sweet the Lord is."[244] The needs of the flesh are a kind of speech, proclaiming in transports of joy the good things experienced. A man who feels this way will not have trouble in fulfilling the commandment to love his neighbor.[245] He loves God truthfully and so loves what is God's. He loves purely and he does not find it hard to obey a pure commandment, purifying his heart, as it is written, in the obedience of love.[246] He loves with justice and freely embraces the just commandment. This love is pleasing because it is free. It is chaste because it does not consist of spoken words but of deed and truth.[247] It is just because it renders what is received. Whoever loves this way, loves the way he is loved, seeking in turn not what is his[248] but what belongs to Christ, the same way Christ sought not what was his, but what was ours, or rather, ourselves.[249] He so loves who says: "Confess to the Lord for he is good."[250] Who confesses to the Lord, not because he is good to him but because the Lord is good, truly loves God for God's sake and not for his own benefit. He does not love this way of whom it is said: "He will praise you when you do him favors."[251]

242. Ps 33:9.                 247. 1 Jn 3:18.
243. Jn 4:42.                  248. 1 Cor 13:5.
244. Ps 33:9.                  249. 2 Cor 12:14.
245. Mk 12:31.                 250. Ps 117:1.
246. 1 Pet 1:22.              251. Ps 48:19.

This is the third degree of love: in it God is already loved for his own sake.

X. 27. Happy the man who has attained the fourth degree of love, he no longer even loves himself except for God. "O God, your justice is like the mountains of God."[252] This love is a mountain, God's towering peak. Truly indeed, it is the fat, fertile mountain.[253] "Who will climb the mountain of the Lord?"[254] "Who will give me the wings of a dove, that I may fly away to find rest?"[255] This place is made peaceful, a dwelling-place in Sion."[256] Alas for me, my exile has been lengthened."[257] When will flesh and blood,[258] this vessel of clay,[259] this earthly dwelling,[260] understand the fact? When will this sort of affection be felt that, inebriated with divine love, the mind may forget itself and become in its own eyes like a broken dish,[261] hastening towards God and clinging to him, becoming one with him in spirit,[262] saying: "My flesh and my heart have wasted away; O God of my heart, O God, my share for eternity."[263] I would say that man is blessed and holy to whom it is given to experience something of this sort, so rare in life, even if it be but once and for the space of a moment.[264] To lose yourself, as if you no longer existed, to cease completely to experience yourself, to reduce yourself to nothing is not a human sentiment but a divine experience.[265] If any mortal, suddenly rapt, as has been said, and for a moment is admitted to this, immediately the world of sin[266] envies him, the evil of the day disturbs him,[267] the mortal body weighs him down, the needs of the flesh bother him,

252. Ps 35:7.
253. Ps 67:16.
254. Ps 23:3.
255. Ps 54:7.
256. Ps 75:3.
257. Ps 119:5.
258. Mt 16:17.
259. 2 Cor 4:7.
260. Wis 9:1ͻ.
261. Ps 30:13.
262. 1 Cor 6:17.
263. Ps 72:26.
264. Cf. Gra 15; OB 3:177; CF 19.
265. Cf. Phil 2:7.
266. Gal 1:4.
267. Mt 6:34.

the weakness of corruption offers no support, and sometimes
with greater violence than these, brotherly love calls him back.
Alas, he has to come back to himself, to descend again into
his being, and wretchedly cry out: "Lord, I suffer violence,"[268]
adding: "Unhappy man that I am, who will free me from this
body doomed to death?"[269]

28. All the same, since Scripture says God made everything
for his own purpose,[270] the day must come when the work
will conform to and agree with its Maker. It is therefore necessary for our souls to reach a similar state in which, just as God
willed everything to exist for himself, so we wish that neither
ourselves nor other beings to have been nor to be except for
his will alone; not for our pleasure. The satisfaction of our
wants, chance happiness, delights us less than to see his will
done in us and for us, which we implore every day in prayer
saying: "...your will be done on earth as it is in heaven..."[271]
O pure and sacred love! O sweet and pleasant affection! O pure
and sinless intention of the will, all the more sinless and pure
since it frees us from the taint of selfish vanity, all the more
sweet and pleasant, for all that is found in it is divine. It is
deifying to go through such an experience. As a drop of water
seems to disappear completely in a big quantity of wine, even
assuming the wine's taste and color;[272] just as red, molten iron
becomes so much like fire it seems to lose its primary state;
just as the air on a sunny day seems transformed into sunshine
instead of being lit up; so it is necessary for the saints that all
human feelings melt in a mysterious way and flow into the will
of God. Otherwise, how will God be all in all[273] if something
human survives in man? No doubt, the substance remains
though under another form, another glory, another power.
When will this happen? Who will see it? Who will possess it?
"When shall I come and when shall I appear in God's pres-

268. Is 38:14.
269. Rom 7:24.
270. Prov 16:4; cf. Rev 4:11.
271. Mt 6:10.
272. Here again Bernard is taking his inspiration from the Mass where placing a
drop of water into the chalice of wine has an important signification.
273. 1 Cor 15:28.

ence?"[274] O my Lord, my God, "My heart said to you: my face has sought you; Lord, I will seek your face."[275] Do you think I shall see your holy temple?[276]

29. I do not think that can take place for sure until the word is fulfilled: "You will love the Lord your God with all your heart, all your soul, and all your strength,"[277] until the heart does not have to think of the body and the soul no longer has to give it life and feeling as in this life. Freed from this bother, its strength is established in the power of God. For it is impossible to assemble all these and turn them toward God's face as long as the care of this weak and wretched body keeps one busy to the point of distraction. Hence it is in a spiritual and immortal body, calm and pleasant, subject to the spirit in everything, that the soul hopes to attain the fourth degree of love, or rather to be possessed by it; for it is in God's hands to give it to whom he wishes, it is not obtained by human efforts. I mean he will easily reach the highest degree of love when he will no longer be held back by any desire of the flesh or upset by troubles as he hastens with the greatest speed and desire toward the joy of the Lord.[278] All the same, do we not think the holy martyrs received this grace, at least partially, while they were still in their victorious bodies? The strength of this love seized their souls so entirely that, despising the pain, they were able to expose their bodies to exterior torments. No doubt, the feeling of intense pain could only upset their calm; it could not overcome them.

**XI.** 30. But what about those souls which are already separated from their bodies? We believe they are completely engulfed in that immense ocean of eternal light and everlasting brightness.

### THE CONDITION OF SOULS AFTER DEATH BEFORE THE RESURRECTION

But if, which is not denied, they wish that they had received their bodies back or certainly if they desire and hope to re-

274. Ps 41:3.
275. Ps 26:8.
276. Ps 26:4.

277. Mk 12:30.
278. Mt 25:21, 23.

ceive them, there is no doubt that they have not altogether turned from themselves, for it is clear they still cling to something of their own to which their desires return though ever so slightly. Consequently, until death is swallowed up in victory[279] and eternal light invades from all sides the limits of night and takes possession to the extent that heavenly glory shines in their bodies, souls cannot set themselves aside and pass into God. They are still attached to their bodies, if not by life and feeling, certainly by a natural affection, so that they do not wish nor are they able to realize their consummation without them. This rapture of the soul which is its most perfect and highest state, cannot, therefore, take place before the resurrection of the bodies, lest the spirit, if it could reach perfection without the body, would no longer desire to be united to the flesh. For indeed, the body is not deposed or resumed without profit for the soul. To be brief. "The death of his saints is precious in the sight of the Lord."[280] If death is precious, what must life be, especially that life? Do not be surprised if the glorified body seems to give the spirit something, for it was a real help when man was sick and mortal. How true that text is which says that all things turn to the good of those who love God.[281] The sick, dead and resurrected body is a help to the soul who loves God; the first for the fruits of penance,[282] the second for repose, and the third for consummation. Truly the soul does not want to be perfected, without that from whose good services it feels it has benefited by in every way.

31. The flesh is clearly a good and faithful partner for a good spirit, it helps if it is burdened; it relieves if it does not help; it surely benefits and is by no means a burden. The first state is that of fruitful labor; the second is restful but by no means tiresome; the third is above all glorious. Listen to the bridegroom in the Canticle inviting us to this triple progress: "Eat, friends, and drink; be inebriated, dearest ones."[283] He calls to

279. 1 Cor 15:54.
280. Ps 115:15.
281. Rom 8:28.
282. Mt 3:8.
283. Song 5:1. Cf. Gra 9; OB 3:172; CF 19; Div 41:12, 87:4; OB 6-1:253,331; CF 46.

those working in the body to eat; he invites those who have
set aside their bodies to drink; and he impels those who have
resumed their bodies to inebriate themselves, calling them his
dearest ones, as if they were filled with charity. There is a difference between those who are simply called friends, who sigh
under the weight of the flesh,[284] who are held to be dear for
their charity, and those who are free from the bonds of the
flesh, who are all the more dear because they are more ready
and free to love. More than the other two, these last ones are
called dearest and are so.[285] Receiving a second garment, they
are in their resumed and glorified bodies. They are that much
more freely and willingly borne toward God's love because
nothing at all remains to solicit them or hold them back. This
neither of the first two states can claim because, in the first
state the body is endured with distress, in the second state it
is hoped for as for something missing.

32. In the first state, therefore, the faithful soul eats its
bread, but, alas, in the sweat of its brow.[286] While in the flesh
it moves by faith[287] which necessarily acts through charity,[288]
for if it does not act, it dies.[289] Moreover, according to our
Savior, this work is food: "My food is to do the will of my
Father."[290] Afterwards, having cast off its flesh, the soul no
longer feeds on the bread of sorrow,[291] but, having eaten, it is
allowed to drink more deeply of the wine of love, not pure
wine, for it is written of the bride in the Song of Songs: "I
drank my wine mixed with milk."[292] The soul mixes the divine
love with the tenderness of that natural affection by which it
desires to have its body back, a glorified body. The soul, therefore, glows already with the warmth of charity's wine, but
not to the stage of intoxication, for the milk moderates its
strength. Intoxication disturbs the mind and makes it wholly
forgetful of itself, but the soul which still thinks of the resurrection of its own body has not forgotten itself completely.
For the rest, after finding the only thing needed, what is there

284. 2 Cor 5:4.
285. 1 Jn 3:1.
286. Gen 3:19.
287. 2 Cor 5:7.
288. Gal 5:6.

289. Jas 2:20.
290. Jn 4:34.
291. Ps 126:2.
292. Song 5:1.

to prevent the soul from taking leave of itself and passing into
God entirely, ceasing all the more to be like itself as it becomes
more and more like God? Then only, the soul is allowed to
drink wisdom's pure wine, of which it is said: "How good is
my cup, it inebriates me!"[293] Why wonder if the soul is inebriated by the riches of the Lord's dwelling,[294] when free from
worldly cares it can drink pure, fresh wine with Christ in his
Father's house?[295]

33. Wisdom presides over this triple banquet,[296] composed
of charity which feeds those who labor, gives drink to those
who are resting, and inebriates those who reign. As at an earthly
banquet, edibles are served before liquid refreshments. Nature
has set this order which Wisdom also observes. First, indeed,
up to our death, while we are in mortal flesh we eat the work
of our hands,[297] laboriously masticating what is to be swallowed. In the spiritual life after death, we drink with ease
whatever is offered. Once our bodies come back to life we
shall be filled with everlasting life, abounding in a wonderful
fullness. This is what is meant by the Bridegroom in the Canticle saying: "Eat, my friends, and drink; dearest ones, be
inebriated."[298] Eat before death, drink after death, be inebriated after the resurrection. It is right to call them dearest
who are drunk with love; they are rightly inebriated who
deserve to be admitted to the nuptials of the Lamb,[299] eating
and drinking at his table in his kingdom[300] when he takes his
Church to him in her glory without a blemish, wrinkle, or any
defect of the sort.[301] By all means he will then intoxicate his
dearest ones with the torrent of his delight,[302] for in the Bridegroom and bride's most passionate yet most chaste embrace,
the force of the river's current gives joy to the city of God.[303]
I think this is nothing other than the Son of God who in passing[304] waits on us as he in a way promised: "The just are
feasting and rejoicing in the sight of God, delighting in their

293. Ps 22:5.
294. Ps 35:9.
295. Mt 26:29; Mk 14:25.
296. Prov 9:1ff.
297. Ps 127:2.
298. Song 5:1.

299. Rev 19:9.
300. Lk 22:30.
301. Eph 5:27.
302. Ps 35:9.
303. Ps 45:5.
304. Lk 12:37.

gladness."[305] Here is fullness without disgust; here is insatiable curiosity without restlessness; here is that eternal, inexplicable desire knowing no want. At last, here is that sober intoxication of truth, not from overdrinking,[306] not reeking with wine, but burning for God. From this then that fourth degree of love is possessed forever, when God alone is loved in the highest way, for now we do not love ourselves except for his sake, that he may be the reward of those who love him, the eternal recompense of those who love him forever.[307]

### THE PROLOGUE FOR THE FOLLOWING LETTER

**XII.  34.** I remember writing a letter to the holy Carthusians some time ago and having discussed in it these same degrees of love along with other matters.[308] Perhaps I made some other remarks in it about charity but not different from what I say here. Hence I am adding the following passage to this tract as it appears useful, for it is easier to transcribe what has already been dictated than to compose something new.

### HERE BEGINS THE LETTER ON CHARITY TO THE HOLY BRETHREN OF CHARTRUSE[309]

I maintain that true and sincere charity proceeds from a pure heart, a good conscience and unfeigned faith.[310] It makes us care for our neighbor's good as much as for our own. For he who cares for his own good alone or more than for his neighbor's, shows that he does not love that good purely, that he loves it for his own advantage and not for the good itself. Such a man cannot obey the Prophet who says: "Praise the Lord, for he is good."[311] He praises the Lord indeed, because

305. Ps 67:4.
306. Cf. Acts 2:15.
307. See SC 83:4; OB 2:300; CF 40.
308. Ep 11; PL 182:108-115; LSB, Letter 12, pp. 41-48. See above, Introduction, pp. 85-90. From this point on, in the Latin text the word *caritas* is used in the place of *amor.*
309. The text here comprises Ep 11:3-9.
310. 1 Tim 1:5.
311. Ps 117:1.

he is good to him, but not because the Lord is good himself. Let him be aware that the same Prophet addresses to him this reproach: "He will acknowledge you when you do him a favor."[312] A man can acknowledge that the Lord is powerful, that the Lord is good to him, and that the Lord is simply good. The first is the love of a slave who fears for himself; the second is that of a hireling who thinks only of himself; the third is that of a son who honors his father. He, therefore, who fears and he who covets do so for themselves. Charity is found only in the son. It does not seek its own advantage.[313] For this reason I think this virtue is meant in the text: "The law of the Lord is spotless, it converts souls,"[314] for it alone can turn the mind away from loving one's self and the world and fix it on loving God. Neither fear nor love of self can change the soul. At times they change one's appearance or deeds, they can never alter one's character. Sometimes even a slave can do God's work,[315] but it is not done freely; he is still base. The hireling can do it also, but not freely; he is seen to be lured on by his own cupidity. Where there is self-interest, there is singularity;[316] where there is singularity, there is a corner; where there is a corner, no doubt there is rust and dust.[317] Let the slave have his own law,[318] the very fear which binds him; let the hireling's be the lust for gain which restrains him when he is attracted and enticed by temptation.[319] But neither of these is without fault nor can either convert souls.[320] Charity converts souls because it makes them act willingly.

35. Then I have said charity is unspotted, it keeps nothing of its own for itself. For him who holds nothing as his own,

312. Ps 48:19.

313. 1 Cor 13:5.

314. Ps 18:8.

315. Bernard employs here a term that has great meaning for the monk: *opus Dei*, the work of God, the almost technical expression Benedict of Nursia employs in his *Rule for Monasteries* to denote the monk's celebration of the praises of God in choir through the day and night. See RB 43; 47; 58:7.

316. Singularity is Bernard's fifth degree of pride: Hum 42; OB 3:48-49; see above, p. 70.

317. Cf VI p P 1:3; OB 5:208; CF 25.

318. Rom 2:14.

319. Jas 1:14.

320. Ps 18:8.

assuredly all he has belongs to God; and whatever belongs to
God must be clean. Therefore, the unspotted law of the Lord
is that love which does not seek what is useful to itself, but
what is good for many.[321] It is called the law of the Lord
either because he lives by it or because nobody possesses it
except as a gift from him. It does not seem absurd for me to
say God lives by a law, because it is nothing else than charity.
What else maintains that supreme and unutterable unity in
the highest and most blessed Trinity, if not charity? Hence it
is a law, the law of the Lord, that charity which somehow
holds and brings together the Trinity in the bond of peace.[322]
All the same, let nobody think I hold charity to be a quality
or a kind of accident in God. Otherwise, I would be saying,
and be it far from me, that there is something in God which
is not God. Charity is the divine substance. I am saying nothing new or unusual, just what St John says: "God is love."[323]
Therefore, it is rightly said, charity is God, and the gift of
God.[324] Thus charity gives charity; substantial charity produces
the quality of charity. Where it signifies the giver, it takes the
name of substance; where it means the gift, it is called a quality. Such is the eternal law which creates and governs the universe. All things were made according to this law in weight,
measure, and number,[325] and nothing is left without a law.
Even the law itself is not without a law, which nevertheless
is nothing other than itself. Even if it does not create itself,
it governs itself all the same.

**XIII.** 36. The slave and the mercenary have a law of their
own[326] which is not from the Lord. The former does not love
God and the latter loves something more than God. They have
a law, I say, not the Lord's but their own, which is subject,

---

321. 1 Cor 10:33; 13:5.
322. Eph 4:3. Does Bernard have the Holy Spirit, the Third Person of the Blessed Trinity in mind here? It is not clear. In the next sentence he does affirm that
he is not speaking of some accidental quality.
323. 1 Jn 4:8.
324. Eph 2:8.
325. Wis 11:21.
326. Rom 2:14.

all the same, to the Lord's law. Each one can make a law for
himself, but he cannot withdraw it from the unchangeable
order of the eternal law. I mean each one wants to make his
own law when he prefers his own will to the common, eternal
law. He seeks to imitate his Creator in a perverse way, so that
as God is for himself his own law and depends on himself
alone, so does man want to govern himself and make his own
will his law. This heavy and unbearable yoke weighs on all
Adam's sons,[327] alas, making our necks curve and bend down
so that our life seems to draw near hell.[328] "Unhappy man
that I am, who will free me from this body of death?"[329] by
which I am weighed down and oppressed to the extent that,
"Unless the Lord helped me, my soul would soon be living
in hell!"[330] The soul struggling under this load laments saying:
"Why have you set me against you, and I am become a burden
for myself?"[331] By the words "I am become a burden for
myself" is shown that he himself is his own law and that nobody but himself did that. But what he said previously, speaking to God: "Why have you set me against you" means that
he has not escaped from God's law. It is proper to God's
eternally just law that he who does not want to accept its
sweet rule, will be the slave of his own will as a penance; he
who casts away the pleasant yoke and light load of charity,[332]
will have to bear unwillingly the unbearable burden of his
own will. By a mysterious and just measure the eternal law
has set its fugitive against himself yet retaining him captive,
for he can neither escape the law of justice which he deserves
nor remain with God in his light, rest, and glory, because he
is subject to power and banished from happiness. O Lord,
my God, "Why do you not take away my sin, and wherefore
do you not remove my evil,"[333] that delivered from the heavy
load of self-will, I may breathe under charity's light burden,
that I may not be forced on by slavish fear or drawn on by a
hireling's cupidity? May I be moved by your Spirit,[334] the

327. Sir 40:1; Acts 15:10.
328. Ps 87:4.
329. Rom 7:24.
330. Ps 93:17.

331. Job 7:20.
332. Mt 11:30.
333. Job 7:21.
334. Rom 8:14.

Spirit of liberty[335] by which your sons are acting, which bears witness to my spirit that I, too, am one of your sons,[336] that there is just one law for both of us, that I must also be as you are in this world.[337] For those who follow what the Apostle says: "May you owe nobody anything unless it be to love one another,"[338] without a doubt they are as God is in this world, neither slaves nor hirelings but sons.

**XIV. 37.** The sons are not without a law, unless a different meaning is given the text: "Laws are not made for those who are good."[339] It should be realized that a law of fear promulgated by a spirit of slavery[340] differs from that of gentleness given by a spirit of liberty. Sons are not obliged to obey a law of fear and they cannot exist without that of liberty. Do you wish to know why there is no law for those who are good? It is written: "But you have not received the spirit of servitude in fear."[341] Do you wish to hear that they are not without the law of charity? "But you have received the spirit of the adoption of sons."[342] Yet listen to the just man affirming of himself that he is not under the law, yet he is not lawless, "I have become," says he, "as if I was bound by the law with those who are bound by the law, although I am not bound by the law; and as if I was not bound by the law with those who are not bound by the law, although I am not without the law of God but bound by that of Christ."[343] It is not, therefore, right to say: "The just have no law," or "The just are without a law," but that "Laws are not made for those who are good,"[344] meaning they are not imposed on them unwillingly but, inspired by goodness, they are given freely to those who accept. Hence the Savior says so fittingly: "Take my yoke upon you,"[345] as if he said: "I do not impose it on the unwilling, but take it on you who desire it; otherwise, you will find toil instead of rest for your souls."

335. 2 Cor 3:17.
336. Rom 8:14, 16.
337. 1 Jn 4:17.
338. Rom 13:8.
339. 1 Tim 1:9.
340. Rom 8:15.
341. *Ibid.*
342. *Ibid.*
343. 1 Cor 9:20-21.
344. 1 Tim 1:9.
345. Mt 11:29.

38. The law of charity is good and sweet. It is not only borne gaily and easily, it also makes the laws of the slave and the hireling bearable, for it does not destroy them but fulfills them, as the Lord says: "I have not come to abolish the law but to fulfill it."[346] It tempers the slave's law and sets the hireling's in order, making both lighter. Charity will never be without fear but it will be a chaste fear; never without cupidity but it will be in order. Charity obeys the slave's law when it imparts devotion; it obeys the hireling's when it sets desires in order. Piety mixed with fear does not destroy fear; it chastens it. The punishment alone is taken away, without which fear could not exist while servile. But chaste and filial fear remains forever.[347] When one reads: "Perfect charity drives away fear,"[348] this must be understood of the punishment which is inseparable from servile fear; it is a figure of speech in which the cause is given for the effect. Cupidity in turn is set in right order by the arrival of charity, which moves one to reject evil altogether and prefer what is better to what is good, desiring what is good only on account of what is better. When this state is fully achieved, the body and all its good things are loved only on account of the soul, the soul on account of God, and God on account of himself.

XV.  39. Since we are carnal[349] and born of concupiscence of the flesh, our cupidity or love must begin with the flesh, and when this is set in order, our love advances by fixed degrees, led on by grace, until it is consummated in the spirit,[350] for "Not what is spiritual comes first, but what is animal, then what is spiritual."[351] It is necessary that we bear first the likeness of an earthly being, then that of a heavenly being.[352] Thus man first loves himself for himself because he is carnal and sensitive to nothing but himself. Then when he sees he cannot subsist by himself, he begins to seek for God by faith[353] and to love him as necessary to himself. So in the second degree of love, man loves God for man's sake and not for God's sake.

346. Mt 5:17.
347. Ps 18:10.
348. 1 Jn 4:18.
349. Rom 7:14.

350. Gal 3:3.
351. 1 Cor 15:46.
352. 1 Cor 15:49.
353. Heb 11:6.

When forced by his own needs he begins to honor God and
care for him by thinking of him, reading about him, praying
to him, and obeying him, God reveals himself gradually in
this kind of familiarity and consequently becomes lovable.
When man tastes how sweet God is,[354] he passes to the third
degree of love in which man loves God not now because of
himself but because of God. No doubt man remains a long
time in this degree, and I doubt if he ever attains the fourth
degree during this life, that is, if he ever loves only for God's
sake. Let those who have had the experience make a statement; to me, I confess, it seems impossible. No doubt, this
happens when the good and faithful servant is introduced
into his Lord's joy,[355] is inebriated by the richness of God's
dwelling.[356] In some wondrous way he forgets himself and
ceasing to belong to himself, he passes entirely into God and
adhering to him, he becomes one with him in spirit.[357] I believe the Prophet felt this when he said: "I shall enter the powers of the Lord; O Lord, I shall be mindful of your justice
alone."[358] He knew well that when he entered the spiritual
powers of the Lord, he would have to cast off all the infir-
mities of the flesh so that he would no longer have to think of
the flesh, but wholly in the spirit he would be mindful of
God's justice alone.

40. Then each member of Christ[359] can assuredly say of himself what Paul said of the Head: "If we have known Christ
according to the flesh, we no longer know him so."[360] Nobody
there knows himself according to the flesh because "Flesh and
blood will not possess the kingdom of God."[361] This does not
mean the substance of the flesh will not be present, but that
all carnal necessity will disappear, the love of the flesh will
be absorbed by that of the spirit and our present, weak, human affections will be changed into divine. Then charity's
net which is now being dragged across the broad and mighty
ocean of time, catching all kinds of fish, will be pulled ashore;

354. Ps 33:9.
355. Mt 25:21.
356. Ps 35:9.
357. 1 Cor 6:17.

358. Ps 70:16.
359. 1 Cor 6:15.
360. 2 Cor 5:16.
361. 1 Cor 15:50.

there the bad will be thrown away and only the good will be kept.[362] In this life, all kinds of fish are caught in charity's net, where, for the time being, it conforms to all,[363] drawing into itself the adversity and prosperity of all. In a way it makes them its own, rejoicing with those who rejoice, weeping with those who weep, as is its habit.[364] When the net reaches the shore, all that has been endured with displeasure will be thrown away like rotten fish, and only what could be a source of pleasure will be kept. For example, will Paul be sick with those who are sick, will he blush with those who are scandalized when sickness and scandal are taken away?[365] Will he weep for those who do not do penance where there is neither sinner nor penitent?[366] In that city whose river's current is a source of joy[367] and whose gates the Lord loves more than all the tents of Jacob,[368] let him never weep for those who have been condemned to eternal fire with the devil and his angels.[369] Even if at times victory causes rejoicing in other tents, one nevertheless must go into battle and often at the peril of one's life. However in that fatherland, no adversity or sorrow is allowed, for one sings of it: "All those who rejoice, dwell in you,"[370] and again: "Everlasting joy will be theirs."[371] Finally, how can mercy be remembered where one is mindful of God's justice alone?[372] Where there is no place for misery or time for mercy, there will surely be no feeling of compassion.

---

362. Mt 13:47-48.
363. 1 Cor 9:19.
364. Rom 12:15.
365. 2 Cor 11:29. Cf. 1 Cor 9:22.
366. 2 Cor 12:21.
367. Ps 45:5.

368. Ps 86:2.
369. Mt 25:41.
370. Ps 86:7.
371. Is 61:7.
372. Ps 70:16.

# ON LOVING GOD:

## AN ANALYTICAL COMMENTARY

by

Emero Stiegman

# THE TREATISE AND ITS AUTHOR

I N THE WORKS of Bernard of Clairvaux (1090–1153) we meet a writer whose engagement in many subjects reveals one literary passion, love. Everything he concerns himself with either leads to love or is explained by love. In his first major work, *The Steps of Humility and Pride*, the God who awaits us at the pinnacle of our climb is 'love itself'.[1] In his most esteemed theological treatise, *On Grace and Free Choice*, Bernard sets out to demonstrate that what he has said about the loving God working within us does not exclude a role for the human lover.[2] In his contemplative masterpiece, *On the Song of Songs*, he celebrates 'the gift of holy love'.[3] In the great body of his sermons, what posterity has cherished is his ability to draw from the Scriptures their spiritual meaning, the revelation of God's love.[4] One small work, not his maturest nor his most polished nor the one most noted by academic theologians, has generally assumed the status of basic Bernard, because it is a brief and comprehensive treatment of the topic which generates all his thinking: *On Loving God* (*De diligendo Deo*). In the opinion of Thomas Merton, 'More than any other single work of his, it gives the deepest understanding of his thought, and it also gives us the key to the theology and spirit of the Cistercian writers of the 12th century.'[5]

A large part of bernardine scholarship is dedicated to the subject of love, and our treatise has never lacked attention.[6] Even so, although its critical importance in the development of this theme has never been doubted, the work itself has never received focused interest in an extended essay. Other than introductions to modern translations, even brief essays which deal directly with the text and reflect the last half-century's renewal of bernardine

45

scholarship are scarce. The manner of all modern studies of *On Loving God* was established in 1934, by Etienne Gilson's classic synthesis of Bernard's mystical theology. There generations of mis-interpretation were set right through the exposition of a cohesive spiritual doctrine.[7] His most urgent objective was to demonstrate, in sufficiently familiar terms, the very orthodoxy of cistercian spirituality. While surveying the saint's thought in its entirety, Gilson understood it to assume the structure of our treatise. Since then, every reading of *On Loving God* has striven to meet the need Gilson correctly perceived: to explain the text in the light of Bernard's other works. As useful as this broad contextual reading is, it fails in one major way. To see our treatise as one more expression of the integral mind of its author is to ignore the work's boundaries, to blur its historical and artistic concreteness—in the end, not fully to understand its specific message. Evidence of how the abbot's thinking developed eludes us and we remain unaware of the literary form that determines an artistic writer's meaning. Bernard of Clairvaux is an essentially artistic writer. We cannot choose to read him for his substance while leaving the shape of his imagination to readers with lesser concerns.

*De diligendo Deo* has suffered in these respects. In the name of clarity, we have so concentrated on showing how Bernard's categories (*affectio/affectus, natura, cupiditas, amor, sapientia, etc.*) can be transposed into those of a more familiar anthropology that we have compromised our ability to receive the benefit he drew from those he actually employed.[8] There may be no quick comfort in learning that such categories are now virtually untranslatable, but this information can lead a reader to the right questions. A similar loss is sustained when such concepts as which are generally part of Bernard's 'mystical theology' (*imago-similitudo, anima capax Dei, similis similem quaerit*)—are relied upon to explain a passage in *De diligendo Deo* even though they do not appear there;[9] or, when themes which have a massive presence in the text (*corpus, necessitas, ratio, infideles, resurrectio generalis, consummatio*) are not perceived as enjoying this rhetorical ponderance, and therefore not given their intended position in the author's thought. Though we can hardly dispense with the syntheses we have received—Gilson's least of all—we need a more analytic reading of this treatise. Only in that approach is something of Saint Bernard, at times a strikingly analytic writer with a passion for literary form, available to us.

As we explore the spirituality of this text, we have no intention of abandoning contextual methods. In *De diligendo Deo* several fundamental theological assumptions must be unearthed; unawareness of them weakens our ability to receive the spiritual substance Saint Bernard wishes to share. How, for example, can we appreciate his vision of the divine Lover working *in* our nature unless we take up his conviction that humans are graced in *creation?* Again, must we not wonder why and with what consequences his concept of the life of the spirit is so thoroughly a matter of love, when for the past several centuries our dominant religious discourse has centered on faith? When we notice that his measure of religious maturity is broadly affective while ours tends to be narrowly voluntary, can we rest content with arbitrary explanations that speak of temperament? In this commentary we will claim that some of his characteristic views depend on a shifting perspective on the condition of human nature and on different readings of 'concupiscence'. Such observations enable us to foresee that attempts to graft bernardine spirituality onto an inhospitable, though orthodox, theological tree will not take. Just as we must fail in any attempt to separate religious *matter* from literary *form,* so we will fail if we try to cull the *substance* of cistercian spirituality while leaving what we imagine to be intellectual *accidents* to the leisure of theologians. The theological underpinning of Bernard's thought is quite visible in *De diligendo Deo,* and the fact that, although not on the surface, it cannot be ignored renders the work suitable as an entry into the thought of Saint Bernard.

'Theology' will engage us only in the way it engaged the author. The clarifications in the notes of this study should not encumber the reader. Students may find them useful; others can safely pass them by. The documentation at times extends beyond the record of discussions among Cistercian specialists. The questions that preoccupied Saint Bernard cannot be surveyed as mere historical data. Because they are our questions still, they must be inserted into the conversation among spiritual writers of our generation. One modern writer claims that 'The greatest need in theology today is to discover and to name [our] pre-religious emotional involvement with God'.[10] But this is in large part the theme of *On Loving God*! The work must be restored to the whole of christian tradition. Its author did not think of it as 'theology'.

Bernard was born in 1090 of the lesser burgundian nobility in the town of Fontaines-les-Dijon. His education was interrupted when, in 1113, with a band of thirty companions—three brothers and an uncle among them—he entered the recently established monastery of Cîteaux. By the witness of his contemporaries, he had a very attractive personality and a genius for friendship. After only two years Abbot Stephen Harding sent him to found the new monastery of Clairvaux. During Bernard's lifetime sixty-eight cistercian communities emanated from Clairvaux.

Though the holy abbot believed monks should pray rather than preach, he found himself engaged continually in the crises of ecclesiastical politics of his generation. When schism pitted pope against anti-pope in 1130, Bernard sided with the supporters of Innocent II against the claims of Anacletus, largely on grounds of Innocent's personal sanctity; and, invited by King Louis VI, he addressed the Council of Etampes on the subject. Though his arduous interventions were in great part successful, the schism ended only with the death of Anacletus's successor in 1138. Bernard was similarly engaged in disputed episcopal elections at Langres and York.

When his close friend William of Saint Thierry, an excellent theologian, reported heresy in the writings of Peter Abelard, Bernard's aversion to the theological manner of the new *magistri* of the schools drew him into action. He instigated proceedings which terminated in the condemnation of Abelard at the Synod of Sens (1140). His opposition to Gilbert of Poitiers came to a less successful conclusion at the Council of Reims (1148). With the fall of Edessa (1145), the last christian stronghold in the Holy Land, Pope Eugene III, one of Bernard's spiritual sons from Clairvaux, commmissioned him to preach the Second Crusade in France. In his zealous compliance, Bernard travelled the length of the Rhine. The Crusaders were defeated at Damascus (1148), and the abbot retreated, humbled and fatigued, to his monastery, where he died in 1153. He was canonized in 1174 and proclaimed a Doctor of the Church in 1830.

Eight volumes of the critical edition of Bernard's writings (all in a remarkably supple and strong Latin), include the following: his great commentary on the Song of Songs, a series of eighty-six profoundly conceived and highly polished sermons; four other sermon collections comprising several hundred homilies and sermon abstracts, some of which have caused his name to be linked with devotion to the Virgin Mary; *The Steps of Humility and Pride*, a development of Saint Benedict's teachings in the Rule; the *Apologia to William of Saint Thierry*, in which he reflects upon a dispute concerning observances among Cluniacs and Cistercians; the treatise *On Loving God*; *On Grace and Free Choice*, a theological study of how merit might accrue to the will; *In Praise of the New Knighthood*, a defense of the military order of the Knights Templars, who engaged in 'malicide, not homicide'; a life of Saint Malachy, whom he presented as a model of the reforming bishop; and five hundred forty-seven letters.

### *Origin and Fortune of* On Loving God

*On Loving God* is an epistolary tract. Letters form the abbot's first writing effort.[11] Among early examples is letter 11 (c. 1124) to Guy, prior of the Grande Chartreuse. In it Bernard breaks new ground as an author. With this somewhat formal essay on the love of God he seems to have felt some satisfaction, for when later asked by another correspondent to address the theme, he joined this letter to his new and more ambitious treatment.[12] In that early letter to the Carthusians the young abbot discovered his vocation as a spiritual writer.[13]

The correspondent to whom the saint responds with our treatise *De diligendo deo* is Cardinal Haimeric (or Aimeric), Chancellor of the Roman See. Asked several sets of questions, Bernard chooses to answer only one and, in responding to it, moves quickly beyond the bounds of the questions to lay out his own agenda. He says,

I DO NOT PROMISE TO ANSWER ALL YOUR QUESTIONS, BUT ONLY THAT WHICH YOU ASK ABOUT LOVING GOD; EVEN THEN MY ANSWER

WILL BE WHAT HE DEIGNS TO BESTOW ON ME. . . . KEEP THE OTHER
QUESTIONS FOR MORE BRILLIANT MINDS.[14] (Prologue)

These are the words of a literary opportunist, pleased to be given
an outlet for what he has long pondered. The ideas that began
stirring in his letter to Guy the prior will be consolidated in this
missive to the Cardinal and set forth entirely on the author's
terms.[15] In De diligendo Deo Bernard will present compactly most
of the foundational themes of his spirituality. He produces a text
laden with imaginative riches; and formulations which were to
become classic appear here for the first time in contemplative
literature.[16]

The treatise spread rapidly in the author's lifetime. Sixty ex-
tant manuscripts make it one of his most copied texts.[17] Already
before the end of the twelfth century it was being circulated
under the title *De amore*; in combination with William of Saint-
Thierry's earlier pieces, *De contemplando Deo* and *De natura et dignitate amoris*. The practice continued in the seventeenth-century
edition of Bernard's works by Horstius.[18] With the triumph of a
different intellectual temperament in the age of High Scholasticism, the treatise lost its vogue. The theological compilation used
by the schoolmen who were closest to Bernard's spirit, those of
the first franciscan school of Paris, contained no fewer than 496
quotations from Saint Bernard's works, but relatively few came
from *On Loving God*. The preferred texts were the abbot's *Sermons
on the Song of Songs* and *On Grace and Free Choice*.[19] Even Saint
Bonaventure, who possessed a closer, more admiring knowledge
of Bernard than did all his contemporaries, and who quoted
fourteen times from our treatise, was not as greatly engaged by
it as by other works of the abbot.[20]

That the Scholastics esteemed Bernard's *On Grace and Free Choice*
is not surprising, nor is their casual evaluation of *On Loving God*.
How to conceive the relation of human freedom and divine grace
is a severe challenge to the theological intellect, whereas how God
is experienced as lovable was not an authentic *quaestio* in the
schools. Today, as the perceived relationship between theology
and spirituality changes, the questions raised by students of both
are in closer accord with the objectives of our treatise.

The questions that occupied Bernard remained a major concern among the mystics of the Rhineland and the seventeenth-century mystics. But, on their side of the divide created by Scholasticism, Bernard's patristic style of reflection had already been replaced by the more objectifying theological treatise, on the one hand, and a more formally poetic discourse on the other. Francis de Sales, writing his great *Treatise on the Love of God* (1616) with an agendum similar to that of *On Loving God*, manifested no direct indebtedness to the abbot's text.[21] Not until the twentieth-century movement to 'discover' and repossess christian classics did *On Loving God* (with the works of Bernard generally) re-emerge as a booklet of startling relevance to a generation that has lost some confidence in christian spirituality's contact with human life.

### A Philosophic Character

Readers approaching Bernard's treatise exclusively as devotional literature will stumble on many passages that may leave them wondering about the fruitfulness of his method. Why does the author discuss at length *nature,* the *necessities* and *possibilities* of human beings, the dynamics of *desire,* the universal *law,* human beings as distinguished from the christian faithful, and (above all) *reason?* These are large philososphical themes. Let us briefly take note of Benard's interest in them.

At the heart of *De diligendo Deo* lies the configuration of that progress toward God which is possible to human nature. That, at least, is what is stamped on the memory of the tradition as the essential treatise. Bernard's four degrees of loving God (23–33) is an original construct, brilliant in its simplicity, comprehensiveness, and experiential plausibility: we first love ourselves for our own sake, then God for our sake, then God for God's own sake, and finally ourselves only for God. The schema arises from two sets of assumptions—first, that God's free, unexacted, but ever-present love works within us; second, that with a nature weakened in its freedom after sin but still open to God, we must begin 'in the flesh'. The assumptions regarding both God and the human condition come from christian faith; but the concept of 'nature' brings with it an orientation to examining possibilities. Although the *possible* is a metaphysical category, the author's bent is to eschew *a priori* approaches such as arguing from abstractions. He considers possibilities in relation to nature as *experienced*. To work deductively from a definition of nature, however theologically sound, would beg the only question that mattered in the spiritual life. What is possible, in his view, is what an observed conscience and pattern of behavior, interpreted in the faith, reveals.[22] In this sense his method is phenomenological.

At the same time, what is observed, both as past and as open future, must be rationalized; it must be shown to proceed from God's love and the human being's nature as both experience and the assumptions of faith have represented this nature. (That Bernard was aware of the circularity of the argument is suggested by his request for confirmation from his reader's own experience.)[23] The on-going necessity of confronting and ultimately resolving doubts that the writer's experience may be idiosyncratic or his interpretations arbitrary produces a rich vein of rationality running through the development of the argument.

The very choice of *self* and *God* as termini of the axis of thought seems to have been made in the name of rationality; better, the choice manifests the level of experience which is most immediate to consciousness. Constructs such as nature-grace, fall-redemption, image-likeness, or the johannine Word-world may organize a conceptualizing of the search for God, but, emerging as they do directly out of christian faith, they could not make equal appeal to the raw data of rational awareness. For Bernard the ultimate and most ready source of the God-and-self duo seems to be the biblical contrast of spirit and flesh (e.g. Gal 5:17); and in that case the removal of the biblical terminology is significant.[24] In its elemental character, the God-self polarity transcends all religious traditions, so that even when addressed to christians it makes minimal demands on their faith. It has an apologetic value, and is, in this psychological sense, foundational.

As the records of various religious cultures and succeeding eras show, the human mind gropes for the nature of the ultimately real and for an understanding of its own relationship to it. Yet something in the quest is found to be irreducible and, therefore, recognizably shared by all traditions: every human self, in meeting what is other, encounters what is larger than self, an Other which confronts the self through the mediation of others, principally other human selves (23).

Like Bernard's sense of the cognitive-affective unity of personality, the first approach to what is other comes through one's desires, and leads to an apprehension of self by which one intuits the Other (6, 18–20). If the phenomenon of thought itself suggests to Anselm a concept of God, to Bernard it was the experience of desire which led to such a conceptualization (18–19). It is hard to imagine that there could be any starting point, any recession to a ground-zero, beyond this. Bernard's monastic drive for simplicity brings him to this position, where, paradoxically, what is most monastic is most broadly shared in human experience and, therefore, most amenable to rational scrutiny. Monasticism in all its forms has always been philosophical, even when denegrating philosophy and transcending it.

But the letter Bernard appended to his treatise strongly suggests that a concrete literary influence was also at work in his mode of thinking. The letter to Guy, prior of the Carthusians, was a response, not only to the holy man's earlier letter, but to his privately circulated *Meditationes*.[25] Thomas Merton illustrated the affinity of *On Loving God* to Guy's work, the heart of which is (in his words) 'the total dedication of the mind to nature and substantial truth'.[26] Guy was a philosopher of the christian life, understanding philosophical pleasure (*voluptas philosophica*) as a knowledge of the creature, even as angelic pleasure (*voluptas angelica*) is the knowledge and love of God. He was concerned with the law of things, and the style of his thought led Merton, who pronounced him 'important as source' for Bernard's anthropology, to suggest an occasional hindu and buddhist parallel. An admiring Bernard put his reply to Guy in the form of an inquiry into the law of love (35–38). Anyone bemused at the abbot's philosophical manner in *On Loving God*, will nod in recognition at reading Merton's ten pages of aphorisms from Guy the Carthusian.

With this cast of mind, Bernard could welcome the inquiries of Cardinal Haimeric, his correspondent. He points out however, that the question 'why' we should love God forces him as author to confront readers who need reasons, rather than those whose experience has preempted the question. In the explicitness of his rational approach, he is addressing novices in the spiritual life.

Let us now, at the beginning, engage in a brief reconnaissance of the treatise to detect the strong thematic presence of this rationality.

*De diligendo Deo* offers at one level the description of a seeker's experience and, at a deeper, interpretive level, the image of a loving God who, though in constant need of being identified, works within. To this two-tiered consciousness and the question of point of view, we shall return continually in this essay. Through most of the treatise the life of the spirit is viewed from the standpoint of those who lack christian faith, the 'infidels' whom we meet early in the second paragraph. In recognition of the restraints this situation imposes on the author, we may speak of his procedure as philosophical. The reason for discussing the consciousness of the infidels rather than that of Christians, is revealed each time *infideles* is replaced by such expressions as EVERY RATIONAL BEING (18) and THE RATIONAL SOUL (21): Bernard refers broadly to the human race.[27] He makes appeal to the experience of every human being.[28]

He goes about the business of a spiritual writer: examining, in the light of the gospel, experiences which he understands to be unambiguously religious. Our focus, for the moment, on his underlining of the rationality of his claims must not be mistaken for an insinuation that he was a closet philosopher. To the contrary, rationality will be recognized as a characteristic of his spirituality.

The *infideles* have a stronger presence in *De diligendo Deo* than seems generally to have been noticed. Bernard addresses Christians, not infidels. His first paragraph, his eloquent pericope on the memory of Christ (7–13), and the concluding image of paragraph 33 are statements of christian faith. This must not prevent us from recognizing that the rest of the work, the largest part, reflects upon the situation of the infidel. The potential significance of this fact is so great that we must verify it in some detail.

In paragraphs 2–6 Bernard speaks of those gifts which constitute human beings, in order to argue that these were quite enough for one to love God completely. There is a break (7–13) in which the author develops the proposition, THE FAITHFUL (*fideles*), ON

THE CONTRARY, KNOW HOW TOTALLY THEY NEED JESUS, AND HIM CRUCIFIED (7).[29] But then the text returns to those who lack christian faith, comparing their condition with that of the faithful (14–15). Paragraph 16 considers the relative positions of God and the human being as such, to emphasize how much God merits human love. There follows a reflection on the spontaneity of love in general (17). The next four paragraphs speak of THE LAW OF MAN'S DESIRE observable in EVERY RATIONAL BEING (18–21)—with a brief interruption on the just man who takes the SALUTARY SHORT-CUT (21) which is Christ. The four degrees of love are introduced by a meditation on prevenient grace (22). The human subject, developing through the entire stretch (23–33) of four degrees of loving God, is the creature gifted with reason, *egregia rationis munere creatura* (4), *homo* (23), every human who is *consors naturae* (23) or of *natura communis* (24).

What emerges from this catalogue, besides a curious ratio of parts, is Bernard's interest in the 'infidel' simply as a type representing the human being as such, humankind in its need for God, universal humanity. We do not imply by this that Bernard is inquiring into essences; his concern is with the historical order, with the human being as graced at creation and as weakened through sin. He affirms this universality by situating his reflections at a point in human consciousness prior to the mind's recognition of God as the source of all good. He contrasts this consciousness to that of the Christian in order to ascertain the human experience that christian faith is to interpret, trying to separate the experience from the interpretation (aware that this is never altogether possible). He addresses himself, not to those who are ignorant of doctrine, but to *insipientes*, those of shallow, undeveloped religious experience, inattentive to God's action within them.

Consistent with his choice of *homo rationalis* as type is Bernard's style of argumentation: except when explicitly acknowledging the fact, he does not argue from faith. His more ordinary appeal is to sheer necessity, a desire for self-preservation (23–26); to the demands of justice, which he associates with reason: JUSTICE IS THE VITAL NATURAL FOOD OF THE RATIONAL SOUL (21).[30] Or, REASON AND NATURAL JUSTICE URGE THE INFIDEL . . . (15).[31] Justice and reason are expressions of that NATURAL LAW (6) which binds infidels to love God and which is the universal LAW OF LOVE (37) that creates and sustains the world. (In a similar way, the young abbot of Clairvaux had spoken, briefly, in *The Steps of Humility and Pride*: humility is the 'law' of truth, given by the Lord.)[32] Arguing from necessity, justice, reason, and law, Bernard brandishes a frontal logic in such expressions as *certissime comperit* (one knows with great certainty) and *demonstrare satagimus* (we labor to demonstrate).[33] With this he is not contributing like Abelard to the disputations of the day, or exulting to the extent Anselm would have done in the beauty of intellectual truth; his objective is more immediately homiletic.[34]

At the same time, the continual recurrence of this appeal to rationality forces us to observe the function of reason in Bernard's spirituality. This is something other than an assumption shared with early scholastic writers. We have become accustomed to comments upon the abbot's 'phenomenological' method and his 'existential' mind-set.[35] Part of the validity of these admittedly imprecise labels derives from Bernard's orientation to the concrete problems of his existence and to his demand that reason forever justify itself against intimate personal experience, a larger human knowing.[36] In view of this difference from what Bernard considered a rationalist mentality, we may fail to appreciate the strong role of reason in his spirituality. The will he later defined as 'a rational movement'; and although he spoke of reason as 'its mate, one might even say its follower', he insisted that the will was 'never moved without reason'. In fact, *sapientia* could not be possessed 'by any means other than by reason'.[37]

The 'law' is amply discussed in Bernard's letter to the Carthusians (34–40), appended to the treatise. We may suspect that the author's wonder over the universality of God's love led him to trace its action in the natural drive of the human being as such. The desire to demonstrate this universality led Bernard, so to speak, to bracket Christian faith in arguing through long stretches of his treatise.

The treatise is an exercise, a form of apologetics.[38] Paradoxically, its intellectual quality depends upon a firm christian faith. The opening lines make the point: the author will answer the question *why* one should love God; but, as we have noted, speaking to those who need reasons for this forces him to build an argument rather than confront the question on its own vital terms. He will be restricted to what his readers are aware of. Beginners, he will tell us, are aware only of themselves and the *affectus* they experience (23). From that he builds a circular argument. At every important juncture he will be guided by christian faith. (Nothing will make this so clear as his wholly unanxious solution to the problem of evil: 'tribulations' are the gift of love, our only hope of moving beyond ourselves [25–26].) But this circular argumentation will put readers of much doctrine and little faith in touch with themselves and with the God working within them.

This discourse, in which spiritual destiny is studied in the sensibilities of the human being as such, presents a monastic doctrine. It assumes the reader is in search of God. What reconciles the monk to the *infideles* of the text is the author's assumption that these latter move to the same destination even though they may not yet know it. Just as the monk may recognize himself in these *infideles*, the monk's quest, in its essence, follows the pattern of all human striving and desiring.

In the sense outlined, then, there is, a strong philosophical tone to *De diligendo Deo*. Although generally professing a hostility towards 'philosophers'—Benedict, the tradition taught, had been *sapienter indoctus*[39]—Saint Bernard was not disinclined to intensely rational thought.[40] What he and the monastic tradition resisted in philosophers was the conviction that eternal truth could be arrived at apart from an integral experience and purity of heart. In our treatise Bernard remains close to the struggling mind and heart of someone who aspires to love; the account he gives of the human quest always suggests the confessions of a writer describing what he has himself gone through at one stage or another of his progress. What he offers the *insipientes* for whom he writes is more than an argument. It is the empathy of a fellow-sufferer, a *consors naturae* (23). It is the overflow of a spirit to whom God speaks. With this, the author moves beyond philosophy. Yet at the same time, as every lover of wisdom, he scans human experience to discern patterns, even as the Stoics had done in their inquiry into cosmic laws. He is not less philosophical for concluding, with the wisdom writers of the Bible, that what the patterns reveal is the eternal

Wisdom which forms and sustains the universe. He has no more interest than these scriptural writers in building a system. His own sense of *sapientia* as religious experience itself does not exclude an intellectual awareness of the great overarching configuration which he, in fact, calls the universal law of love (37).

Hans Urs von Balthasar observes that the vision of a universal *eros* struggling toward the One was broadly classical, and that Augustine's *desiderium* was a christianized version of it.[41] Throughout the *Confessions*, one reads about *caritas*, a love for God (not God's love for us as in 1 Jn 4) which is conceived as a synthesis of *eros* (*desiderium*) and the *agape* of the New Testament.[42] In his rich biblical language, Saint Bernard makes it difficult for us to recognize this geneology; but he shares it with the entire patristic and medieval period. What makes him a witness of great importance is, not only his genius for recording human experience, which he interprets religiously, but an optimism with respect to the concrete reality of human nature, which he sees as open to grace.[43] In this— though it is easy to exaggerate differences—he is not altogether augustinian.

The value of the specifically philosophical thought of Saint Bernard, and generally of the patristic, monastic tradition he represents, is demonstrated in the work of a critically important christian philosopher of this century, Maurice Blondel (d. 1949). The phenomenology of human development found in this philosopher's great work *L'Action* is, in its foundation, that of Bernard's *De diligendo Deo*; in major ways—however partially—it can be traced by direct literary filiation to our treatise.[44] Blondel's germinal influence has been crucial in returning the thought of Saint Bernard and of other experiential contemplative writers of the era, anonymously, into the mainstream of christian awareness.[45]

After Blondel, it was easier to arrive at a new reading of (for example) Aquinas, where static essentialism gave way to the concept of a dynamic continuity of God's action in humanity: for many, this Transcendental Thomism has provided the intellectual legitimation of a spirituality suprisingly in accord with Bernard's *On Loving God*.[46] Awareness of Blondel's debt to our treatise would eliminate the surprise. For others today, the current of Saint Bernard's mind feeds the broad stream of psychological realism in spiritual matters, repossessed by those who have attended studiously to the Hebrew Scriptures and to Oriental religion. In either case, what in this century has most commended the thought of the abbot who routinely warned against *philosophi et heretici* has been its philosophical validity.

These remarks address the lower experiential level of Bernard's work, and if we were to see nothing else we would read him poorly. The double level of consciousness we have mentioned includes a continual reference to christian faith. The abbot makes a determined effort to universalize the experiential validity of his subject by removing it from the consciousness of the Christian as such, by declaring that what he experiences is not limited to the *interpretation* his faith affords. Yet at the same time, we encounter a continual proclamation and exposition of christian faith. In this, Bernard disengages the two levels conceptually and attempts to expose human experience and render it recognizable to a prosaic and secular consciousness. Here, he means to tell us, here is where the Spirit is at work within you.

What we are calling a philosophical element in Saint Bernard, nowhere so prominent as in *De diligendo Deo*, is what modern spirituality has seized on. Although this treatise is but one nugget from a rich vein of christian tradition, it provides a privileged beginning point for those who would clarify for themselves the precise meaning of Christian spirituality, both as life and as literature.

## The Place of the Treatise in Bernard's Works

The editors of the *Sancti Bernardi opera* declined to narrow the dating of *De diligendo Deo* to anything less than a fifteen year span.[47] In letter 18, written in the summer of 1126, Bernard lists the works he has published to that time, and this treatise is not mentioned.[48] Cardinal Haimeric, to whom the tract is addressed, died in 1141. No convincing case has been made for locating the date more precisely.

Haimeric was a canon regular from Burgundy, and a critically important person in Bernard's ministry. Pope Callistus II, son of the Count of Burgundy, called Haimeric to Rome early in his pontificate, and at the first opportunity made him chancellor, a position he kept under three popes. Holding one another in high esteem, Haimeric and Bernard became close allies. The bond was well known. The burgundian pope, the burgundian chancellor, and the burgundian abbot worked well together. We possess fourteen letters from Bernard to Haimeric, all on business matters but all written in a tone of confident friendship.[49] At the death of Honorius II in 1130, Haimeric was pope-maker in the contested succession, and it was probably at his request that Bernard set out to defend the claim of Innocent II.[50] The composition of *On Loving God*, unfortunately, can be tied to none of these numerous interactions.

Some commentators look for help in the association of the treatise with the work of Bernard's close friend William (d. 1148), the Benedictine who left the abbacy of Saint Thierry to join the Cistercians. We have noted that William's first two writings, *De contemplando Deo* and *De natura et dignitate amoris*, were circulated with Bernard's *De diligendo Deo*.[51] Dom Jacques Hourlier believes that Bernard's work came shortly after William's and places all three texts between 1119 and 1124.[52] This accords approximately with earlier studies on William done by André Wilmart and Jean-Marie Déchanet.[53]

The absence of *De diligendo Deo* from Bernard's catalogue in letter 18 remains a difficulty to such early dating. The close association of William of Saint Thierry and Bernard antedated their literary production and blurs the time lines of their relative development.[54]

Working from a different direction, Ermenegildo Bertola has recently claimed that Bernard's treatise should be dated sometime after the beginning of the papal schism of 1130. He reads a deliberate ambiguity in the word *orationes* of the prologue. Bernard writes to Haimeric: 'Up to now it has been your custom to ask me for prayers (*orationes*) and not for answers to questions'.[55] These *orationes* can mean either prayers or oratorical efforts to counter his correspondent's adversaries.[56]

Bertola's ingenious suggestion is not to be ignored, though it labors against a reader's strong impression that the development of the paragraph concerns only prayer: there is an echo of prayer in the text but none of oratory.[57]

Finally, Bernard McGinn, though not arguing this issue, inclines with many other authors to consider the treatise as slightly before *On Grace and Free Choice*, i.e. before 1128, the date accepted from Elphege Vacandard by the *Sancti Bernardi Opera*.[58] Vacandard's '*vers* 1126' for *On Loving God* pushes the date to the earliest possible point.[59] One reason for inclining toward this opinion would be the plausibility that the treatise presumed to be later would take up in a more analytical way issues arising out of the earlier one. Bertola's inversion of the sequence lacks this strength.

Our search for internal evidence of a sequence, however, leads us to a phenomenon of larger import than precise dating. An attentive reading of *On Loving God* reveals no literary presence in this text of the theme which forms the founding concept of Bernard's anthropology as we know it from subsequent works. We look in vain for the relationship between God's image and likeness in the human being; the teaching that we are made in God's image but have lost our likeness to God in sin, and that through the conformity of our will to God's will, the likeness will be restored.[60] *On Grace and Free Choice* is the first of Bernard's works to develop this theme, which becomes, from that point on, the principal construct of his spiritual doctrine. In that treatise the idea organizes an important part of the work.[61] In *The Steps of Humility and Pride*, in the *Apologia to William of Saint Thierry*, and in the sermon-series *In Praise of the Blessed Virgin Mary*, the three works Bernard mentions in letter 18, it is completely absent. In the *De moribus et officio episcoporum* (letter 42), generally dated 1126–1128, it is likewise absent. In *De diligendo Deo* there is one reference to image and likeness:

> WHO, AGAIN, CAN BE WICKED ENOUGH TO THINK THE AUTHOR OF
> HIS HUMAN DIGNITY, WHICH SHINES IN HIS SOUL, IS ANY OTHER
> THAN HE WHO SAYS IN THE BOOK OF GENESIS: LET US MAKE MAN
> TO OUR OWN IMAGE AND LIKENESS? (6)[62]

This reflection is irreplaceable in the treatise; no christian anthropology can dispense with it. It is the biblical manner of asserting that God is the source of what is distinctively and essentially human. Rather than call attention to the fact that Bernard cited this passage from Genesis, we might match its popularity in the era with the character of his argument in *De diligendo Deo* and wonder at the small play it receives there. Most significantly, for our purpose, the sentence does not distinguish between image and likeness, as Bernard will always do, in the tradition of Origen and Augustine, but simply quotes from Gen 1:26, where image and likeness are undifferentiated as an hebraic parallelism. There is nothing here of the characteristic dynamism arising out of the distinction. This use of the theme has not yet entered the abbot's works, though, common among spiritual writers of the times, it was certainly known to him.[63]

He does mention 'likeness' in the letter to the Carthusians (32) attached to the treatise; but the usage is not in accord with the traditional use of *likeness* in conjunction with *image*.[64] Bernard writes of the soul 'passing into God entirely, ceasing the more to be like itself as it becomes more and more like God'.[65] In the image-and-likeness tradition, as the likeness to God increases, the true self is established; here, instead, likeness to God is measured by unlikeness to self.[66]

In Bernard's sermons, chronology is difficult to discern; but, to the extent that early placement in the collections signifies an early date, we may single out the third sermon *De diversis* (2), where we find the same unthematic use of the likeness-to-God idea as in the letter to the Carthusians, repeated in our treatise.[67] Then, in the first of three sermons *In annunciatione* (7), a simple statement of what we have referred to as the dynamism of the image-and-likeness idea occurs, undeveloped.[68]

Image-and-likeness is not one motif among many in the collected works of Saint Bernard; it functions as a conceptual model for the process according to which much of the spiritual life is accounted for. To show the centrality of free choice, its priority over *intellectus*, for example, Bernard will say that this *liberum arbitrium* is the place where the divine image in the soul is situated (Gra 9.28). In our treatise, where he makes the claim for the priority of free choice for the first time, he does not state the case this way. He says instead that free choice is the soul's *dignitas* (2), a terminology to which he will never return.[69] Again, Bernard's usual manner of describing significant spiritual progress uses the language of a gradual restoration of the soul's divine likeness. In this work, however, where the soul's journey to God is very schematically and comprehensively sketched, the advance is never referred to as a restoration of divine likeness. Bernard generally explains a human being's capacity for God by noting that we are made in God's image; e.g., 'Only God's own image receives God'.[70] In our treatise, however, the soul's transformation is not spoken of in this way.

To this 'silence' of image and likeness in the works before *On Grace and Free Choice,* we must join another: the four-degrees-of-love scheme at the heart of *On Loving God* is never again repeated after this treatise.[71] This double silence suggests inferences beyond a problem of dating, though it may also affect one's tendency to date the treatise. Consider that, in the wake of *On Loving God,* Bernard has recourse to many schemes of gradation which have the function of charting, in various perspectives, the process of spiritual maturing. His first such scheme had been the steps of humility, which, as he read in the Rule, were the monk's path to love.[72] Among those that followed are the three kisses of Sermons 3 through 8, on The Song of Songs, the *amor carnalis, rationalis, et spiritualis* of SC 20.9, and the seven-point progression, from the correction of faults to the enjoyment of God, of SC 85.1.[73] None of these, however, plays so dominant a role as the differentiation of image and likeness, the regular fulcrum of his anthropology.[74]

Much is made clear by the application of the image-and-likeness scheme to major portions of *The Steps of Humility and Pride,* the *Apologia to Abbot William,* and *On Loving God.* In fact, interpreters tend to explain the spiritual doctrine of these works in that language, though the language is not to be found there. Our treatise is handled that way by such writers as Etienne Gilson, Edgar DeBruyne, Pacifique Delfgaauw, Aimé Forest, Jacques Hourlier, Rowan Williams, and Robert Dresser.[75] This type of contextual reading is doctrinally correct, for just as the God-and-self axis of *On Loving God* had provided Bernard with a dialectic which he preferred over an elaboration of the tensions of grace-and-nature, so the image-and-likeness axis to which he later moved performed a similar function. His concept of the graced 'nature' of the self allowed him to revel in God's immanence, which was even more clearly present in the concept of God's image in the human being—though one need not imagine that Saint Bernard evaluated the situation in this self-conscious and abstract manner.

In fact, the end of Bernard's reflection upon four degrees of love, postulated upon the duality of God and self, marks the beginning of his reflection on a more easily nuanced transformation postulated upon the duality of image and likeness. Although a satisfying explanation has yet to be worked out, it seems clear at this point that Bernard's two early treatises, *On Loving God* and *On Grace and Free Choice*, lie on either side of a seam in the development of his thought. Such ideas may offer more interpretative value than would a precise dating of the treatise; but they contribute as well to a dating solution. *On Loving God* should be set, then, between the following terminal dates: the summer of 1126, time of the composition of letter 18, and the end of 1127, the date currently favored for the composition of *On Grace and Free Choice.*

What we know of the date of Bernard's earlier letter to the Carthusians can only confirm this view. Damien Van Den Eynde, in studying the setting of letter 11, finds a wide divergence of opinions on its composition and a lack of certain data.[76] From what both the letter and other documents reveal of the situation at Clairvaux—the press of administrative duties and the lack of means in the community's first several years—he concludes to a date no earlier than 1124 nor later than 1125; and emphatically not later than the end of 1127, when Bernard entered a new and broader phase of his ministry.

Readers will not fail to observe that the largest part of what we suggest as new evidence for dating *De diligendo Deo* just before *De gratia et libero arbitrio* constitutes merely an argument from silence in which reasons for the phenomenon observed may be more than one. To claim some attention to the absence of image-and-likeness, however, is to indicate a degree of probability that our treatise adheres in this respect to *all* of the early works. While the case made provides one more element in a suggestive accumulation pointing to the date we propose, we will argue (even at the expense of that case) *another* reason for the silence: the absence of an interpretive scheme (such as image-and-likeness) arising immediately out of christian faith, and the presence instead of the God-self scheme, which in reference to religions generally is more elementary and trans-traditional, indicates the rational and foundational level at which the author pitched his reflection.

The abbot detects a certain depth of insight in this God-self duality, as we said earlier. Yet, it is questionable—and Bernard does question—whether the many persons who think in these terms get clear of a spiritually primitive concept of the problem of self-realization (our *fulfillment,* the *consummatio* of paragraph 9).[77] Bernard says as much, even as he decides to accept the terms of his correspondent's question, which is in effect, 'Why should *I* love *God'*? Pastoral possibilities are opened by working from such a point of departure. Bernard describes the process of spiritual development in the language of a God-self tension—just as 'the unwise' conceive of it—and leads his readers to discover the deeper tension to be found *within* the self, between a self that is the locus of God's action and a self diminished through its clinging to what is not God, to what is its own (*proprium*). When asked the logically subsequent question—If it is all God's work, what part do I play? (cf. Gra 1.1)—Bernard will answer in *On Grace and Free Choice* by describing this inner tension in another terminology, that of the abiding divine image in the soul, as distinguished from the lost divine likeness.[78]

Each of these two sets of terms, God-self and image-likeness, attaches to the same process of growth. Students of bernardine spirituality can enrich their understanding of the classic patristic anthropology of image and likeness—Bernard's later preference— by matching it to the earlier, psychologically more analytic and theologically more elementary approach of *On Loving God.* Not the smallest of gains from the comparison would be an observation of the extent to which the earlier schema perceives divine action within the soul to be of the order of creation, while the image-and-likeness conception, keeping the loss of divine likeness in the foreground, defines a process of redemption. The first is always to be assumed in the second.

Although Bernard's early treatises do not engage in theological controversy—the abbot seems in this to be like Gregory the Great, resting comfortable in the conviction that all significant doctrinal matters had been settled in the patristic era—they are

highly organized arguments addressing fundamental questions.[79]
Awareness that *On Loving God* belongs to this literary setting and
to this stage of Saint Bernard's development may assist readers,
warmed in the glow of affective language, not to leave aside their
intellectual sensors. When the abbot of Clairvaux published this
book, he was in his late thirties. He had been an abbot already
for about twelve years, and was writing in the growing strength of
early maturity—making the only explicitly systematic approach of
his career to his single most important subject.


Before beginning my commentary, let me outline the treatise to
highlight its structure. (Parenthetical numbers refer to paragraphs
of the treatise.)

PART ONE: WHY AND HOW GOD SHOULD BE LOVED, RESPONSE TO CARDI-
NAL HAIMERIC (1–22)
I.  Why God should be loved (1–16)
    —Nothing is more just than loving God.
    A. The gifts of God to the human being as such (2–6)
    B. The gifts of God to Christians (1 and 7–15)
II. How God should be loved (16–22)
    —Nothing is more to one's advantage than loving God.
    A. God must be loved without measure (16).
    B. God must be loved for God's self (17).
    C. Yet, loving God is to our advantage (17).
       1. The nature of love
       2. The nature of human desire (18–21)
          —God alone fufills our natural desires (20–21).
    D. God's love precedes ours as its cause (22).

PART TWO: FOUR DEGREES OF LOVE (23–33)
I.   First Degree of Love: loving oneself for one's own sake (23–25)
     A. Carnal love (23)
        —Either growth or self-destruction
     B. Loving others, carnal social love (24)
        1. The needs of others, justice
        2. Your neighbor as yourself
           a) In God
           b) The necessity of loving God first (25)
II.  Second Degree of Love: loving God for one's own sake (26).
III. Third Degree of Love: loving God for God's sake (26).
     —The sweetness of God's love, experience
IV.  Fourth Degree of Love: loving oneself only for God's sake (27–33).
     A. Losing oneself in God (27)
     B. Deification: the human substance remains (28).
     C. The role of the body in this state (29–33)
        1. The fourth degree of love is not fully possible until the resurrection (29).
        2. Souls separated but awaiting the resurrection (30–33)
           a) The soul's desire for its separated body (30)
           b) The body as faithful partner (31–33)
              —Three phases of the body-soul relationship

PART THREE: COMPLEMENTARY ARGUMENTS, FROM A LETTER TO THE CARTHUSIANS (34–40)
I.   Three ways of relating to God (34)
     A. Loving God out of fear: servile love (34, 36)
     B. Loving God for a reward: mercenary love (34, 36)
     C. Loving God as God's child: filial love (34, 37)
II.  Love as universal law (35–38)
     A. Law of (for) God: 'God lives by a law' (35).
        —In God love is substantial: God is love.
     B. Law of the slave and mercenary: fear and cupidity (36)
        —Bondage of the will
     C. Law of the sons of God: love for God and neighbor (37)
     D. Charity's relation to the laws of fear and cupidity (38)
III. Recapitulation (39–40)
     A. Four degrees of loving God (39)
     B. Heaven: 'Nobody there knows himself according to the flesh' (40).
        —Charity's net pulled onto the shore of eternity

PART ONE

ON LOVING GOD:

WHY AND HOW GOD SHOULD BE LOVED (1–22)

*On Loving God* may be conveniently considered as falling into three parts, though no such division is found in the manuscripts. First, an answer to Haimeric's questions, why and how God is to be loved; second, a development of four degrees of loving God—a further elaboration of the quesion of how God is to be loved; and third, arguments that complement the case made to that point, taken from letter 11 to the Carthusians. (See An Outline of *On Loving God*, pp. 66–67).

Bernard begins part one (1–22), by saying that THE REASON (*causa*) FOR LOVING GOD IS GOD (1), and that the measure, or manner, of loving God is without measure.[80] This would be a sufficient answer for the wise, but for the unwise (*insipientibus*), those who have not experienced this to be true, the writer must try to build a case—even though his evaluation of this kind of reflection is that it will add profusion rather than profundity (*profusius quam profundius*) to the truth. To the extent that one loves God, there is *sapor*, the experience of taste, rather than the *quaestio* of a treatise. The profundity of Bernard's tract must never allow readers to lose sight of the mindset to which he addresses it: it is aimed at beginners, the unwise; in fact, the spiritually slow-witted (*tardiores*). In blunt charity, the author must inform those who ask for reasons that, in attempting to communicate with them—standing as they do outside the love relationship—he must disavow his answer in advance, for one cannot represent the mystery of God's incredible love from the perspective of human need. An anthropological legitimation of christian faith is never adequate. We simply love as we are loved; love's *causa* is God. That Bernard does commit himself to the labor of communication can only be out of compassion for the hesitant human lover—out of a desire to remove fears that the gift of self may become the loss of self.

Love's *causa* has a felicitous double meaning: in this early part of the work, it refers to the motive or reason for loving God; but when the discussion turns to the four degrees of love (23–33), with preparatory reflections on prevenient grace (21–22), this *causa*, which is God, will be pronounced THE EFFICIENT AND FINAL CAUSE

OF OUR LOVE (22)—in an explicit recall of this original statement that the *causa* of loving God is God.[81] In the concept of God as cause, all the parts of the treatise are bonded. Should someone take *love* to mean a human attitude, then, as the latin title *De diligendo Deo* (Concerning God to be Loved) declares, the topic of the work is not love but God.[82]

At the same time, readers will not fail to take account of some early clues regarding the method of the author, who will later declare that love is a natural passion (see our discussion on 'natural affection' at paragraph 23). The method does not always conform to his protestations. He has undertaken to write about the 'reason' for loving God. The double-edged *causa* with which he responds to *quare* (why) allows him to discuss, at a surface level, what human consciousness grasps as motive, and, at a deeper level, God's action in the world—that true 'cause' with which the true 'reason' must, in the end, coincide. The coincidence is discovered only as love matures. His choice of the category *causa*— not as inevitable as Bernard has made it seem—allows him safely to explore the phenomenology of religious development without placing in jeopardy a reader's understanding of the agency of divine grace. In several parts of the text, he will reason his way through the world of human motivation and experience in what we have called a philosophical manner.

Moving on to the creation of his argument, Bernard finds two reasons why God should be loved for God's self: NO ONE CAN BE LOVED MORE JUSTLY, AND NO ONE CAN BE LOVED WITH GREATER BENEFIT (1).[83] The first reason is developed largely in the answer to *why* God should be loved (1–16), and the second (contrary to the plan Bernard seems to announce here) in the next answer, to *how* God should be loved (17–22).

That God merits our love is seen first in God's gift of the Saviour (1). This is the gift of God's *self*: HE GAVE HIMSELF TO US (1).[84] The assertion is echoed continually (paragraphs 7 through 15), until Bernard concludes that, having received God's self, I owe God myself. The polarity of self and God is established at the start. The contents of the treatise will be hinged to this. Here we find only an introductory development on the theme of God's self-gift. The author employs ardent poetic and biblical language and makes clear the position from which he functions: his 'reason' for loving God is Christ, the witness to God's self-giving love and the gift itself.

After one paragraph he breaks off, backtracking to a more elementary idea and creating the occasion for presenting the rudiments of a theological anthropology. Even those who do not know Christ, he says, can see God's gifts—in bread, sun, and air, or in our nobler gifts of dignity, knowledge, and virtue (2). The reason of easiest access which men and women have for loving God is that all persons preserve a sense of indebtedness; all are aware of their status as receivers. The author insists upon the inevitability of this in a properly functioning mind, upon its sheer rationality.[85]

The first topic to be elaborated, then, is the human situation in the world. Bernard's language becomes sober and analytic. Consider

> MAN'S NOBLER GIFTS—DIGNITY, KNOWLEDGE, AND VIRTUE: . . . MAN'S DIGNITY IS HIS FREE CHOICE (*liberum arbitrium*). . . . HIS KNOWLEDGE IS THAT BY WHICH HE ACKNOWLEDGES THAT THIS DIGNITY IS IN HIM BUT THAT IT IS NOT OF HIS OWN MAKING. VIRTUE IS THAT BY WHICH MAN SEEKS CONTINUOUSLY AND EAGERLY FOR HIS MAKER(2).[86]

Dignity, knowledge and virtue are in the soul. But, despite the *corpus-anima* terminology of these sentences, we cannot conclude that Bernard means that the seat of our higher gifts is the animating principle of the body. Elsewhere he will situate *liberum arbitrium* in the *mens*, as contrasted to *caro*—an augustinian dichotomy closer to the biblical notions of spirit and flesh.[87]

In the patristic era, the *mens* had been understood as the higher part of the soul; it was volitional as well as rational. Augustine granted preeminence to the intellectual element—*ratio, mens, intelligentia*.[88] In *On Loving God*, Bernard declared instead, 'Man's dignity is his free choice' (2). Bernard's stress on free choice, however, does not represent the degree of difference from Augustine that one might at first suppose. The two views are, in a sense, complementary.[89] Bernard could speak of free choice— '*free* referring to the will, *choice* to the reason' (Gra 3.6)—as 'the eye of the soul . . . arbiter in discerning and free in choosing', even as Augustine (in situating the divine image in the human person) had at times underlined freedom.[90] McGinn is right in concluding that, although 'Bernard did not lack for predecessors who had stressed human freedom as the true location of the *imago Dei* [human *dignitas* in our treatise] . . . his own understanding of this was conditioned by the role that love played' in his life and thought.[91] In the context of history, the abbot's opinion that *liberum arbitrium* is the very dignity of the human being is significant.

Dignity is the first among God's three 'nobler gifts' to the human being.[92] EACH OF THESE THREE GIFTS HAS TWO ASPECTS (3).[93] On the one hand, since they are what we *are*, they are natural; on the other hand, each of them is supplied by God and must be seen as grace (though at this juncture Bernard does not use a nature-grace terminology). To have the gifts while not recognizing their source is to have a certain glory, BUT NOT BEFORE GOD (3).[94] In the double aspect of these gifts we particularly see the character of their mutual dependence; for example, in knowledge we understand our dignity, and in virtue we not only inquire after God but reach God: WE ADHERE TO HIM SO CLOSELY WE BECOME INSEPARABLE FROM HIM (3).[95]

Toward the end of his life, Saint Bernard was to make an even clearer statement of this double aspect of God's essential gifts to human nature and of the mutual dependence of his three gifts. As his example he took knowledge from that underside of what he speaks of as essentially human. He writes of reason, of the relationship between reason and the virtue or strength by which it achieves its true end:

> You have need of strength (*virtute*), and not simply strength, but strength drawn from above. For this strength, if it is perfect, will easily give the mind (*animum*) control of itself, and so it will be unconquered before all its adversaries. It is a strength of mind which, in protecting reason (*ratione*), does not know how to retreat. Or, if you like, it is the strength of mind standing steadfast with reason and for reason. Or again, it is a strength of mind which gathers up and directs everything towards reason.[96]

In creation, then, God gives us knowledge directed to and open to the divine, and in a continuing assistance God freely gives the strength, or virtue, needed to achieve this end. After sin, our need is greater; our very mind needs to gain 'control of itself'; reason needs to be protected.

The knowledge God breaks in upon us first as self-knowledge. THERE ARE TWO FACTS YOU SHOULD KNOW: FIRST, WHAT YOU ARE; SECOND, THAT YOU ARE NOT THAT BY YOUR OWN POWER, LEST YOU FAIL TO BOAST AT ALL OR DO SO IN VAIN (4).[97] This self-knowledge, so prominent in the abbot's works—so easily misinterpreted as the self-help, self-absorption of an introspective disposition—is presented here as an extended gloss on God's gifts. It is one of the three gifts that constitute a human being as such. As something received, the self-knowledge of the spiritual person is an essentially passive condition. As the treatise traces God's action in the soul, all religious experience will assume the guise of self-knowledge, a recognition of what is happening to us and an identification of our benefactor and lover. More and more we will possess the knowledge that what we 'are' we are not by our own 'power'. Even our DIGNITY WITHOUT KNOWLEDGE IS UNPROFITABLE (3).[98] Tragedy for human beings lies either in not recognizing their dignity and living like animals, or vainly glorying in that dignity and living like demons. But to live as a human being (*homo*) one needs virtue, which is given by God (5).

Discovering, therefore, in natural law itself (*per legem naturalem . . . moneri*) that they receive all that they are, human beings— even those who do not know Christ—ought to love God for God's own sake.

> WHO CAN BE SO IMPIOUS AS TO THINK THAT THE AUTHOR OF THE HUMAN DIGNITY WHICH SHINES IN HIS SOUL IS ANY OTHER THAN HE WHO SAYS IN THE BOOK OF GENESIS: 'LET US MAKE MAN TO OUR OWN IMAGE AND LIKENESS'? (6)[99]

Human beings may not know Christ, but they know themselves (*etsi nesciat Christum, scit tamen seipsum*). AN INNATE JUSTICE, NOT UNKNOWN TO REASON, CRIES INTERIORLY TO MAN THAT HE OUGHT TO LOVE WITH HIS WHOLE BEING THE ONE TO WHOM HE OWES ALL THAT HE IS (6).[100] Nevertheless, since their feelings and thoughts are inclined to evil (Gen 8:21), ALL SEEK WHAT IS THEIR OWN (6). This pauline phrase, *quaerere quae sua sunt* (Phil 2:21), more than any other words of Scripture, functions as Bernard's characterization of a self that keeps God at bay.

The reader cannot fail to notice the sudden collapse in Bernard's concluding utterance. As he leaves his discussion of the position of infidels, he remarks,

NEVERTHELESS, IT IS DIFFICULT|IMPOSSIBLE, IN FACT|FOR ANYONE, EVEN BY THE NATIVE POWERS OF HIS FREE CHOICE, TO CONVERT HIMSELF COMPLETELY TO THE WILL OF GOD RATHER THAN TO TWIST HIMSELF TO HIS OWN WILL, RECEIVED FROM GOD, AND HOLD TO IT AS TO SOMETHING TRULY HIS OWN (6).[101]

However essential this assertion is as doctrinal qualification of the abbot's subject, it is not a change in direction: the point of the discussion has been human nature's orientation to God. This remains true even for someone who does not know Christ.

Bernard's 'infidels' are those who do not know Christ. Although in the Christendom of Bernard's era it was not conventional to use magnanimous language in regard to non-Christians, we should not misread these texts. The author writes, with respect to the christian mysteries, 'If these things remain hidden from infidels, it is easy for God, with his innumerable benefactions, to confuse those who are not thankful'.[102]

The curious literary manner of this sentence invites reflection. If one speaks of a lack of gratitude in those who have been given no knowledge of their benefactor, one speaks of a fault in a merely material sense.[103] Yet, Bernard has God strike them, so to speak, 'with his innumerable benefactions'. This is an action of divine love, yet, one that allows the recipients to remain in the confusion that such good fortune causes. Those who do not know what the world has been given are left without an explanation (faith as noetic) for the wonder of human existence; and, as the text will suggest, they lack a special knowledge to assist them in the common human effort to avoid claiming as their own (*ad propriam retorquere*) what is given by God. Obviously, Bernard is attempting in these words the christian mind's identification of its own special blessing. The nature of this blessing of christian faith is discovered in the fact that those who lack it may yet love God with all their hearts. EVERYONE, THEREFORE, EVEN THE INFIDEL, the author writes,

IS INEXCUSABLE IF HE FAILS TO LOVE THE LORD HIS GOD WITH ALL HIS HEART, ALL HIS SOUL, ALL HIS MIGHT (6).[104]

Although indirectly, Bernard explains why infidels have this responsibility for loving God totally. The entire treatment of the text is a reminiscence of Rom 1 and 2, where Paul writes of the unevangelized gentiles who do not keep God's law. The infidel is obliged to love God because he is INFORMED BY NATURAL LAW, and because AN INNATE JUSTICE, NOT UNKNOWN TO REASON, CRIES INTERIORLY TO HIM (6).[105] The 'natural law' the author cites cannot be simply the ethical norm by which we know right from wrong. In this context, what we discover in the essential human gifts under discussion, and its message is that all are OBLIGED TO LOVE GOD FOR HIS OWN SAKE (6).[106] This 'natural law' is really the universal and eternal law of love which is expounded in the letter to the Carthusians appended to the treatise (35–38). The 'innate justice not unknown to reason' cannot be reason alone, therefore—at least not in the narrow sense of a later literature—because what is declared by this justice is THAT HE [the infidel] OUGHT TO LOVE WITH HIS WHOLE BEING THE ONE TO WHOM HE OWES ALL THAT HE IS (6).[107]

Saint Bernard did not address the problem of defining *faith* more broadly than 'christian' faith. But the meditation he makes here forces on us the reflection that what he describes as the eternal destiny of all human beings presumes an ultimate faith. His argument is not really the same as that of Rom 1 and 2, where Paul holds gentiles responsible for their bad morals in so far as they might have known God's law 'in the things that have been made'. Bernard holds infidels responsible, instead, TO LOVE GOD FOR HIS OWN SAKE (6)[108]—a love which he will speak of as the third degree (26), the highest he believes that can be stably attained in this life (39). Denis Farkasfalvy has noticed that Bernard never attributes to human beings the possibility of knowing the significance of the created world and arriving *in concreto* at a true knowledge of God without conversion. To know God in any way other than as loving and lovable is to know an idol: *facit sibi idolum pro eo quod non est* (SC 38.2).[109] Bernard's *infideles*, therefore—among them those who love God—are people of faith. When they are contrasted with the *fideles* (7), the latter are believers in Christ. We shall see that this observation has some importance in preserving the central insights of *De diligendo Deo*.

The treatise speaks much about what we can know from God's gifts. Does it suggest thereby that the knowledge of God precedes the love of God? More than anywhere else, Bernard here speaks of the knowledge of God in seeming separation from the love of God, somewhat in the manner of a philosopher's appeal to reason alone. Yet, when we notice the extent to which this knowledge of God's gifts is kept within the context of self-knowledge, we realize that the author is not marking off human rationality as a preliminary to religious experience but integrating it into this experience. The 'innate justice' which calls someone to love God is 'not unknown to reason'; the apprehension of this justice, then, *includes* reason. The claim that to know oneself (*etsi nesciat Christum, scit tamen seipsum*) is to be placed in the moral necessity of loving God can stand only on the perception of that divine presence within the human being explained as God's image. Bernard has less to say of that in *On Loving God* than in any of his extended works that follow. But there is sufficient information on the character of the knowledge spoken of to make clear that the knowing subject is not an observer but one who, in the subjection of faith, responds to the concrete God. This is the Bernard for whom the light by which we see God will always be love. He did not believe that the knowledge of God can arise from any other act than one which engages the whole person as an act of love; that is to say, we know God concretely (which is Bernard's meaning) only in religious experience and only within a context of conversion. The flourishing dialectics of our treatise must not lead us into mistaken notions of Bernard's sense of the function of reason or of the nature of human knowing.

After his initial survey of the situation of the infidel (2–6), Bernard turns to a comparison: THE FAITHFUL, ON THE CONTRARY, KNOW HOW TOTALLY THEY NEED JESUS AND HIM CRUCIFIED (7).[110] He speaks of the faithful as such, not as the identifiable population of Christendom. Those who realize they are more loved will more easily love. As the writer enters this second topic, the pace of the argument slows, his language becomes markedly more lyrical and recaptures the warmth of his first paragraph. Reminiscences from the Song of Songs and the psalms are blended with images of the passion of Christ. The soul longs for the visit of the Bridegroom (7,9,10): CUSHION ME ABOUT WITH FLOWERS, PILE UP APPLES AROUND ME, FOR I LANGUISH WITH LOVE (7).[111] Planting a motif which will flower late in the work, Bernard writes that the bride expects the fruit of the Resurrection only at the future general resurrection (8), when Christ returns FOR OUR FULFILLMENT (9), *ad consummationem nostram.*

This consummation will be the perfect love of God, complete unity with God in eternal glory. In the context of the introduction to this section—'The faithful, on the contrary', (7)—this suggests that true 'fulfillment' of the human being is not what the *infideles* are capable of envisioning, although it is the end of a process in which they feel themselves caught up. Bernard's treatise defines the process. In the concept of *consummatio* there is an affecting appeal to the logic that the happiest state of affairs lies in things finally becoming what, along the way, they potentially *are.* Since the idea is in great vogue today, we might underline its attractiveness to Bernard.

His first statement of it (9) situates *consummatio* within the faith. The next occurrence plays *consummo* (to sum up, to perfect, to complete) against *consumo* (to take, to consume, to waste, to annihilate): the lives of the wicked are NOT CONSUMMATED [completed] IN A BLESSED END BUT CONSUMED [wasted] IN EMPTY STRIVING; and this is because they fail to see their destiny as CONSUMMATION RATHER THAN CONSUMPTION (19).[112] The word-play underlines the difference between a transcendent becoming and a futile self-aggrandisement. The self-reliant drive to develop possibilities of an illusory self ends in a wasted life. God alone, the abbot insists, CONSUMMATES [fulfills, completes] OUR DESIRE (22).[113] The paragraph concludes with an opening onto a four-step description of the process: LET US NOW SEE WHERE OUR LOVE BEGINS, FOR IT HAS BEEN SHOWN WHERE IT ENDS (*ubi consummetur*) (22).[114] Later, in the recapitulation of the whole process, OUR LOVE ADVANCES . . . UNTIL IT IS CONSUMMATED IN THE SPIRIT (39).[115] A quite literal rendering of Bernard's *consummatio,* both lexically and contextually, is *fulfillment,* a fact made the more interesting by the ambiguities latent in a certain ideological vision of *self*-fulfillment at which Bernard hints.[116]

Closely related to the author's concept of human fulfillment is the question of when such a fulfillment can be expected to be complete. Although the theme does not move to the foreground until paragraph 30, already at this early stage of the treatise we read that the fruit of a Christian life will come forth IN THE END AT THE FUTURE GENERAL RESURRECTION (8), and that the risen Christ WILL SOME DAY RETURN FOR OUR FULFILLMENT (9).[117]

To some Christians there are problems attaching to any conceptualizing of humanity's destiny in God as a fulfillment, the satisfying of human desire, and we cannot pretend to lay these questions to rest with one or another tidy distinction. But, since views of the human end are tied to views of its beginning, we may postpone an evaluation of Bernard's *fulfillment* until we have seen how he conceives the source of desire (21–22), the character of eros (17–21), and that *nature* underlying the 'natural affection' of which he will write (23–25).

Returning to the poetic incantation on the flowers of the bridal couch (8), we note the statement, THE HEAVENLY BRIDEGROOM . . . ENTERS WILLINGLY AND OFTEN THE CHAMBER OF THE HEART (*cordis thalamum*) HE FINDS DECKED WITH THESE FLOWERS AND FRUITS (8).[118] The divine Word's visit to the diligent contemplative soul will occupy a large part of Bernard's masterwork, *On the Song of Songs*.[119] Here, however, the focus is on the irresistible lovableness of God, known in Christ. This Bridegroom wishes to find in the chamber of the heart LAST YEARS'S FRUIT (8) and THIS YEAR'S FLOWERS (8)—tokens of the passion and signs of the general resurrection—i.e., a spirit possessed of the kind of *memoria* that Bernard will explain in the following paragraphs (10–13).

Until we reach our fulfillment in the risen Christ, we have memory: MEMORY IS FOR THE CONTINUING AGES, PRESENCE IS FOR THE KINGDOM OF HEAVEN (10).[120] Bernard dedicates a long unit to memory (10–13). The faithful may delight in remembering eternity (*recordatio illos delectet aeternitatis*).[121] MEMORY IS A PLEASURE FOR THOSE WHO SEEK AND LONG FOR GOD'S PRESENCE (10).[122] At the same time, the memory of the passion is necessary if we are to glory in the cross and to experience (*probare*) that the Lord is sweet (12). Memory generates hope, a confidence arising out of both a hallowed past and a treasured promise. This memory which looks both ways in time, is seen in the figure of the Bridegroom's embrace: HIS LEFT HAND IS UNDER MY HEAD AND HIS RIGHT HAND EMBRACES ME (10).[123] The left arm, on which the spouse rests her head, LEST IT SHOULD BE BENT DOWN (*incurvetur*) AND INCLINED TO CARNAL AND WORLDLY DESIRES, is the awareness of Christ's continuous victory over all spiritual heaviness in the human condition; and Bernard refers to this heaviness as the body (13).[124] The right arm is the promised union in eternity. The activating force of this memory is the Holy Spirit: THE PARACLETE . . . WILL TEACH YOU ALL THINGS AND WILL MAKE YOU REMEMBER ALL I HAVE SAID TO YOU (13).[125]

Clearly Bernard does not see the divine Spouse's presence as reserved for a future life. The devout soul can collect, not only 'last year's fruit' (the tokens of the Passion), but also 'this year's flowers' (9)—i.e., moments in that awareness of the risen Christ which faith makes possible. These flowers of meditation strewn about the soul are a condition for receiving frequent visits from the Bridgroom.

Developing this idea of Christ's presence to us, the author appeals to the New Testament image of eating the Lord's body, but in a manner less familiar to today's readers than that of the sacramental piety of a later era. He refers to Jn 6:55: WHOEVER EATS MY FLESH AND DRINKS MY BLOOD HAS LIFE EVERLASTING (11), and, in his long paragraph of explanation, elaborates a meaning that does not explicitly include the Eucharist: WHOEVER MEDITATES ON MY DEATH AND, FOLLOWING MY EXAMPLE, MORTIFIES HIS MEMBERS, WHICH BELONG TO THIS EARTH [Col 3:5], HAS ETERNAL LIFE (11).[126] Never questioning the real presence in the sacrament of the altar, Bernard was intent on cultivating a readiness for the presence of the Word through meditative and ascetical preparations for the unmerited 'visit' of the Bridegroom in contemplation. The passage is neither incidental nor exceptional but typical of Saint Bernard.[127] In his mind, the sacramental presence of Christ was to be distinguished from the high possibilities of the Word's presence to human awareness (in Bernard's integrative sense). Inevitably, this conviction emerges in a pericope on the *memoria Christi*.

Jean Leclercq underlines the moral intent in this treatment of what exegetes generally consider eucharistic allusions in the New Testament: in the abbot's view, he believes, Christ is both *exemplum* and *sacramentum;* if the faithful separate imitation of Christ from the sacramental mystery, there can be no divine union.[128] We will return to this subject in connection with the 'triple banquet' of paragraph 33.

Most of his treatment of God's gifts to the faithful is presented in the imagery of the Song of Songs 2:5, flowers and fruit (7–13). What does this apparently extravagant literary approach accomplish? The writer contrasts the consciousness of the human being as such (2–6) with that of the faithful, those who have a memory of the passion of Christ (7–15). The first he presents in the analytic manner which he will resume at the heart of the treatise in discussing the four degrees of love; the second, with an exuberant lyricism. He finds in the flowers and fruit of the Song an image pattern in which several postulates of the Christian life coalesce. First, there is the playful irony of prevenient grace: the human being tries to win the attention of its divine Lover with flowers—NOT BY HER OWN MERITS, BUT WITH FLOWERS PICKED IN THE FIELDS THE LORD HAS BLESSED (8).[129] Since flowers are to fruit as promise is to fulfillment, the encounter with the God who loves will be complete only in the fruit of the general resurrection (8). Gathering flowers and resting on flowers represent the absence of care and the quiet of contemplation. These are a few indications; an analytic precis of the full meaning which Bernard demonstrably intends in his imagery is rarely possible. In the present context what is projected is the contrast between a placid acceptance of all dimensions of this rich meaning and the poverty and rational struggle of the human being who lacks the *memoria Christi.*

Bernard concludes his answer to the question why God should be loved by recapitulating his comparisons between the situation of those who know Christ with those who do not (14–15). Those lacking faith in Christ cannot know either the Father or the Holy Spirit; and they love less what they know less. But, since all they are aware of having is known to be from God (*sui totius . . . auctorem*), they know that all is due to God. Reason urges total love of God. Faith, on the other hand, can only sing in astonishment at what it sees of God's goodness. The most compelling reason why God should be loved is God's self-gift in Christ. Anticipating his most graphic development of the God-and-self polarity, in the four degrees of love, Bernard concludes: WHEN HE GAVE ME HIMSELF, HE GAVE ME BACK MYSELF (*Ubi se dedit, me mihi reddidit*) (15). The distinction between a true and false self derives from the concept of the human being made, as Bernard said (6), in the image and likeness of God. The self-gift of God in Christ is the revelation of true human nature. In Christ we find the model and the empowerment for the restoration of humanity. The author's concrete way of saying this results in powerful poetry.

We must acknowledge, then, that God merits our love; but, when we consider how God merits it, we are overwhelmed. TO WHOM IS THE DEGREE OF THIS MERIT CLEAR? (16)[130]

LET US NOW SEE TO WHAT ADVANTAGE OF OURS (*quo nostro commodo*) GOD IS TO BE LOVED (17).[131] The author marvels at how far from reality is our vision of our own advantage![132] He continues: GOD IS NOT LOVED WITHOUT A REWARD, ALTHOUGH GOD SHOULD BE LOVED WITHOUT REGARD FOR ONE (17).[133] This distinction introduces a series of observations, seemingly on the nature of love, where *caritas* and *amor* are used interchangeably.[134]

> IN LOVE (*caritas*) THERE IS ATTRACTION (*affectus*), NOT A CON-
> TRACT. LOVE DOES NOT DRAW UP A PACT NOR CAN IT BE DRAWN
> FROM ONE. IT MOVES OF ITSELF AND ALLOWS ONE TO ACT OF ONE-
> SELF (*spontaneum*). TRUE LOVE (*amor*) IS CONTENT WITH ITSELF: IT
> HAS A REWARD IN WHAT IT LOVES. FOR, REGARDLESS OF WHAT YOU
> MAY SEEM TO LOVE BECAUSE OF SOMETHING OTHER THAN ITSELF,
> WHAT YOU LOVE IS THAT TO WHICH YOUR LOVE FINALLY TENDS,
> NOT THAT THROUGH WHICH IT TENDS (17).[135]

Even for readers not anxious about scholarly precision, some problems of translation require urgent attention here. Our concern is not with an academic refinement but with fundamentals.

Does Bernard mean to define charity—his word is *caritas*—merely as the experience of 'attraction'? Does 'attraction' truly translate his term *affectus*? First of all, it should be clear from the context that the author's intention is to offer, not a definition of the soul's love for God, but of some of love's characteristics. True, he calls love *caritas*; but, when we observe that in the following

lines the word immediately changes to *amor*, that in the fuller
analysis of love's four-stage progression (23 ff.) it becomes *affectio,*
and that in his recapitulation of the process (32) he calls it *cupiditas* (*cupiditas vel amor noster*), we are sure that Bernard does not
use *caritas* here in the same way—in the same technical sense, we
may say—as we find it in 1 Jn 4:10 ('In this is love, not that we
loved God but that he loved us'). What he points to in love is an
element which he refuses to identify with those movements of the
soul that issue from calculations of personal benefit, from logic,
duty, or obligation. Loving God *is* of personal benefit; it *is* our
duty; but, in these dimensions it cannot be properly explained,
for neither advantage nor obligation can extract it. Love moves to
its object only because of the object. Love is, indeed, a decision of
the will, an act of freedom; but, the volitional cannot be what the
author singles out here as he *contrasts* this to a transaction and to a
pact (*contractus . . . pacto*), both of which are eminently volitional.
When, among his many remarks, he states that love moves of
itself (*sponte*) and makes one spontaneous (*spontaneum*), he asserts
that love is not compelled from without; but, if he wished to say
nothing more than that love was an act of the will, this would be
a strange and novel formulation. All told, the quality he points
to is the natural leaning of the subject toward the object of love,
or something in the object which accounts for this experience of
being drawn.

What word does he choose to indicate this characteristic? Love,
he says, is *affectus,* the term that refers to a personal state produced by some influence. This state comprises the action of the
will together with feelings and emotions, or what we now call
affective movements—i.e., the entire response of personality to
that which affects it. We have no modern-language equivalent for
this, and scholars intent on sketching Saint Bernard's spirituality
have rightly insisted that the *affectus* or *affectio* which we find
in his writings is not to be misread as mere sentiment. On the
other hand, we cannot indicate what Bernard means in a specific
context by invariably translating the word *affectus* in such a way as
to preserve the role of the will—at the cost of all other dimensions
of *affectus*—because we cannot emphasize one of the components
of this category while passively including the others—as Bernard

does. We must, then, survey this paragraph (17) looking for indications of that element in *affectus* which receives the writer's special attention.

The paragraph develops the proposition that the reward for loving God is God; what is said about the nature of love serves that idea. The author compares THE UNWILLING, the *invitos* (17), those who need to be lured with rewards, to those who have no such need—THE SPONTANEOUS, *spontaneos* (translated narrowly by Walton as THOSE WHO ARE WILLING): the love of such spontaneous persons is, he says, like the appetite of the hungry, the thirst of the thirsty, the attachment of a mother, or the material concerns of vintners and householders. In this instance, affectivity is not simply included with the will in Bernard's *affectus*; affectivity is emphasized. We drop all hesitation about this as we continue on into paragraph 18 and find the proposition developed through reflections on human desire.

If the mismatch of languages forces us to choose the least inadequate word for *affectus*, we should choose here 'attraction'. To a translator's grief, the word is not sufficiently inclusive: 'attraction' seems to leave out the *will* of THE SPONTANEOUS (17). (Translators of Saint Bernard always read over the entrance to their project, 'Choose your heresy'.) The quality the author points to is the natural leaning of the subject toward the object of love, or something in the object which accounts for this experience of being drawn.[136] Here the reader may have to reflect that the lover experiences a pull upon all faculties. While safeguarding the irreducibility of human freedom, we may say that the will too suffers an inclination. Even so, we are aware that our language itself is the crystalization of a psychology alien to Bernard's (see the discussion at paragraph 23) and that we must set our imprecise formulations into a context that will rectify them.

Could we avoid the danger of misunderstanding by reading [*caritas*] *affectus est* as 'love is a decision' or, with Walton, 'love pertains to the will'? With this we would say something safely orthodox, even something profound—but something which would be deliberately deaf to the rhetorical development of the paragraph, passing over the starting point of Bernard's psychology and, accordingly, missing the direction or intentionality of his thought. Increasing familiarity with this treatise will show that nothing is more crucial to its understanding than ascertaining the point of departure for the author's concept of growth in love.

We conclude that a disciplined paraphrase of [*caritas* ] *affectus est* may come closest to the author's meaning. We read, IN LOVE THERE IS ATTRACTION (17).[137]

When Bernard becomes more explicit about his starting point, in his exposition of four stages of love, he will virtually repeat this assertion, in the words LOVE IS NATURAL AFFECTION—or, as we will translate his sentence in its new context, LOVE IS ONE OF THE FOUR NATURAL PASSIONS, *Amor est affectio naturalis una de quattuor* (23). This *affectio* will re-introduce the language problem we have seen in *affectus*[138] and at that point we will offer further clarifications.

It would be unfortunate if, caught up in the difficulty we have discussed, we missed the beauty of paragraph 17. The thought is developed in an epigrammatic manner, with brilliant rhetorical clarity and force. It is an example of the philosophical strength we have spoken of: Bernard discloses the rationality of what he has both traditionally received and personally experienced. He explicates the thesis with which he opened the treatise: THE REA-SON FOR LOVING GOD IS GOD (1). His analysis of it can hardly be improved upon, for by implication he draws atention to the fallacy in conventional thinking about the reason or motive of love—i.e., the assumption, difficult to uncover, that this is something other than the very object of love. Unless this assumption is abandoned, all love must prove a delusion.[139]

Thomas Merton argued, plausibly, that the text referred not to the *object* of love as the lover's reward but, in a surprisingly existential way, to love itself; he translates *Habet praemium, sed id quod amatur* (17) as 'The reward is in the fact that love is exercised'. His understanding of Bernard's meaning is set in this paraphrase: 'The dynamic of love contains within itself sufficient reason for its existence and is its own fulfilment, because God is love and when we love we are living as He lives, we are like Him, we are participating in His inner life'.[140] This view has the significant advantage of further clarifying the argument that even the lowest levels of love—e.g., Bernard's first and second degrees, below (23–26)—can be the love of 'God'.

That love moves to its 'object' invites from Bernard a lengthy philosophical reflection on the nature of human desire (18–21). As the biblical allusions diminish, his thought takes on a dialectical shading.[141]

> WITHIN EVERY RATIONAL BEING THERE IS A NATURAL AND PEREN-
> NIAL DESIRE TO HAVE WHAT COMES CLOSEST TO SATISFYING ITS
> MIND AND WILL, AND NEVER TO REST CONTENT WITH ANYTHING
> TO WHICH SOMETHING ELSE MIGHT BE PREFERRED (18).[142]

The key verbs in the paragraph (18) are *appetere* and *concupiscere*; the *summum* or *optimum* that is sought is simply the satisfaction of *appetitus.*

After giving many illustrations, Bernard remarks, BY THE VERY LAW OF MAN'S DESIRE, WHICH MAKES HIM WANT WHAT HE LACKS . . . HE WILL HASTEN TOWARD THE ONLY ONE WHO IS MISSING, THE GOD OF ALL (19).[143] The abbot, however, delays his insistence upon a turn to God. He concludes the paragraph wryly: SO, AS I SAID, WHOEVER DESIRES THE GREATEST GOOD (*id quod optimum est*) CAN SUCCEED IN REACHING IT, IF HE CAN FIRST GAIN POSSESSION OF ALL HE DESIRES SHORT OF THAT GOOD ITSELF (19).[144]

Life is too short for that (20). Human beings are possessed not only of sense (*sensus*), but of spirit (*animus*). They are capable of foreseeing the futility of following the law of desire. They suffer frustration because they receive their soul (*hoc est animam ratio-nalem*) in vain, allowing reason to lie idle. A TWISTING ROAD AND AN ENDLESS ROUTE IS THIS WILL TO EXPERIENCE ALL THINGS (20).[145]

The theory Bernard will later offer to account for what he describes in this work as our insatiable desire is that, in its very creation, the soul is like God and hungers for God: 'There is such a relatedness of natures that one (the *Verbum*) is the Image and the other is made in the image'.[146] Although our treatise restricts itself more to the sheer data of experience, the concept of human 'nature' it reveals calls out for this lofty explanation.

The twisting road of desire is not followed by the just. THEY TAKE A SALUTARY SHORT-CUT AND AVOID THE DANGEROUS, FRUITLESS ROUND-ABOUT WAY, CHOOSING THE SHORTENED AND SHORTENING WORD (*verbum abbreviatum et abbrevians eligentes*). . . . (21).[147]

At this point we must pause, leaving the author's sentence incomplete, to take special notice of this seemingly incidental remark, set within the study of human desire and at the threshold of a new unit that will follow desire's laborious advance toward God. Enter this ascent of the four stages of love toward which I am moving, Bernard seems to say, but know from the start, first, that it is actually experienced as a labyrinth—a DANGEROUS, FRUITLESS, ROUND-ABOUT WAY (21)—and, second, that people of Christian faith do not take this course. In following Christ, the infinite Word made small in the Incarnation (*verbum abbreviatum*), they take a short-cut (*verbum . . . abbrevians*), a royal road, to their destination in God. About his concept of the disparate situations of Christians and *infideles*, the author could not be clearer. About the difference between his faith and this exercise in apologetics, he could not be more direct.

Again, we interrupt Bernard because this remark occurs in a paragraph (21) dedicated to another matter, justice. This *iustitia* faces two directions simultaneously in a thematically complicated paragraph. First, the just person has a characteristic attitude toward material things—to one side, detachment, and to the other, a recognition of the poor. Second, it is those who follow Christ who are the just (*Hi sunt qui . . .*). The reader finds coherence by inferring that, if JUSTICE IS THE VITAL, NATURAL FOOD OF THE RATIONAL SOUL (21) in general, then Christians in particular are just simply by the gracious ease of their short-cut (*verbum abbreviatum*)—SELLING ALL THEY HAVE AND GIVING IT TO THE POOR (Mt 19:21) (21).[148]

There is nothing complicated in the author's designation of those whose desire is governed by wisdom as 'the just'. Those who hunger for justice will be filled. Corporeal things and self-seeking attainments cannot quench the thirst of the spirit. The remark transposes into the language of rationality what the author knows more deeply: God is the satisfaction of human desire.

That indeed is a major conclusion of the treatise; and, as he restates the thought, Bernard locks it into an epigram which is the alpha and omega of his spirituality: HE MAKES YOU DESIRE, HE IS WHAT YOU DESIRE (21).[149] Both members of this declaration witness to a wisdom beyond human ken; they affirm the final answer, beyond philosophy, to all questions of the heart. Until this point, he has spoken of God as the end of human desire. He turns now and asks how this *desiderium* originates and develops, though in the maxim which marks the transition he has already provided the conclusion. He will trace the unfolding of desire in human experience as the progress of 'natural affection' (*affectio naturalis*) through four degrees (23–29). Faith's great testimony, 'He is what you desire', allows the author to name the process, from the start, four degrees of loving *God*; and faith as well has the first word on the source and cause of this desire: 'He makes you desire'. In the end is the beginning known—even though the end is not yet fully seen, not yet attained.

Bernard is careful to mark the entrance into his psychologizing account of the human advance toward God with a radiant christian *credo*. Paragraph 22, on prevenient grace, expands the thought; it is the touchstone of Christian understanding for all that follows.

Finished with his long examination of human desire and with his answer to the question how God is to be loved, Bernard is ready to turn to the second part of his treatise: the four degrees of loving God. His exposition of prevenient grace (22) emphasizes a principle already referred to in paragraphs 1 and 21.[150] The development is fitted into the paradoxical language with which he opened the treatise: 'God is the reason for loving God' (1). He repeats this, and follows with a succession of short sentences made up of balanced phrases in series, building a rhetorical tension which he will release in a concluding prayer. He has said that God is the reason or *causa* for loving God. This *causa* is now declared to be *efficiens et finalis*. His examples of this include an advance clarification of how our natural affection (which he will next trace through four degrees of transformation) relates to God and God's grace: God CREATES THE AFFECTION AND CONSUMMATES THE DESIRE (22).[151] The nature out of which these arise is graced at creation.

He has spoken of God as lovable. Now the assertion is: HE MAKES HIMSELF, OR RATHER HE HAS BEEN MADE, LOVABLE (22).[152] In this reflection on God's gracious action, Bernard is intrigued by the notion of God's *making*, and he will return to it (25). God is 'made', or 'has been made' to be loved (*ut amaretur*), not only in the sheer 'efficient' causality the abbot has referred to, but in the manifestation of God's lovableness. The reminiscence of the Word made flesh in John's Gospel (Jn 1:14) does not exhaust the meaning, for the treatise is here speaking of God simply. God 'makes' God lovable in the prevenient grace which causes human beings humanly to perceive the divine goodness.

HIS LOVE PREPARES AND REWARDS OUR OWN. [Compared to us] HE IS MORE CARING AS HE GOES BEFORE, MORE JUST AS HE RECOMPENSES, MORE PLEASANT (*suavior*) AS HE WAITS UPON US (22).[153] *Justice* is an unthreatening appeal to order and rationality. The writer, then, can exclaim, LORD, YOU ARE GOOD TO THE SOUL THAT SEEKS YOU. WHAT, THEN, TO THE ONE THAT FINDS YOU? (22)[154] The seek-and-find dialectic provides a model for prevenient grace:

> MORE WONDERFUL STILL, NO ONE CAN SEEK YOU WHO HAS NOT ALREADY FOUND YOU. YOU WISH TO BE FOUND THAT YOU MAY BE SOUGHT FOR, AND SOUGHT FOR THAT YOU MAY BE FOUND. YOU MAY BE SOUGHT AND FOUND, BUT IN THIS NO ACTION CAN PRECEDE YOUR OWN (22).[155]

Finally, balancing *oratio* and *inspiratio*, Bernard protests that every genuine prayer is incited by divine inspiration: LUKEWARM IS EVERY PRAYER THAT IS NOT PRECEDED BY INSPIRATION (22).[156] Here too it is by the specificity of the chosen word that he makes a theological point, however cursively: the redemptive act of *inspiration* is itself the work of the creative breath of God.[157] As he now turns to speak about what is *natural*, Bernard has prepared his meaning.

PART TWO

ON LOVING GOD:

FOUR DEGREES OF LOVING GOD (23–33)

In the second part of the treatise Bernard discusses four degrees of loving God. Earlier in the letter to the Carthusians (Dil 39) this schema appeared in a brief form which may be the abstract Bernard decided to develop here. He had a penchant for organizing his thought in precise numerical patterns. His collection of sermon sketches called *Sententiae* demonstrates this: 'The breasts of the spouse are two . . .' (1.9); 'The divine mercy is threefold . . .' (2.18); 'The windows of the contemplative are three . . .' (2.127); 'Four fountains irrigate the garden of God . . .' (2.128); 'The wings of the Seraphim are six . . .' (2.134); 'The divine mercy is threefold . . .'. (3.18)[158] Leclercq, seeing these sentences as notes either for projected sermons or from delivered sermons, comments that the conception of the abbot's discourses seems to occur in these sharp distinctions.[159] Although listing seems to be, in most instances, a rhetorical device for winning the attention or aiding the memory of listeners, the four degrees of divine love is an intensely analytic effort.[160]

LOVE, the author begins, IS ONE OF THE FOUR NATURAL PASSIONS, *Amor est affectio naturalis una de quattuor* (23).[161] In the Sermons on the Canticle, he will offer an illuminating image of these passions as four horses drawing 'the chariot of the mind':

> It [the soul] will gain force by struggling with itself and, becoming stronger, will impel all things towards reason: anger, fear, covetousness, and joy; like a good charioteer, it will control the chariot of the mind, bringing every carnal affect into captivity, and every sense under the control of reason in accordance with virtue.[162]

Covetousness (*cupiditas*) is, as we have seen, the word he uses later in the treatise as a near synonym for love, or *amor* (39). If we read 'in accordance with virtue' in the context of his remarks on virtue in paragraphs two and five, above, we will see how, in this late sermon (SC 85), the abbot's understanding of 'every carnal affect' (*affectus*) has the same meaning in the life of the spirit as the 'natural passions' (*affectio*) we are studying here.

It is not that Bernard was careless with terminology in his inter-changeable use of many words for love; it is rather that in his vision the several states of desire are energized, at a common source as he has explained (21–22), and their final meaning—their direction—is the same. This meaning in experience overrides other intel-lectual, and even moral, concerns. In some settings, then, we may have *amor* = *affectio* = *affectus* = *caritas* = *dilectio* = *cupiditas* = *desiderium*.

If the love of God begins in a *natural* disposition, it is possible to say, as the author does, that, like all nature, this disposition is directed, of itself, toward the Creator of nature. For that reason, *unde et dictum est*, to love God is the first of the commandments. In this *unde*, one notices, the treatise argues for the validity of the first commandment from its rationality.

### Discussion: 'natural affection' (*affectio naturalis*)

Further reading of the treatise will make clear that 'natural passion', *affectio naturalis*, is intended not as a definition of love but as one perspective from which love can be observed. Three others will be discussed: love as relationship (34), as substance (35), and as universal law (35–38). At the heart of the work, however, is *affectio naturalis*, a concept which, since the era of Scholasticism, eludes all our familiar anthropological categories (it is neither passion, attraction, affection, nor act of will) and which alone can account for most misunderstandings of Bernard's treatise. It is, the text implies, what a secular literary tradition meant by the *affectiones*—ONE OF THE FOUR (23)[163]—but, as the qualifying assertions accumulate with the transformation of *affectio*, we realize the writers of classical antiquity meant much less than this.

So much of Bernard's optimism about human nature shines through his concept of *affectio naturalis*—i.e., through its openness to transformation by grace—that it becomes necessary, not only to indicate what he meant by it and how he stressed its goodness, but also to demonstrate his awareness of those darker possibilities which he more frequently chose not to dwell on. These we find in paragraphs 34–36, taken from the letter to the Carthusians which Bernard appends to his treatise. The love of a slave and that of a hireling spring from fear and desire for gain—two *affectus* which he excludes from any part in charity. CHARITY, he writes, IS FOUND *ONLY* IN A SON (34).[164] It is that eternal law which must be contrasted to Paul's 'law of sin'. Later, in the *Super Cantica*, he will develop this meaning of *affectio*:

> There is an affection which the flesh begets, and one which reason controls, and one which wisdom seasons. . . . The first is pleasant, of course, but shameful; the second is emotionless (*sicca*) but strong; the last is rich and delightful. (SC 50.4)[165]

His manner of speaking of this first affection, *quam caro gignit*, follows explicitly Rom 8:7, where we read, 'The mind that is set on the flesh is hostile to God'. Our natural drives are seen in the context of 'the law of sin which dwells in my members' (Rom 7:23). Bernard contrasts this *amor vitiosus* with an affection governed by the *ratio fidei*, and with that experience of God which he calls *sapientia*. At bottom is an understanding of concupiscence which sees humanity's present weakened condition—where, as Bernard says, the *affectio* springing from the flesh (cf Rom 8:7) is sin, the result of sin, and the danger of further sin.[166]

We must not press too hard. Bernard does not make a doctrinal statement in these passages, saying that concupiscence *is* sin, but, his adjectives (e.g., *turpis, vitiosus*) suggest he conforms to that side of Augustine's reading of Paul where concupiscence is strongly bonded to sin. Even more, the antithetical rhetoric leads to that conclusion; SC 50.4, quoted above, for example, contrasts *affectio* as found in *caritas affectualis* with carnal self-indulgence. What Bernard says of the concupiscence of *caro* must be understood within its context. Not all examples are as simple as that of SC 20.9, where the sinful nature of *vita carnalis* is clearly indicated: 'This carnal love [of Christ] is good, because through it the carnal life [*vita carnalis*] is excluded and despised, and the world is evercome'.[167]

Such a meaning for *affectio naturalis* offers no promise for an elaboration of the four-degrees schema of our treatise. But, another point of view is possible, one in which the natural movements of the psyche are seen as not in themselves sinful and, just as importantly, as open to being set in order by divine grace. In their disordered state resulting from sin, they are called concupiscence. The different meaning bears a different set of connotations. In *De diligendo Deo* we move from one view to the other. In the letter just quoted, Bernard dedicates a paragraph (38), which we shall consider below, to the transition. It is as if *cupiditas* were viewed, first, concretely in its present destructive direction; then, secondly, and by way of explanation, as a force which has been divinely planted in nature but which is operating now after sin in the wrong channel: it can be rechanneled.[168] The cupidity which Bernard excluded from love is now spoken of in a new way: OUR CUPIDITY *OR LOVE* MUST BEGIN WITH THE FLESH (39).[169] In sin, human nature, with its *affectiones*, did not lose its ordination to God and its capacity to receive the divine love which can put it in order.[170] It is this second view which establishes the terms of reference for Bernard's outline of our maturing in the life of the spirit. *Affectio* as we will encounter it here is God's human creation, open to being gradually possessed by the divine *Sapientia*.

This latter *affectio naturalis* challenges three of our relatively conventional distinctions—first, between nature and grace; second, between the faculties of the psyche; and, third, between matter and spirit. We must consider each of these.

A twofold conception of the relation of nature and grace prevailing among the Latin Fathers may be observed in Augustine. He discovers human *nature* in the history of salvation, the way the Eastern Fathers do: it is what God *in fact* created, what was later weakened in sin. But, sometimes he considers nature more abstractly, apart from sin and in contrast to grace.[171] The first view predominated in the tradition until a more aristotelian sense of nature among the Scholastics gave dominance to the second. That Bernard's *natura* is what God makes, in the order of history, emerges clearly from our text. We read that the essential dignity of the human being, its free choice, deriving from the image of God in which it is made and according to which it is capable of responding to God (SC 80.2), is a prerogative of nature, *naturae praerogativa* (3). The *iustitia* which calls all persons to love God is made known in the NATURAL LAW described as INNATE and NOT UNKNOWN TO REASON (6). The true self given back to us in the Redemption is the same though weakened, self which God created

(15).[172] The *affectio* which moves us to God through four degrees is characterized, therefore, as *naturalis*.

Bernard is explicit: this sense of the natural includes divine grace. He speaks of a 'creating grace', *gratia creans*. God, as THE EFFICIENT AND FINAL CAUSE OF OUR LOVE, . . . CREATES THE *AFFECTIO* (22). With *affectio*, we have the ability to love; to love *God*, however, requires the addition of *gratia salvans*. With this, one understand that *gratia creans*[173] has already established the groundwork for further graces. Divine grace works within our *affectio* to bring us to God. In the Rule of Saint Benedict (Ch 7), Bernard had encountered a beautifully simple version of all this: 'We must believe God is present even in our bodily desires'.[174]

It is important at this point in the treatise to recognize that, in the mind of Saint Bernard, grace is all. Of love he says, NOBODY POSSESSES IT EXCEPT AS A GIFT FROM HIM (35).[175] He emphatically distinguishes grace from nature. Here we discover always a concrete nature (not the abstraction 'pure nature') in which the danger exists that an abused freedom may arrogate God's gifts as its *proprium*. For example, in desiring to recover its true self, the human being must act 'by grace, not by nature nor, indeed, by effort'.[176] The difference is marked in the relation of the *affectio naturalis* to *virtus*. In his *On Grace and Free Choice* we read,

> Mere affections live naturally in us, *as of us*, but those additional acts, *as of grace* [our emphasis]. This means only that grace sets in order what creation has given, so that virtues are nothing else than ordered affections (Gra 17).[177]

We may wonder why Bernard, who believes that the *affectio* described as ordained to God by creative grace and as loving God only in the force of a further grace, insists nevertheless on calling this *naturalis*. The treatise established its idea of 'nature' very early—and of necessity. The exposition of God's gifts began with those things that make us what we are (2). The image we reflect is God's (6), and the glory in us is of God (4); yet, we must become aware that what is from God is what we *are* (4). Bernard's notions of nature and grace are encapsulated in the strong simplicity of the pronouncement, THERE ARE TWO FACTS YOU SHOULD KNOW: FIRST, WHAT YOU ARE; SECONDLY, THAT YOU ARE NOT THAT BY YOUR OWN

POWER (4). If cistercian spirituality places great emphasis upon self-knowledge, it is because Saint Bernard was overwhelmed by the realization that our highest spiritual possibilities are, not a matter of what we may or may not choose to be, but of what we simply are. All human becoming which does not begin in a recognition of a true self to be restored will be a frustration of our very nature. Our treatise is not interested in laying claim to some metaphysical territory as the domain of humanity rather than of God. *Natura* here is the field of God's loving activity; within it and through it *gratia* leads us to love God.

The author discusses *affectio* as *naturalis*, we must remember, only after having emphasized that grace forever precedes even our desiring and leads us finally to God's eternal embrace. He marked the transition: LET US NOW SEE WHERE OUR LOVE BEGINS, FOR WHERE IT ENDS HAS BEEN SHOWN (22).[178] This statement helps us understand how Bernard conceives of 'grades' of love, or of a continuity between the lowest and the highest. The continuum he envisions is not a metaphysical *tertium quid* between finite and infinite but the divine action itself, grace—God's uninterrupted love. Even that willing of the good seen in the first degree of love will emerge in Bernard's schema as a love of God.[179]

A second set of distinctions put under stress by *affectio naturalis* concerns the faculties of the soul. Briefly, Bernard writes out of a tradition older than that of the Scholastics, whose 'faculty psychology' was accepted by the Enlightenment and remains in vigor among us. In the Platonism of the Fathers, the knowledge that one spiritual being had of another, or the love it had for another, was explained (in the Pythagorean maxim) as like seeking like; the nature of the agent, in its entirety, explained the possibility for mutual access.[180] Accordingly, Bernard's *affectio*, or *affectus*, is not essentially 'affection' nor an 'attraction' (nor the 'natural passion' of our translation), though it does not *exclude* these meanings; all operations of the psyche—cognitive, volitional, and affective—are predicated of the whole human subject. While distinguishing the functions of intellect and will, even in contemplative experience, Bernard insists upon the unity of the soul.[181] One finds expressions in his work such as *affectus animi, affectus mentis,* and *affectio in voluntate est.*[182] These are statements of what is emphatically to be included. Though the will is preeminent, *affectio* (or *affectus*) is not simply volitional—as we have noted with reference to paragraph 17, above.

At times Bernard stresses the spiritual character of *affectio*: Love for God, which at the end of our treatise is still an *affectus*, is in the *Super Cantica* called *amor spiritualis*.[183] In yet another work he will gloss 'God is love' in an unusual manner—*Deus affectio est* (Csi 1.15).

The spirituality of *affectio* is no warrant for excluding the influence of human embodiment. The principal benefit the abbot seeks in dwelling on love as *affectio* is the experiential character the word suggests. He gives his readers no complex of theories about love, like a thinker subjecting an object to speculative inquiry; he gives a description of what he undergoes in his life and of what his readers may observe in their own hearts. 'Instruction makes one learned', he reminds us, 'while *affectio* makes one wise' (SC 23.14).[184] Such wisdom (*sapientia*) is a direct contact with the object of knowledge (*sapor* means *taste*). It is receptive of what lies outside our free control. These are the meanings we want to communicate in speaking of the experiential character of Bernard's writing.

What emerges for the interpreter is the necessity of staying in touch with the context of *affectio*. What a writer in Bernard's tradition means to predicate of it at one stage of its transformation is applied only incorrectly to another stage. At its beginning, before it is set in order by grace, *affectio* is an almost instinctual force; when, later as a virtue, it is directed by grace, it pertains to the order of the Spirit.

The superior value of that *sapientia* which is reached in *affectio* is the wholeness of its knowing, its engagement of all dimensions of the subject, the partial recovery, therefore, of those aspects of our native freedom lost in sin. At the beginning of the four degrees, the abbot establishes the earthier parts of *affectio naturalis* as those which come most easily into play for a weakened nature and, for that reason, those to which he gives a certain importance. He writes of *amor carnalis*, which is really *animalis* —*cupiditas* (38, 39). Bernard's *affectio* is, then, also simple affection—the experience of attraction—or (as the Walton translation has it) a natural passion.

When this cohesiveness of the concrete order is transposed into intellectual model—this is the case with the ancients—it eludes the categories of a later psychology.

A third way in which Bernard's *affectio naturalis* disrupts a later pattern of Christian reflection lies in the meaning of *spiritual*, particularly in the association of this concept with the two sets of distinctions we have just reviewed. The *affectio* which loves God is natural, and at the same time it is spiritual, by which we mean, not immaterial, but of the Holy Spirit. This is the New Testament sense (cf. 1 Cor 15:46).

To what has been said about the spirituality of *affectio* we can add something that emerges clearly from the abbot's remarks on virtue. VIRTUE, he says, IS THAT BY WHICH MAN SEEKS CONTINUOUSLY AND EAGERLY FOR HIS MAKER AND WHEN HE FINDS HIM, ADHERES TO HIM WITH ALL HIS MIGHT (2). *Virtus*, then, refers to what empowers both *liberum arbitrium* and *scientia* (that which acknowledges God's gifts). Yet, Bernard does not use the technical term which highlights otherness in the origin of what is received: *gratia*. He speaks instead of *virtus*, a correlative term which underlines the already-received character of what is given by God, of what is IN THE SOUL (2). Proper to God's human creature, in the divine plan—before sin—there is *virtus*. It accompanies that free choice (our *dignitas*) which is the prerogative of our very nature, *naturae praerogativa* (3). Nevertheless, when we reflect that virtues are *affectiones ordinatae* (Gra 17), we understand them to be natural in a different sense: they belong to the restoration of our nature. We understand them to be spiritual, also in a different sense: they signify an operation of the Spirit for which *affectio* is merely ordained. *Affectio* is, indeed, both natural and spiritual, but in ways which this context clarifies.

William of Saint Thierry is more typical than Bernard of the era and of the augustinian tradition in preferring to reserve the concept of love to a condition of spirit for which he makes greater demands than *affectio naturalis*. For William, ordinarily, love requires a will which is good, well-ordered, and vehement (*vehemens voluntas*).[185] Nevertheless, when we observe, as we shall, that Bernard's *affectio*, even in the first degree, is both good and ordinate, we may conclude that his difference from William is not significant.

Bernard, while establishing the spiritual, or graced, character of *affectio*, is intent on keeping its natural, spontaneous, reliable quality in the foreground. As nature, *affectio* does not exact grace, but is open to a grace which Bernard trusts is always freely present to it. *Affectio* is *appetitus*.[186] It is equivalent to *cupiditas*: OUR CUPIDITY OR LOVE MUST BEGIN WITH THE FLESH (39).[187] CHARITY . . . WILL NEVER BE WITHOUT CUPIDITY, BUT IT WILL BE IN ORDER (38).[188] One bernardine enumeration of the four *affectiones* reads: *cupiditas* (cf *amor*), *timor, tristitia, laetitia* (QH 14.9).[189] The abbot's objective is to focus on the observable dynamism of the human psyche, which, he tells us, possesses a triple force, *rationalis, concupiscibilis, irascibilis* (Div 74).[190] When the *anima concupiscibilis* responds to God in *affectio*, it is not a moral sense alone which functions. Bernard envisions a love of God in which we human beings respond, not because we wish to please God, but because God pleases us.[191] Although this is not the totality of love, it is the point of view Bernard chooses—not as one intellectual option among several, but as the record of experience. At the same time, this point of view allows him to demonstrate two coordinate ideas: first, that grace works through our very nature to bring us to the perfect love of God (or, seen from the human side, that loving God is our only possible self-realization); and second, that God, who is love, is perfectly and unimaginably lovable.

Critics misread the four degrees of love when they fail to perceive *affectio naturalis* as Saint Bernard's experiential point of departure. Pierre Rousselot and Anders Nygren represent, respectively, Catholic and Protestant interpretations of this *affectio* which neglect to locate it in the context we have described. To Rousselot, 'love' in our treatise was physical, which is what he meant by natural.[192] Nygren, too, read *affectio* as natural, in a meaning wholly irreconcilable with supernatural charity.[193] Bernard's modern apologists, on the other hand, have risked neutralizing the greatest strength of *De diligendo Deo*—its closeness to a recognizable and felt reality—in their very determination to defend its orthodoxy. Gilson's technical cautions led him virtually to eliminate the first degree of love: 'This "vicious self-love" is an adventitious corruption, and it can, in consequence, be eliminated'.[194] For Delfgaauw, this was 'une maladie de la nature', 'pas un amour authentique', and only in the third degree of love did he think the soul would be converted.[195] Clarifications of this kind (they are not meant as strictures) can unfortunately make it difficult for a reader to accept the central intuitions of the four-degrees schema as anything but invalidated, reduced to a rhetorical contrivance.

Bernard's intuitions regard a simplicity characterizing the human situation, which he represents, not as good against evil, but as the struggle between the self and God, somewhat in the manner of Jacob wrestling with the angel. He configures four degrees in the victory of divine love, with the love of self first and last, and the love of God at the pivotal center—God on either side, now as sustainer and now as lover. This chiasmic configuration preserves for Saint Bernard both the simplicity of the confrontation, as grand design, and the complexity of it in our experience.[196] The double meaning we have noted in his *causa* for loving God (1)— the evolution of perception and of motive and the unique fixity of cause—serves this configuration. Unless we, with the author, see four degrees in the receiving of God's love—accepting the assumptions which warrant this view—we do not see through to the wellspring of his thought.

The defensive theological atmosphere in which this treatise has been read in the recent past has been dissipated. Seminal thinkers, recovering the perspective of graced nature in which a large part of the christian heritage of spiritual writings was conceived, have prepared a new era in the study of christian spirituality. Bernardine studies have shared in this recovery. Theologians have repossessed the insight of Saint Bernard's *affectus*: 'The capacity for the God of self-bestowing personal love', writes Karl Rahner, 'is the central and abiding existential of man as he really is'.[197] It should be easier today to avoid confusion, not only regarding Bernard's position in a grace-nature reconstruction of the human condition, but regarding faculty psychology as well. There is no need to react so desperately to the misreading of *affectio* or *affectus* as 'feeling' that we then assign it to another 'faculty', the will—accepting in the process an anachronistic assumption that vitiates the reading. The affective motion which Bernard calls *affectio* engages the whole psycho-physical subject.

With these essential clarifications, we can rejoin Bernard's text. Love is natural, he writes, and must be, therefore, AT THE AUTHOR OF NATURE'S SERVICE (23).

### The First Degree (23–25)

BUT, SINCE NATURE HAS BECOME MORE FRAGILE AND WEAK, he continues, BY THE RULE OF NECESSITY ONE IS COMPELLED TO SERVE IT FIRST (23).[198] The beginning of love will be found, then, in human beings loving themselves, for their own sakes.[199] From the context it is clear that such love is not disordinate (though it may become so). This is the first degree of loving God, for the love of self is the norm of every other love.[200]

It is called carnal love (*amor carnalis*), in keeping with the pauline distinction, FIRST WHAT IS OF THE LIVING CREATURE [*quod animale*] AND THEN WHAT IS OF THE DIVINE SPIRIT (23).[201] The human being, to this point, has an experiential knowledge of (*sapit*) nothing but itself; its love is carnal of necessity. LOVE IS NOT IMPOSED BY A PRECEPT; IT IS PLANTED IN NATURE (23).[202] Gilson comments that this is 'what we should call the instinct of self-preservation'.[203] But, we must go further than that, recognizing that the 'self' to be preserved in this paragraph is a human person with resources that transcend instinct. Bernard begins his process of ascent with a subject that already experiences a conscious need to discover its significance and to feel worthy of survival. This groping for self-affirmation is already at its start a *love* of self. Although the lover is seen as unable to name the object toward which he or she reaches, our author pronounces the attitude a love of God—just as in our day the initial reaching out for self-validation has been called a 'pre-religious love affair with God'.[204]

Thomas Merton glosses PLANTED IN NATURE (23) as 'rooted in our psychic automatism', and, with Bernard, argues that this natural love of self is 'a service owed to God *the author of nature*'.[205]

But what is this "self" that we love? Rather than define it, Bernard studies the acts in which it is affirmed. In this, says Aimé Forest, he suits our own times, where a reflexive manner of philosophizing has come to prevail.[206] The self emerges cumulatively in the abbot's essay as an agent capable of freedom, knowledge, and virtue (2), similar to God in that is is made in God's image (6), the subject of necessities, needing 'bread, sun, and air' (2), and the object of God's love (1). What clearly impresses Bernard about this agent, short of a definition, is the difficulty with which it relinquishes an illusory claim to what is its own (23–25, 30). What is illusory in the constitution of a *proprium* is, not that there are elements necessary to its essence, but that the agent itself is the final guarantor of its survival. The abbot discusses this self-deception in the first degree of love; in the fourth degree, before the general resurrection, when the self is concerned about its integrity in the absence of its body, other subtleties enter the reflection, as we shall see.

While each step of the exposition is crucial here at the start of love's development, the writer moves so rapidly as to make clear he has no apprehension of theological resistance or torpor in his readers.[207] Within the same first paragraph (23), he explains why carnal love must advance from self to neighbor. The principle has already been stated: nature in its weakness must be served first. The same nature, however, is shared among all humans. Therefore, in the name of justice (*read* rationality), we must meet the necessities of others as well as our own.

In advance of this *iustitia*, a simple operation of *affectio* will incite a move to others. Seeing ourselves in others, we are affectively inclined to them by that love which the treatise speaks of as PLANTED IN NATURE (23). Elsewhere Bernard remarks that, with those who share our nature, it is more natural 'by a certain law of humanity' (*iure quodam humanitatis*) to be compassionate than to be angry.[208] Merton seems to have had a text of this kind in mind when he interpreted Bernard's metaphor of the river bursting 'the banks of necessity' (23). Our 'surplus' of love must go to those who share our nature, he wrote: 'One might see it as universal man loving himself—Adam loving himself in all men—[a] capacity to become 'one Christ loving Himself' (Saint Augustine)'.[209]

'Necessity' (necessitas)

The sanction discovered for this rationality is self-destruction; *necessitas* is the governing concept. Love that fails to move beyond

the self destroys the self.[210] The author organizes the leading
categories of the thought in an image:

> YET, SHOULD LOVE, AS IT HAPPENS (*ut assolet*), GROW IMMODERATE,
> AND, LIKE A SAVAGE CURRENT, BURST THE BANKS OF NECESSITY,
> FLOODING THE FIELDS OF DELIGHT, THE OVERFLOW IS IMMEDIATELY
> STOPPED BY THE COMMANDMENT WHICH SAYS: 'YOU SHALL LOVE
> YOUR NEIGHBOR AS YOURSELF (23).[211]

We notice here that the source of knowledge about what the
commandment comes to heal is personal experience rather than
a teaching. Throughout the exposition of the first degree of love
(23–25), the treatise will appeal to Scripture, and it is important to
see the sense intended: first, by way of assumption, the beginner
whose consciousness is described and who is addressed is a person
of faith; and second, the general approach to Scripture is that
of apologetics—i.e., it is the rationality of the revealed word (or
the fact that something of it is demonstrably validated in nature)
which Bernard employs to build his argument. The writer's insistence is not on the assent of faith, but on attention to the data of
consciousness, to experience.

The recognition sought at this juncture is of the exocentric
nature of the human being. We are so constituted, our experience
shows us, that we must go out to others.[212] That Bernard is impressed by this truth is evident especially in the strikingly concrete
language he employs to depict movements of human compassion.
In SC 44.4, for example, he will speak with the graphic imagination of a botanist dealing in moisture and warmth and the miracle
of first growth, as he describes the genesis of the love of neighbor:

> It is in intimate human affections like this that fraternal love
> finds its origins; and, from the natural inbred gentleness with
> which a man cares for himself, it takes on, as if from the moisture
> of the soil, the force of vegetation, through which, as grace
> breathes down from above, it bears the fruit of a caring concern
> [*fructus pietatis*].[213]

This is a beginning. One works first from the creaturely human
side of the love of neighbor—where what is of the essence of the
human being wins respect, though it is not yet fully discerned—
and then through to the far side, where the neighbor is loved, as

Bernard will say, IN GOD (25). The discovery of others is not a new
degree of divine love, for Bernard posits a simple polarity of self
and God—something already suggested in the two-sided character
of neighborly love. There is a parallel between the deepening
relationship of the self and the neighbor, on one side, and the
self and God, on the other. The self loves the other (neighbor or
God), first, for itself and then, WITH PURITY (25), for the other.
The love of a sharer in one's nature progresses to the love of
another person as such, another I; but now the other is perceived
and loved as a unique and inviolable other, not in virtue of a
shared nature, but in God.

Exposition of the necessity of loving others continues: What
you subtract from luxury to add to your needy neighbor will
temper your love and make it just (*temperans erit, et iustus*). IT IS
ALTOGETHER RIGHT THAT WHAT SHARES A NATURE NOT BE CUT OFF
FROM WHAT IS BESTOWED (*gratiae*) UPON THAT NATURE, ESPECIALLY
OF THAT GIFT (*gratiae*) WHICH IS GRAFTED INTO NATURE (23).[214]
Recall that, in paragraph one, the author identified God as the
one who had no necessities.[215] Nature in Bernard's conception of
it here, is the subject of necessities.[216] Humans have needs.

We look in vain for a further word on the gift grafted into human
nature. This somewhat cryptic clause, in the context of nature's
necessities, seems to refer to the image of God in the human
being, who is made able, by something which comes with that
nature, though is not of it (the gift is grafted), to respond to God.
The word Bernard chose for God's gifts to nature is *gratiae*—
meaning here the goods of the earth which one is exhorted to
share (cf. *voluptas* and *superfluitas* in the preceding sentence) and
also something more intrinsic to human nature, something set
within it. But how is the reader to associate Bernard's admonition
about not depriving others of the graces given to our common
nature with that added caution, ESPECIALLY OF THAT GRACE WHICH
IS GRAFTED INTO NATURE (23)? In the answer to that question one
finds much of the force of the author's insistence on material
sharing and the love quality of this sharing.

Earlier in the treatise (2.3), Bernard said that the essential dignity of human beings is their freedom of choice; and he linked this
freedom to the image of God in which they are created (6). When

later, in *On Grace and Free Choice*, he elaborates these ideas, he will
define free choice, in an original phrase, precisely as 'freedom
from necessity'; and he will specify that this is the locus of the
divine image in the soul.[217] But here he has said what is essential to
his thought: he has bonded the sharing of material necessities to a
respect for what is the most special of God's gifts to human nature,
that freedom of choice which is humanity's very dignity. One may
infer that to neglect the necessities of others is to curtail their
freedom from necessity and thus to deface what is most sacred
about them.

The ascertaining of *necessitas* has something of the character
of revelation for Bernard. A monk could assume this attitude
from familiarity with the Rule (Ch 7): 'It is said that "self-will has
its punishment, necessity its crown." '[218] The abbot's observations
began in the *necessariora* which God provides for our physical life
(2). In self-knowledge he discovers that we are, above all, free
act, but this free act arises out of that necessary act which is the
love of self.[219] Loving ourselves first from a necessity of nature, we
move outside ourselves from a necessity to preserve the self; we
love our neighbors, sharing the necessities of life, from a desire
to protect that dignity which is their freedom from necessity, as it
is our own. Until we succumb to the pull of God's charm at the
highest level of love possible in this life, it will be the engine of
*necessitas* which pushes us forward (*urgere*) to maturity.[220] Bernard
will lament below (27) that the enjoyment of even the most advanced love must be interrupted by the necessities of our situation
(*sollicitat carnis necessitas*). When, ending the treatise, he speaks of
a new human condition in the beatific vision, he does so with
the affirmation, ALL CARNAL NECESSITY WILL DISAPPEAR (40).[221] In
the meantime, a respect for necessities preserves human beings
from the violation of their nature.[222] If necessity knows no law, as
he repeats elsewhere (SC 50.5), this is because necessity is nature
itself, a manifestation of the divine plan or law. It is then logical
for him to pray: 'Direct our actions, in the manner which our
temporal necessity requires'.[223]

There is a curious balance here. The source of self-realization
is the divine action, the creative force directed toward unique-
ness and expressive originality, while the existential demarcation

between the possible and the self-destructive is the experience of need, that *necessitas* which the abbot construes as the index of a law for humans. The equilibrium of this vision contrasts as much with certain dull, pseudo-biblical derogations of humanity as it does with a modern heterodox exaltation of self-creating personhood.[224]

*Necessitas*, to the exclusion of *superfluitas*, became Bernard's guide in architecture and the arts, just as it was in the acquisition and use of all material things.[225] *Necessitas*, rather than *curiositas*, determined what he studied and wrote about.[226]

To receive what is in the text of *On Loving God*—what is simply there, not an imaginative reconstruction of it—the reader has to work with an affecting paradoxical composition: Bernard exalts freedom from necessity as the human being's essential dignity, and at the same time he establishes the necessity that binds and limits humanity as the touchstone of rationality. Elsewhere, to address the issue, the abbot speaks in the language of obedience, of conformity of the human will to the will of God. But it is here in our treatise that the question is answered most clearly, in terms of the polarity of self and God: to love self *for* self (the first degree of love) is to answer to mere necessity, to be not yet free; whereas to love self only for God (the fourth degree) is to be finally perfectly free.[227] The human person achieves an uncompromised freedom only in assuming the same position toward nature (which includes the self) and its *necessitas* as is found in the Author of nature, who *is* freedom. Freedom from necessity and respect for necessity form a double criterion of wisdom, which, in the tradition of the Fathers, is both deeply philosophical and guided by biblical faith.

The perspective in which *necessitas* virtually defines the reality of the creature may help account for the assurance with which Bernard resists the mainstream proposition of his augustinian tradition that what is most God-like in the human person, our essential dignity, is *intelligere*: for Bernard it is the will's freedom from necessity.[228]

This conviction uncovers something of our author's motive in moving immediately from the beginnings of love to a reflection on justly sharing the goods of the earth: to deprive others of material things is to menace their spiritual nature. His development of the idea is so economical that he can avoid leaving his discussion of nature and hold to the course of his present topic: the love of self which fails to open to others destroys the self.

Bernard is more intent on describing the human situation than on moral exhortation. He speaks of carnal love as natural but warns against CARNAL DESIRES WHICH WAR AGAINST THE SOUL (23).[229] His sense of the problem of affirming the self involves an inexorable choice: share what you have equally with those who share your nature or give it to unregulated desire, the destroyer of the self.[230] His rationale here is not the avoidance of sin: if one becomes a *transgressor* by slighting the needs of others, what is transgressed is the integrity of the self. In the hoarding of luxuries what stands to be violated is not an optional asceticism: LET HIM INDULGE HIMSELF AS MUCH AS HE WISHES, we read, AS LONG AS HE REMEMBERS THAT HIS NEIGHBOR IS TO BE TREATED EQUALLY (23).[231] The moral register here is the simple acknowledgment of the way things are, discernible to someone at a primitive stage of spiritual reflectiveness. It is the avoidance of self-destruction. In a later sermon, the abbot would say again that at stake in the orderly regulation of *affectio naturalis* is the survival of nature.[232] Human beings are preserved in their nature when they discover and respect that same nature in others—when carnal love becomes social.

We must not skim too quickly over the solitary monk's case that the love of self for self is *essentially* social. The argument transcends exhortation. It issues from an insight which we are inclined to arrogate to twentieth-century explorations into mental health.

The recognition of the essentially social character of our humanity produces the first disciplinary restraint upon the self's natural passion for itself. This is a remarkable concept (neither conventional nor inevitable), for already the first advance toward the preservation of the self is a move, not so much *from* the self to the other, as *toward* that larger self discovered in the other. When perceived in Bernard's four degrees as reaching for a more integral self, this move anticipates in effect the resolution of the polarity of self and God. God is the ultimate other.

*Affectio naturalis,* which in our weakened nature has no principle of order or measure, begins now to be put in order. Bernard exclaims,

> THE LAW OF LIFE AND ORDER (*DISCIPLINA*) IMPOSES ON YOU THE RESTRAINT OF TEMPERANCE, TO GUARD YOU AGAINST THE DESTRUCTION OF FOLLOWING YOUR CONCUPISCENCE AND AGAINST SERVING, WITH THE GOOD THINGS OF NATURE, THE ENEMY OF YOUR SOUL, YOUR LIBIDO (23).[233]

*Libido,* or *concupiscentia,* is not a drive toward evil but an unregulated drive; in that sense, it is a danger to the self. Bernard's *amor* shares in this character. *Amor carnalis* is not to be destroyed, therefore, but set in order. Acknowledgment of the needs of others, which the treatise argues is rational, is the first step in the *ordinatio amoris.* Elsewhere Bernard designates *ratio,* or *discretio,* as the principle of order in human affections.[234] He offers the beginner, in the first stages of love, the reassurance that what God asks is what our very nature requires.

Just as grace works through the affections in Bernard's view of nature, so it is grace which acts within human rationality, setting the affections in order. The abbot is elaborately clear about this in the two paragraphs on prevenient grace which prepare his discussion of the four degrees (21–22). Later, in *On Grace and Free Choice,* he sums up the case this way: 'There are within us, naturally, as if from us, simple affections . . . ; grace sets in order what creation has given'.[235]

Bernard's discussion of the love of neighbor is instructive of his entire conception of how grace works in the soul leading it to love God. The love of neighbor, as all love, has a mystic dimension (as we would say) but it is a progressive one. Our sense of what the love object is deepens. In the first degree we begin by seeing ourselves in the other; in the second and third, we see in ourselves, first God the sustainer, and then God the lover; in the fourth, we see ourselves in God alone. Nevertheless, even the love of others which fails to transcend the self cannot be dissociated from God, who is love. In a later work the abbot entertains the question whether love of neighbor precedes or follows love of God, and he answers that an incipient (*incipiens*) love of God precedes, while a developed (*nutrita*) love of God follows.[236] The reader bent on appraising the early stages of the process in our treatise principally from the viewpoint of what they lack will encounter unnecessary difficulties, for Bernard's focus is upon the wonder of God's positive action.

We will observe here, incidentally, a similarity between Bernard's thought and that strain of present-day psychology which propounds the necessity of self-love. Although modern psychology very early absorbed popular versions of that part of the christian ethic which demands moving beyond the self, it has more recently discovered the value of loving the self.[237] In its dependence on empirical science, psychology cannot absorb Bernard's mystic vision in which is resolved the dichotomous tension of self and other, even to that ultimate other which is God. Nevertheless, our generation's reflection on the goodness of the self, at least as a pragmatic concern, finds a distant precedent in Bernard. *On Loving God* cannot appeal to our knowledge of the unconscious or to patterns of childhood development, but its method is psychological in a deeper sense: its point of view is that of the self's felt necessities. Bernard's christian justification for thinking in this vein is his conviction that God acts within the human person to bring about the fulfillment of a graced nature.

Consider Bernard's description of the religious consciousness of those who are advancing but remain still in the first degree of love, those who do not yet see God as the object of this love (24). Such people share their goods with others to the point of accepting the privation of necessities; they pray for God's help with confidence; they see all good things as provided by God; they believe that in acting justly towards others they seek the kingdom of God; they *love* their neighbor; they affirm that their deprivation of others would be the destruction of the self in the reign of sin; they acknowledge their creaturely condition as they read of it in God's revealed word. To observe such faith in those spoken of as not yet loving God is to be forced back, in the name of consistency, to repossess Bernard's designation of love as a natural passion. In their approach to God, these people of faith do not reject God, but they are not yet affected by God in the whole of their nature. Since they love themselves, they replicate something of the divine attitude towards themselves and respond to an object which, though they fail to recognize it as such, is godly; and, in this sense, they are on the path to loving God.[238] But what is directed to God is not yet a love characterised by any self-conscious response to its divine Object. Here we discover the weight Saint Bernard throws behind the psychological inclusiveness of *affectio naturalis.* Unless this *affectio* is whole, a person will not mature in the love of God.

*Affectio* or *affectus* means, of course, more than feeling, and Bernard does not isolate feeling as the dimension of affectivity essential in love; but he does find it natural that the entire affective human being, as the object of God's love, be the lover. Human beings love as they experience.[239] To have experience of nothing but oneself and of the nature shared with others—*nondum quippe sapit nisi seipsum* (23)—is to be confined to the lowest level of the love of God.

The idea of a God working to solicit distinct spiritual acts of believing and willing in human beings is foreign to Bernard. He grounds love in *affectio naturalis* because he understands God as the lover who plays to the response of integral human beings as they are in fact created. Our treatise describes, not what human beings can or should do, but what God is doing in creation. Saint Bernard's God, wanting to be experienced humanly by human beings, is forever cultivating an affective response in that nature which he created affective.

The perspective of creation is repeatedly made evident. We see it play on *nature.* IT IS ONLY RIGHT TO SHARE NATURE'S GIFTS WITH HIM WHO SHARES THAT NATURE WITH YOU (24).[240] Identifying human nature with the nature permitted to human use is proper of such parts of the Hebrew Scriptures as Bernard cited a few lines earlier in speaking of the Creator who FILLS WITH BLESSINGS EVERY LIVING BEING (24).[241] God desires that every part of nature answer according to what is natural to it.

The quality of faith that the treatise describes as characteristic of the first degree of love regards God as the protector of nature, the ultimate principle upon whom all depends: NATURE WAS CREATED IN A WAY THAT IT MUST HAVE ITS CREATOR FOR ITS PROTECTOR (25)—or, regarding the question in hand, the human being as a creature depends on the Creator to preserve the integrity of its nature.[242] This is biblical faith: the God affirmed and trusted is, not an intellectual construct (however much of the argumentation is from reason), but the God of revelation. And yet this God is not yet known as God wishes to be. The roles we allow to God are reduced to those which a self-preserving human rationality demands of deity, and at the start this does not include the lover God. Closing his account of this first degree with an exhortation to faith pitched at what he understands to be the level of the beginner in divine love (24), Bernard makes clear that even the love of self brings us to an encounter with God: loving ourselves for our own sakes, we find that the only safeguard of our nature is God.

This conclusion—its upward dynamism flowing from the assumption of historically graced nature—is lost on the reader intent on plotting the four degrees of love on a nature-grace graph. However important it is to recognize love's incompleteness in the first of the four degrees, a mistaken emphasis here will cast a shadow on what Bernard most wants to illuminate—the loving action of God within our created nature, the lovableness of God to the most creaturely eyes, God as the initially unknown goal of the human quest. Without a strong sense of this point of departure, the schema of four degrees loses its cogency.

### THE QUESTION OF FAITH AND CONVERSION

Nevertheless, the approach to God is incomplete, and a question regarding the moment of conversion has been raised. Pacifique Delfgaauw, following a precedent in Gilson, calls attention to a potential source of confusion by offering a forthright opinion: one is not justified, he claims, until the third degree, loving God for God's sake.[243] Justification is by faith, and it may not be obvious how faith fits into the four degrees of love. When our relatedness to God is conceived in terms of three theological virtues, these may be distinguished but not separated. Saint Bernard follows a johannine tradition in seeing this relatedness more frequently from the point of view of love than of faith. While love, in this usage, includes faith and hope, faith frequently suggests a more restricted cognitive scope, (as suggested already in Heb 11) and a trusting self-surrender as the merely initial turn to God.[244] Many Christians, however, from the time of Luther have suspected that schemata of growth in divine love imply a self-congratulatory attitude; they have insisted on a pauline faith perspective, seeing in this a clearer affirmation of God's agency.[245] These two languages can be understood as compatible—in fact, coordinates. An example showing Bernard's ease with both may be seen below in his passing remark on the relation of faith to love, where two reminiscences of Paul guide him: WHILE IN THE FLESH, IT [the soul] MOVES BY FAITH (2 Cor 5:7), WHICH NECESSARILY ACTS THROUGH CHARITY (Gal 5:6).[246] The abbot frequently enters into Paul's reflections, that 'love believes all things, hopes all things' (1 Cor 13:7) and that 'when the complete [charity] comes the partial [faith and hope] will come to an end' (1 Cor 13:10); and he is confirmed in his johannine manner.[247]

Comparing the two manners may be a necessary exercise, however for those firmly set in the more pauline perspective. Using the present treatise for this comparison is opportune, for Bernard, more than any medieval figure, was deeply respected by the great Reformers.[248] In the abbot's model of maturing love, is there a point in the development before which there is no faith?

We have already noted the attention Bernard calls to the dispositions of faith proper to souls in the first degree of love (24). From this account, we can conclude that the four degrees describe the experience of someone of initial faith. But we have also seen that the advancing soul's perception of God in others is only gradual. In the *Super Cantica* Bernard takes up some issues of the relation of faith to love. We may look there briefly for assistance.

The primordial rise of an *affectio* for others, Bernard tells us, takes place when we see ourselves in them (SC 44.4).[249] When we see God in others, carnal love develops into rational love and then spiritual love (SC 50.4).[250] He links rational love in a special way to faith: it is governed by *ratio fidei* (SC 20.9).[251] But, discussing love for Christ, he writes of a carnal love which is already so characterized by faith that the advance to a rational love gains nothing more to faith than a self-conscious validation of its ecclesiatical orthodoxy.[252] Clearly, Saint Bernard's mind is organized along the lines of the biblical dichotomy of flesh and spirit (e.g., 1 Cor

15:46), and his *amor rationalis*, in keeping with the practice of many of his contemporaries, is merely a kind of parenthetical link between the two rather than a distinct stage.[253] If we wish to trace the way to God in relation to a conversion to faith, or to an arrival point at the faith which saves, Bernard's vision of a maturing love will disappoint us. *De diligendo Deo*, from the start, presumes faith in the subject who progresses through four degrees—a miminal faith comparable to the feeble love found in the first degree, and needing the same development as that love.

'Conversion' is a metaphor quite different from 'grades' of development. Briefly, the terms represent reflections on two different truths. Since the Reformation, questions of christian theology have focussed on justification and on the discontinuity between nature and grace: one is saved in the merits of Christ, by the faith which accepts them. Christian faith as a decision is a simple transit from rejecting to affirming, where what is affirmed is not a proposition but Christ himself. Faith in God generally is defined by the same simple transit. At any point in the changing psychological landscape of the four degrees of love, we may ask: Does this move give entry to the faith in which we are justified? In the faith perspective spiritual development occurs, but it is conceived in relation to a conceptual and volitional line that one crosses, to an irreducible decision. This conception is manifest when Delfgaauw restricts the love of God to the third degree. If we eliminate the first two degrees and place the fourth on the far side of death, we have salvaged the notion of faith as a boundary—and obliterated the construct of degrees. Bernard's monastic agenda is different. Viewing the approach to God from the perspective of love rather than of faith, of God's action within a graced nature rather than of human striving, of religious experience or spiritual awareness rather than of systems of belief, the abbot contemplates the unspeakable gentleness with which God, in loving respect for the human creature, works within human nature to be known and loved—through such degrees as that wounded nature can bear.

Nygren may explain the later preference for the pauline perspective of faith, especially in Protestant Christianity, when he writes: 'Faith includes in itself the whole devotion of love, while emphasizing that it has the character of a response, that it is reciprocated love'.[254] It is incumbent on readers of Saint Bernard, therefore, to be alert to his sense of love as a response. He is an heir of Augustine's integration of *eros*, an affective drive planted in the human by the Creator, and *agape*, God's act of love, which may be accepted responsively by the human. Conversion in Bernard's scheme is *agape's* progressive transformation of *eros*, which he never disavows.

As we press our question upon the four degrees, we become aware of a double level of operation. First, Bernard describes the progress of a committed Christian—of the monk or of the prelate to whom the treatise is addressed or of his spiritual charges—as his exposition of this person's initial faith shows (see 24). Second, he describes the progress in a religious primitive, someone who is, as we read, 'only aware of himself', at the *animalis* rather than the *spiritualis* level (23). Bernard is not explicit about this double register. At one point, his presuming faith in the soul whose ascent he is following (24) may even strike us as inconsistent. This manner is common to the tradition of spiritual writing, where veterans are never considered as secure against the delusions or the weakness of beginners, and where whatever is said at the lower level echoes in the higher. But our being explicit about it here can shed light on the question of conversion.

The christian concepts of faith and conversion relate to one another with reverberating subtleties. With seeming inconsistency, the tradition affirms two propositions: that there is no life of the spirit until one is converted, and that the most spiritually alive souls pray and strive for their own conversion. These ambiguities may be seen in the opening lines of Bernard's sermon *Ad clericos de conversione*, written in 1139: Committed christian students have come avidly (*avidae concursionis*) to hear the voice of the Lord: and the preacher declares they cannot enter the kingdom of heaven unless they are converted (Mt 18:3).[255] Bernard's definition of conversion is partially clarified when he advises: 'Flee the environment of Babylon, flee and save your souls; fly off to the city of refuge'.[256] Conversion means entering monastic life.[257] Accepting that as an archaic or time-bound view, we must still find its sense in a conviction that transcends the appraisal of institutions. The body of Bernard's sermon makes plain that conversion is a whole-hearted and effective turning about toward God; and this is associated with faith, in one sense as effect and in another as precondition. Both faith and conversion are conceived on multiple planes.

   Advanced souls are forever in quest of a radical turn-around; the 'conversion' they long for is loving God as God should be loved. Already loving God for God's self, they may look back in grateful recognition at their progress as they read of the first two degrees. Beginners described as loving themselves for themselves, are said to be in the first degree of loving, not themselves, but God. They do not read about themselves here, for the ability to understand their lives in the religiously objective terms found in these lines would be proper only to the vision of faith. In Bernard's eyes, the strength to call things by their real name comes only from great wisdom.[258] These beginners have, as we would say, good will, but a lowly situation in the ascent of love. The faith which Bernard concedes them has to be seen largely in a restricted, cognitive sense: they are believers whom he can exhort to trust in God, but their faith is weak. It is not yet that experience of God found in a full affective love, a love which has taken possession of their *affectio naturalis*. Descriptions of this weakness play, as we have said, to the higher level of advanced souls, who periodically fall back and who recognize themselves in Bernard's account of the first and second degrees of love. Their actual, occasional, functioning at a lower level does not deprive them of their status as aspirants to the complete love of God.

   That Bernard writes of 'conversion' as a change from loving God for oneself to loving God for the sake of God (34)[259] does not settle the issue of the relationship of this conversion, which we have described as having a higher meaning, to that conversion which implies arriving at the act of saving faith. Truly to love God *only* for God is the effort of holy souls who are conscious of their regular falling off from this purity. They pray to be 'converted' because they perceive their failings as demonstrating that something at the center of their consciousness, from which they might expect a motive power, is not yet wholly operational. Their failings are not incidental errors: these holy souls know they simply do not yet love God only for God.

Neither for these advanced souls nor for beginners are the first two degrees of love definitively restrictive attitudes. To be responsive to the author's obvious compassion for the striving but feeble aspirants to mature love represented in the first two degrees, to perceive the encouragement of his tone, but most of all to respect a divine intentionality in the process delineated as gradual, we must interpret the qualifying motive of love—FOR THE SAKE OF, FOR THE BENEFIT OF (*propter*)—as a stage of growth rather than as a deliberately and finally exclusive condition. In fact, caution should be exercised speaking of this as a 'motive' in any sense which would make of it exclusively the *formal object* of the action in a scholastic sense. It refers, rather, to limited experience, in an augustinian usage.[260] Caution here leads us to recognize the difference between what, in the upper reaches of the will, we wish should move us and what, on the other hand, effectually does move us. We may indeed *formally* love God for God's sake, while retaining a lamentable degree of self-interest.

Bernard highlighted this ambiguity earlier in the treatise when he recognized in the question why God should be loved two meanings: what is the attractiveness of God; and what is our advantage in loving God. By the remark WHATEVER YOU SEEM TO LOVE BECAUSE OF SOMETHING ELSE, YOU DO NOT REALLY LOVE (17) he wishes to eliminate self-interest as a motive and to center upon God's lovableness; and yet, he will develop the recognition and acceptance of the human need for God as itself a 'degree' of divine love. Someone who loves God in the first degree—loving the self for the sake of the self—does not yet see God as the object of love, but is not someone who refuses to love God. The *experience* of God will, by degrees, displace the self-centered motive of the soul that experiences only itself. The continuity of the ascent is specified in the latin formula of the second degree: human beings love God, BUT IN THE INTERVAL, FOR THEIR OWN BENEFIT (26), *sed propter se interim.*

In his summation of the four degrees, the abbot speaks of the first advance from total self-absorption as a movement of faith: WHEN HE SEES HE CANNOT SUBSIST BY HIMSELF, HE BEGINS TO SEEK FOR GOD BY FAITH AND TO LOVE HIM AS NECESSARY TO HIMSELF (39).[261] The four stages Bernard chose represent stop-action

points, as it were, in the unfolding of love which God brings about
in us. In each, we respond to God. In all there is a saving, justifying
faith. Even in the first, a conversion has already occurred.[262]

Were we to abstract some elements from the first degree in
order to produce the mindset of the religious primitive we spoke
of, without sustaining the context of a process, we would read
Bernard's treatise incorrectly. In this disorientaton, we would be
inclined to look ahead to a point marking the true beginning
of the life of the spirit, the acceptance of God in faith. Such a
perception of Bernard's struggling lover would exclude what he
has said early in the treatise of the awareness of God given to all
human beings in the essential gifts of their nature (2–6). We have
had to conclude to faith in some of Bernard's *infideles*, on the
grounds that they love God.

Beyond that, consideration of the 'advanced' condition of those
in the third degree forces on us to the realization that this state
may not be the minimum requirement for salvation. In Bernard's
view the monk spends the entire maturity of his spiritual life,
except for rare brief moments, at that stage (29). What the treatise
discusses later as loving God out of fear or for a reward (34, 36)
is rejected as inadequate: it does not 'convert' the soul.[263] The
conversion spoken of here takes its meaning from that higher level
we have just seen. From what we read in the treatise, we must infer
that even an imperfect love mixed with fear and venality may contain the faith which saves. The fear of the Lord is the beginning of
wisdom and, as Bernard says, *initium caritatis*.[264] Although the first
degree of loving God is driven by a fear of self-destruction, and the
second by a desire for God's gifts, we recognize in them the *caritas
actualis* which Bernard sees as 'performing deeds', loving 'in deed
and in truth', and 'consenting to the law of God'.[265] Bernard's
beginner shares the goods of creation to meet the needs of others
(23).[266] Once this soul loves God for God's self, this disposition
towards others will be perfected (26); it functions, nevertheless,
already in the first degree.

Essential to the nature of love for God is a developing mystic
dimension. In the beginning stage Bernard describes, the awareness of God in others may seem non-existent, but to accept this as
the whole truth would require eliminating Bernard's first degree

and pronouncing the claim of his schema—that it is in some way the love of God—a simple error. Perhaps what has saved some from this drastic move is a suspicion lurking on the perimeter of their minds that the abbot who alludes (23) to the gospel of Matthew, 'You shall love your neighbor as yourself' (Mt 22:37), had reflected also on the contents of the next page—the *surprise* of those saved from among 'the nations' on the last day: 'Lord, when did we see you hungry and feed you?' (Mt 25:37)

We have spoken of faith as the acceptance of God. Doing so forces us to confront a problem linked to the preceding one. Is christian faith not the acceptance of the lordship of *Christ?* Although our treatise is profoundly christian, the specific schema of four degrees in the growth of divine love regards the self and God. It is a conception of the human situation which the author regards as the most elemental. The first answer to his correspondent's question, Why should we love God? is that Christ shows the lovableness of God (1, 7, 8, 11, 14, 15). But Bernard thinks of the plight of human beings who do not know Christ: they do not have the noetic benefits of this divine self-revelation. FAITH he says, BIDS ME LOVE HIM ALL THE MORE WHOM I REGARD AS THAT MUCH GREATER THAN I, FOR HE NOT ONLY GIVES ME MYSELF, HE ALSO GIVES ME HIMSELF (15).[267] In the understanding of the non-Christian, God has not given God's self. Before Christ, THE AGE OF FAITH HAD NOT YET COME, Bernard writes. [GOD] HAD NOT YET COMMENDED HIS GREAT CHARITY IN US, ABOUT WHICH I HAVE SAID SO MUCH (15).[268] The treatise then, operates again on a double register— the approach of human beings to God, simply, and the approach of those who know God in Christ. The resonance between these will be similar to the other two-tiered functioning just described. As Bernard reveals a pattern in the coming together of the self and God, there will always be the implication of a conclusion that must be drawn *a fortiori* by those to whom it has been made known that God has given God's very self: WHEN HE GAVE ME HIMSELF, HE GAVE ME BACK MYSELF (15).[269]

Christian insistence on faith in Christ as the act through which one is justified is a demand for orthodoxy made of those who know Christ in faith. It is only through his merit and intercession that sinful humanity is restored to friendship with God. It is by accepting one's unity in Christ that one shares in his merit before the Father. Bernard's four degrees gives an exposition of the approach to God through love made by human beings who are not described as possessing this knowledge of Christ in faith. Not even when they love God for God's sake are they described as making an act of christian faith (26).

In the four degrees, then, in the explicit lower register, THE AGE OF FAITH has not yet come. The restrictive christian meaning of this becomes clear when we see how often the author appeals to a faith, nevertheless, in the God who is revealed in the living of a human life. All love implies faith, even to the mind which interprets neither in a theistic manner. Love in any degree, conceived as an approach to God, implies faith in God;[270] but, as may be observed in our treatise, this does not necessarily mean faith in Christ. Cognizant of Bernard's treatment of this distinction, readers will understand why he leaves the *amor carnalis Christi* outside of the four-degrees schema. (A passing reference to Christ, at the third degree, as the example of not seeking what is one's own, is a corroborative illustration.) The author has chosen to think through his subject at the level where its universal human validity can be most easily secured.

Students of comparative religion will delight in this dimension of *On Loving God* and will be confirmed in their regret that the christian community regularly fails to uncover such elements as this in its tradition—testimonies from the saints to the deepest, though most generic, meaning of faith among human beings. Something of this approach is present, in fact, throughout the treatise, though its upper level insistently dwells upon the *memoria Christi.*[271] As a consequence, *On Loving God* can be considered a vehicle of that wisdom tradition which issues from the Bible: its vision, though deriving from experience interpreted in the light of revelation, may be argued for in terms of sheer rationality.

This discussion, associating faith and conversion with the four degrees of love, has involved neither a chain of technicalities nor a refinement of details. We have been attempting to reconcile the four degrees with the clearly biblical vision of simple alternatives implied in the concepts of both faith and conversion. This vision of simple alternatives, we remind ourselves, is the ordinary content of Bernard's imagination. Historically what is challenged in any schema of gradual spiritual 'ascent' has been, not its psychological verisimilitude, but its christian orthodoxy. This is, we may presume, the preoccupation and the merit of Delfgaauw's question, with which we began. That a love perspective on christian growth is open to the danger of seeing growth as a human achievement is true. That a faith perspective is open to a different danger, that of dissociating faith and conversion from efforts at growing, is also true. Today, when writings on christian spirituality move with the broad current of interest in human development as explored in psychology, the question of the relationship of this development to faith becomes irresistible, for there can be no double truth. What we discover in *On Loving God* is an acccount of spiritual growth, stage by stage, which vindicates rather than challenges the claims of faith.

Only with difficulty, then, could we consider the first degree of love in the light of a faith lacking to it, or with respect to a future moment of justification, without losing sight of the objectives of the treatise. But as the author moves to the second degree of love, he presents, in a transitional paragraph (25), his own concept of the inadequacies of the first. These regard, not theological concepts of creatureliness and grace and sin, but concrete failures, known by experience, to achieve what so far has been established as necessary for the wellbeing of those who love themselves. They know they should love God and should love others as themselves, but they do not succeed. The author suggests reasons for the failure. To love others as they should be loved (*pure diligere*), we must love them IN GOD (25).[272] To love only ourselves in others would not be truly to love them; to love them in themselves would require that we affirm their dignity, as Bernard would say, as deriving not from ourselves but from God. IT IS NECESSARY, THEREFORE, TO LOVE GOD FIRST; THEN ONE CAN LOVE ONE'S NEIGHBOR IN GOD (25).[273] The author's argument for loving God is addressed *ad hominem*, to someone who remains in the first degree of love: the nature one loves can be sustained and preserved only by God. It is as if Bernard were offering a rebuttal to the serpent in paradise. He elaborates the total dependence of all being on God. But rather than insist immediately upon humility and subjection, he points out (to beginners, struggling to love) that this God who makes everything to be what it is, also makes *God* to be beloved of human beings.[274] This unusual expression, a play on the notion of God's 'making'—we have seen it earlier (22)—attempts to capture the insight that the God who is love and who brings about the act of love makes the lovableness of all things—making God loved because God is 'made' lovable. Though the abbot does not wish to say that God makes God, he is reaching for the words which can suggest here what we will find elaborated toward the end of the treatise (35) as the universal 'law' of love. At the same time, he realizes, the presence of the creative act of God in the world, as explanation of the goodness of what we desire, is difficult for human pride to acknowledge affectively—i.e., in RENDERING DUE HONOR TO GOD (25).[275] To assist us in this, BY A DEEP AND SALUTARY COUNSEL, THE SAME CREATOR WILLS THAT MAN BE DISCIPLINED BY TRIBULATIONS (25).[276] Only repeated experiences of our inadequacy and of God's assistance will open us to God. IN THIS WAY, MAN . . . STARTS LOVING GOD FOR HIS OWN BENEFIT (26). And the motive is made explicit: BECAUSE HE LEARNS FROM FREQUENT EXPERIENCE THAT *HE CAN DO EVERYTHING THAT IS GOOD FOR HIM* IN GOD (25).[277]

With this the author has moved from an initial point—the love of self for one's own sake—to the experience of the destructive potential of human desire, to moderating efforts at sharing with others and loving them justly, to failures in these and other efforts, to successes recognized as God's assistance, to the cumulative discovery and acknowledgment that one cannot bolster the beloved self without God. This first *gradus amoris* is obviously neither a single grade nor a static condition. The literary swiftness with which Bernard moves through this series of advances hardly conceals the distance he has traveled, the challenge of the journey he proposes, or the richness of his analysis of love's transit from self to God. Still, within the schema of Bernard's four degrees of love, the love of oneself for oneself, however multiple its postures, is one attitude.

### The Second Degree (25–26)

The attitude changes in the second degree, when, for their own benefit, human beings love God (26).[278]

Bernard explained the consciousness proper to his second degree when he spoke of the progress yet required for the love of self (25). Now, under the caption of this second degree, his exposition is an advance upward from the new grade announced, not a description of its content.[279] Here one loves God, he says, not yet for God's sake:

> NEVERTHELESS, IT IS A MATTER OF PRUDENCE TO KNOW WHAT YOU CAN DO BY YOURSELF AND WHAT YOU CAN DO WITH GOD'S HELP TO KEEP YOU FROM OFFENDING THE ONE WHO KEEPS YOU FROM DAMAGING YOURSELF (26).[280]

In the rhetorical finesse of the latin sentence, the author seeks a form which might disclose, gently, the crudely disparate character of the principal elements in that relationship to God which he defines as the second degree of love. He is overwhelmed to the point of amusement by the absurdity of the contrast between the endemic selfishness of the weakened creature and the abiding love of the Creator. There is compassionate irony in the expression WHAT YOU CAN DO BY YOURSELF (26) and in the empathetic assuming of the point of view that the progress of love is A MATTER OF PRUDENCE (26).

The abbot's protectiveness can go only so far. The way out lies in more frequent tribulation. We turn repeatedly to God who frees us (and, we recall, the experience of being free is a contact with the *dignitas* of the true self). Gradually we end by REALIZING THAT IT IS GOD'S GRACE (26) which frees us.[281] The breakthrough in awareness regards, not information, but the eventual recognition of what has been resisted. The clear connotation of 'grace' in the text is, not that of a technical term, but the 'graciousness', or attractiveness of the one we find freeing us. When a new grade of love is reached, the heart has come into play. Saint Bernard conceives the move to loving God for God's sake as the softening of a resistance in the human heart, the center of personality where the faculties operate in concert, and where he can trace the transformation of *affectio naturalis*.

As we notice this tenet that God's lovableness is revealed in the experience of God as liberator, we must mark the difference between the christian doctrine explaining our liberation in Christ's redemption and what Bernard represents as a human experience universally verifiable, even in the *infideles*. The first liberation of human beings is from the imprisonment within themselves—from their incapacity to be truly rational, respectful of their nature both in themselves and in others. The first divine graciousness they recognize is that of the God who enables them to become themselves. As the author said earlier, what the 'faithful' know (*quod plane fideles norunt*) is the role Christ has in this process (7).[282]

### *The Third Degree* (26)

The third degree of love consists in loving God for God's sake.[283] The cumulative occasion bringing it about is, as we have seen, the *tribulatio* from which human beings seek relief in God (26). But, as Bernard prepares to cross over into that highest perfection of love which he believes habitually possible on earth, he recapitulates what has gone before under the rubric of the *necessitas* which pushes us to God: the frequency of our recourse to God brings about an intimacy in which we TASTE AND DISCOVER HOW SWEET THE LORD IS (26).[284] In his summation at the end of the treatise, the abbot will say simply, WHEN MAN TASTES HOW SWEET GOD IS, HE PASSES INTO THE THIRD DEGREE OF LOVE (39).[285] But this, we are told, happens 'gradually', as God is revealed (*paulatim sensimque Deus innotescit*).

Bernard explains the gradualness of our entry into this love as a transit from the push of necessity. Only slowly do we abandon reliance on ourselves, for the pull of God's charm (*suavitas*). Up to this point he has chosen an approach to match the limitations of those who require continuous verification of the rationality of their faith—those whose faith is tenuous and ineffectual until the human necessity of its demands is demonstrated. But by and by, TASTING GOD'S SWEETNESS ENTICES US MORE TO PURE LOVE THAN DOES THE URGENCY OF OUR OWN NEEDS (26).[286] Awareness of these two forces functions either simultaneously or alternately, at least for a while. The transit is not a road-to-Damascus experience. In summarizing his thought, Bernard points to a process of reaching out and accepting:

WHEN FORCED BY HIS OWN NEEDS HE BEGINS TO HONOR GOD AND
CARE FOR HIM BY THINKING OF HIM, READING ABOUT HIM, PRAYING
TO HIM, AND OBEYING HIM, GOD REVEALS HIMSELF GRADUALLY IN
THIS KIND OF FAMILIARITY AND CONSEQUENTLY BECOMES LOVABLE
(39).[287]

Even while loving God for God's sake, however, we express
our joy in God in the language of human needs, for THE NEEDS
OF THE FLESH ARE A KIND OF SPEECH (26).[288] God is construed
with reference to our desires.[289] Bernard calls attention to the
anthropomorphism. Nevertheless, the human being now attends
to God, NOT BECAUSE HE IS GOOD TO HIM, BUT BECAUSE HE IS
GOOD (26).[290]

Bernard's amplification of this discovery is quite limited. The
effort to say concretely what THE SWEETNESS OF GOD (26) consists
in was spent in that earlier part of the treatise where he described
specifically christian experience (7–15). There the exclamation of
psalm 33:9 on tasting the sweetness of the Lord (11) was associated
with the recurring discovery that God loves us—i.e., with the
memory of Christ as the revelation of God's love and with images
of visits from the divine Bridegroom. These supply the real content
for the passage,

IT [THIS LOVE] IS JUST, BECAUSE IT RENDERS WHAT IS RECEIVED.
WHOEVER LOVES LIKE THIS LOVES THE WAY HE IS LOVED, SEEKING
IN TURN, NOT WHAT IS HIS [1 COR 13:5], BUT WHAT BELONGS TO
CHRIST, THE SAME WAY CHRIST SOUGHT, NOT WHAT WAS HIS, BUT
WHAT WAS OURS, OR RATHER OURSELVES [2 COR 12:14] (26).[291]

'Tasting God's sweetness', then, means experiencing God's love
for us. We must compare the tone of this paragraph on God's
love for us with the handling of this theme in the earlier part
of the treatise. In the context of a celebration of christian faith
(7–15), Bernard's manner was exuberantly poetic—elsewhere he
comments that God's love is called sweet 'because he took on a
body'[292]—whereas here, in the perspective of possibilities open
to human beings as such (the four degrees), the development is
rather cooly rational. A portrayal of the soul who loves God now,
NOT BECAUSE HE IS GOOD TO HIM, BUT BECAUSE HE IS GOOD (26)
marks a clear and telling distinction, but is not so affecting as an

illustration of the difference between needing God (the first two degrees) and revelling in the knowledge of God's love. The two styles present the same reality. Yet Bernard has reserved the vivid experiential portrayal of God as our lover to a setting in christian faith, and in place of alternatives in religion, he offers an account of God's action in humanity in a philosophical manner—even though it might be said that religions in general claim the insight that God loves us.[293]

The attitude proper to this third degree of love gives rise to a new situation. Our response to God in faith is activated no longer by witnesses to God but by the direct experience of the divine presence. Until now it has been the very limitations of our creatureliness (*caro nostra*) which in God's assistance to Them, have spoken for God. We no longer depend upon this testimony. The love of others no longer requires a vision of ourselves in them; we love them as we love what is of God (*quae Dei sunt*). The commandment to love them need no longer be supported by a reflection upon its rationality; in our new freedom, we answer with THE OBEDIENCE OF LOVE (26).[294] The justice previously appealed to as rational order is now seen as a desire to reciprocate love. Now LOVE IS PLEASING BECAUSE IT IS FREE (26) (*gratus quia gratuitus*). Recall an earlier reflection upon love: 'It moves of itself and allows us to act of ourselves' (17).[295] So far, love's freedom has been qualified by the *necessitas* which pointed to self-harm as the alternative. Recalling Bernard's view of the *dignitas* of human beings—their freedom—we may reflect that the freedom found in loving God is the freedom of the true self. And yet, selflessness is of the essence of such love: it SEEKS NOT WHAT IS ITS OWN (26).[296] The model in this is Christ.

At this stage the true nature of Bernard's quest is revealed. The need and the search for God is one of the major themes of all religion in antiquity and receives a special identification in Christianity. The particular form of it found in *De diligendo Deo* can be distinguished from those yearnings for an end to finitude or for unity in the One; it has the stamp of Augustine's restless *desiderium* for the God of love which one finds as well in William of Saint Thierry and Richard of Saint Victor. In fact, with so particularized a focus upon God as lovable Lover, rather than as omniscient

Orderer of the universe, Bernard gives to the classical drive of *eros* a biblical coloring of love that can also be distinguished, to some extent, from the thought of Augustine.[297]

## The Fourth Degree (27–33)

The ultimate advance in selflessness is the fourth degree of loving God, in which one NO LONGER EVEN LOVES HIMSELF EXCEPT FOR GOD (27).[298] Bernard introduces this new state with a marked change of tone. It would be difficult to find a better example of Bernard's famed biblical language than the beginning of this pericope, where in nine lyrical lines he makes eleven biblical allusions, most of them to the psalms. This absorption in God where you LOSE YOURSELF AS IF YOU NO LONGER EXISTED (39), is offered not as the author's personal experience—I CONFESS, IT SEEMS IMPOSSIBLE (39)—but as a goal derived from personal aspiration—WHEN WILL THIS SORT OF AFFECTION BE FELT? (27)— and doctrine: OTHERWISE, HOW WILL GOD BE ALL IN ALL? (Cf 1 Cor 15:28) (28).[299] The abbot is composing a document for a public outside the intimacy of his community.[300] But, there is an ambiguity: the experience he projects he seems to know well. It is all too brief and rare, he laments. The needs of the flesh and brotherly love call him back to the world of cares. Though the return is necessary, it MOVES HIM BACK TO HIMSELF (27) and to what is his own.[301]

As the soul longs for the experience of BECOMING ONE WITH HIM IN SPIRIT (27), it looks forward to a condition in which THE MIND MAY FORGET ITSELF (27).[302] This ecstasy is seen as a freedom from the misery which sin brings into the world and which Bernard experiences in the very act of consciousness. The freedom from sin which the ascetical life strives for is a progressive freedom from misery and all of a piece with contemplation. Ascetical effort is itself a form of contemplation, an idea to be developed in the *Super Cantica*.[303] Here already the meaning and implications of ecstasy are clear. Gilson reflects on the profundity of this integration of the spiritual life and calls it 'a real stroke of genius'.[304]

Saint Bernard is writing about the highest level of contemplation, about how far God takes our human possibilities, not only in heaven, but in this life. We notice, however, that aside from the forgetting of self nothing is said, even at this point, to describe those special states of consciousness which a later literature associates with 'mysticism'. Bernard's only concern is with loving God and, therefore, resting in God. There is, of course, an always closer knowing of God, but in Bernard's tradition this was the light of charity: 'He who loves . . . knows God' (1 Jn 4.7).[305]

The inevitable return to the world of cares would of itself suggest that the degrees of love are not contrasts.[306] Important differences from the preceding stage of love seem necessarily over-stated, and Bernard doubles back to qualify them. He has said of the ineffable fourth degree that it is NOT A HUMAN SENTIMENT (*affectio*) BUT A DIVINE EXPERIENCE (27); now he says of it, O SWEET AND PLEASANT AFFECTION (*affectio,* 28)![307] Then, the self is not truly 'lost'; THE SUBSTANCE REMAINS, THOUGH UNDER ANOTHER FORM (28).[308]

This highest love produces a new awareness: THE SATISFACTION OF OUR WANTS, OUR CHANCE HAPPINESS, DELIGHTS US LESS THAN TO SEE HIS WILL DONE IN US AND FOR US (28).[309] The comparison is to love's beginnings. At its pinnacle there is still *affectio* (God's will 'delights us'), still joy in the satisfaction of wants and in the awareness that God's will is 'for us'. But our deepest delight is that HIS WILL (28) is done. The new form (*forma*) of the self that survives conforms (*conformet et concordet*) to God's will.[310] The cognitive element of this *affectus* in the human being is called the INTENTION OF THE WILL (28).[311]

When we love ourselves only for God, we love ourselves as God loves us; we love the self that God loves, the self cleansed of what Bernard refers to as the *proprium* of a false self. This identification of our human will with the divine will constitutes our 'union' with God. Yet, such conformity is never a true identification: in loving purely what God loves, my created will is not annihilated: it remains my own. Still, at that moment, the self I love becomes eternally secure, affirmed in the irrevocable creative will of God; its quiet is no longer threatened by attachments to what is not of the divine image—*nulla mordente cura de proprio* (32). I am one with God in positing myself. Conversely, until the choice of God is set in ultimate confrontation with the self, it remains unproven.

In the fourth degree, the *affectio naturalis* with which God has endowed the self is so transformed as to express God's own loving; and the created will, rejecting in itself all that is not of its divine origin, chooses God alone in its love for its very self.

All that Bernard has said so far defines the meaning of deification, as in the expression, IT IS DEIFYING TO GO THROUGH SUCH AN EXPERIENCE (28).[312] To look for further meanings is to fabricate problems. Anchored in the assertion that 'the substance' of the human subject remains, Bernard exults in the intimacy with God of this supreme degree of love: it produces, he says, the closeness of a drop of water to the wine which receives it, of molten iron to the fire, of clean air to the sunshine. The deification theme comes from Eastern Christianity and reached the author possibly through Maximus the Confessor (d. 662).[313]

Bernard's stress here on the closeness of the self and God and on the difficulty such a relationship poses to the human lover has led some scholars to contend that his fourth degree of love is the beatific vision itself.[314] If this means being in heaven after death, however, it misrepresents the text. The abbot is explicit: reaching this level is SO RARE IN LIFE (27); and IF ANY MORTAL . . . IS ADMITTED TO THIS, . . . THE NEEDS OF THE FLESH BOTHER HIM, . . . BROTHERLY LOVE CALLS HIM BACK (27).[315] Statements about the rarity and brevity of the experience are themselves declarations of its possibility in this life. When later he writes in the *Super Cantica* more extensively of the highest reaches of love and their effects, he makes plain that he is urging his monks to strive for them now—e.g., 'If any of us . . . wants to depart and to be with Christ [Phil 1:23], with a desire that is intense . . . he will certainly meet the Word in the guise of the Bridegroom . . . even while still a pilgrim on earth [2 Cor 5:6], though not in its fullness and only for a time, a short time'.[316] The fourth degree of love, like the three preceding, is not a stationary level; it has degrees within itself, as is evident. Though Bernard would agree with Augustine that the highest love and fullest vision is reserved for heaven, he does not restrict loving oneself-only-for-God simply to that level.[317]

Bernard's dwelling upon the consciousness of the human being in glory is essential in fixing the directionality of love in the four degrees; it is not an academically theological exercise. What he

describes here, he reflects, is what we pray for daily: YOUR WILL
BE DONE ON EARTH AS IT IS IN HEAVEN (28). And yet there are
subtleties in his account which may seem to work at cross purposes:
he insists on the inviolable integrity of the individual in its relation to God, but he represents human self-awareness as virtually
obliterated; for there you LOSE YOURSELF AS IF YOU NO LONGER
EXISTED; you CEASE COMPLETELY TO EXPERIENCE YOURSELF (27). At
this point we may ask whether the ontological survival claimed
for the individual—THE SUBSTANCE REMAINS (28)—has any recognizable human meaning.[318] Perhaps this difficulty underlies a
classic but unseeing objection raised to the abbot's concept of
the consummation of divine love: i.e., that the human person is
absorbed into God and therefore lost.[319]

Consider, first, Bernard's defense of the necessary integrity of
the human person, body and soul, in glory. It is this survival
he argues for when (30) he concludes that our love cannot be
complete until we receive our resurrection bodies. Though affectivity (*affectio*) is not essentially a function of the body (and
is not restrictively emotion), it is, we repeat, the operation of
the whole human creature and *includes* the body. Andrew Louth
correctly remarks that Bernard's affectivity is the greatest accentu-
ation of human individuality in the God-self relationship.[320] In his
concept of consummate love's effect on the human subject—*Sic
affici, deificari est* (28)—does Bernard destroy the individuality for
which he struggles in his argument concerning the resurrected
body?[321] In western culture reflexive self-consciousness is so central to an image of selfhood that we may wonder whether one can,
with consistency, conceive of a personal survival in which this is
not enjoyed.

Bernard, however, has not said that in the fourth degree of love
we will enjoy God rather than the self. In the end, we love the self:
*Homo diligit se propter Deum.* The author's attempts to expand on his
proposition cannot be construed as a denial of it. If there is love
of self, there is also awareness of self: we have seen Bernard's idea
of the *intentio voluntatis.* But it is at least questionable whether
the survival of the self in awareness requires the kind of self-
contemplation which the habit of our culture construes as reflexive self-consciousness. What Saint Bernard describes may indeed

contradict certain broadly shared assumptions about self-identity, but they were not his asssumptions.

Using language that, as he acknowledges, cannot claim to express personal experience of so pure and total a love for God as this fourth degree, the abbot is not satisfied with his own explanations of loving self only for God; he modifies original statements. Behind what we are construing as a popular uneasiness with Saint Bernard's 'heaven', is there some inadequacy in his language? Many may have to acknowledge, for example, a personal struggle against the statement that 'nobody there knows himself according to the flesh' (40). Certainly Bernard's vision of the individual's state of consciousness in a blessed eternity has not informed the communal imagination of Christians. And yet, his attempt to describe psychologically the great consummation in which God will be ALL IN ALL (28) (1 Cor 15:28) is derived from patristic sources and is frequently reproduced among contemplative writers. Measuring our own mind against it can lead to a discomforting conclusion: the idea is traditional, it is orthodox, and it is very little known.[322]

If the fourth degree of love follows the commandment to love God with all our heart, soul, and strength (Mk 12:30), then, Bernard believes, it cannot take place (at its highest reaches) UNTIL THE HEART DOES NOT HAVE TO THINK OF THE BODY AND THE SOUL NO LONGER HAS TO GIVE IT LIFE AND FEELING AS IN THIS LIFE (29).[323] His opinion arises out of his experience: *affectio* has regularly been compromised by *necessitas*. The perfection of love requires AN INTEGRAL BODY . . . SUBJECT TO THE SPIRIT IN EVERYTHING (29).[324] 'Integral body' (*in corpore integro*) is an arresting expression. It suggests a more plausibly normal unity of the human person than that which Bernard actually knew in life. He is speaking of the lamentably fragmentary character of human experience, about the dividedness we suffer at the deepest level of consciousness. Bernard does not long for a heaven of the disembodied.

It is impossible in our present condition to withdraw the care of heart and soul from our bodies; but the martyrs in dying accomplish this at least partially. They must, then, AT LEAST PARTIALLY (29), experience the fourth degree of love while still in their bodies.[325] Bernard finds the meaning of pain in the model of those who give witness of their love for God through a trusting acceptance of it. Martyrs are those who perfect the human response to the 'tribulations' (25) which the author declared to be God's loving way of drawing us beyond the first degree of love.

### The General Resurrection

BUT WHAT ABOUT THOSE SOULS WHICH ARE ALREADY SEPARATED FROM THEIR BODIES? (30)[326] They desire their bodies BY A NATURAL AFFECTION (*affectu naturali*), and therefore STILL CLING TO SOMETHING OF THEIR OWN (*de proprio*). In this condition they are not yet completely free to love. Before giving his views on the full consequences of what he reads to be the prolonged separation of body and soul, the abbot states that these souls are COMPLETELY ENGULFED IN THAT IMMENSE OCEAN OF ETERNAL LIGHT (30).[327] But the highest state of rapture cannot take place BEFORE THE RESURRECTION OF THE BODIES (30).[328] How can the two statements be made compatible? One senses a certain intellectual discomfort in the author, an awareness that what seems to be the received belief is in tension with a conviction that claims an even higher warrant in the faith.

For a preview of this resurrection theme, we might return to the long pericope on the flowers and the fruit early in the treatise (7–13): the flowers of Christ's resurrection do not bear fruit until the general resurrection (8); and Christ WILL SOMEDAY RETURN FOR OUR FULFILLMENT (9).[329] Bernard has already alluded to Phil 3:20–21, which speaks of waiting for our likeness to Christ's glorified body (14). A Christological understanding of the general resurrection has already been well established.

Bernard's opinion regarding the delay of full glory is repeated several times in his works.[330] It is his only departure from the eschatological thought of his era.[331] He gathered this archaic view from traces in the Fathers—Origen, Augustine, Ambrose, and Gregory the Great—passed on by Bede and the Carolingian commentators.[332] Ambrose's *De fide resurrectionis* (Bk 2 of *De excessu fratris sui Satyri*) established the precedent for our treatise.[333] The idea, exhumed by Bernard from his patristic sources, had never become the tradition, and not even his closest cistercian disciples followed him in it. Two centuries later, when Pope John XXII appropriated it out of Bernard's *De diligendo Deo*, theologians took note and in 1336 the following pope, Benedict XII, a Cistercian, officially condemned the thesis of his predecessor.[334]

What premises in our treatise led Bernard to his proposition regarding the general resurrection?[335] In this final stage, he continues to treat of love as *affectio naturalis*. This *affectio*, he knows, in its association with our earthly bodies cannot love with perfect purity—i.e., *ob solam ipsius videlicet voluntatem, non nostram voluptatem* (28). It needs the spiritual body of the resurrection, SUBJECT TO THE SPIRIT IN EVERYTHING (29).[336] But since he sees the *affectio* of the present life as receptive of grace, why would he not envision a condition, even before the resurrection, in which grace could overcome the 'heaviness' of our present embodiment, a state in which the soul was not encumbered by the body? Bernard's *affectio*, remember, is never rejected, only possessed and informed progressively by grace. An answer is suggested by his sense of the necessary cooperation of the body in the operations of the self— the necessity, for human fulfillment, of a *corpus integrum* (29): THE BODY, he says, IS NOT . . . RESUMED WITHOUT PROFIT TO THE SOUL (30).[337] Much of the enthusiasm of his argumentation in the four degrees is inspired by the conviction that loving God is the purpose for which God has made us, an expression of a 'nature' graced in creation and capable of receiving God's leading action. He does not divide or abstract the human subject's actions from its essential embodiment. The self that loves God is the integral self. But, how can one love God with all one's strength, *tota virtute*, as long as one's material condition requires the soul's strength to supply life and sentience (29)?[338] To be a body, then, is to be distracted from God (*corpori intenta et distenta*) or, as he explains elsewhere, to be in some measure 'absent' from God.[339] To overcome this condition, grace cannot destroy the human person; it supplies, instead, a new kind of body, A SECOND GARMENT (31).[340] Until then, love is imperfect. The invaluable experiential perspective in which the author has studied love creates a difficulty here where he must describe an advance beyond the possibilities, as he says, of present experience.

A later theology, speaking metaphysically of the *formal object* of love and the *supernatural* character of charity, was able to move past the speculative barrier, though we may lament that, as a mode of christian reflection, it failed to incorporate the richness of Bernard's existential concerns.[341]

His first concern was that we elicit all the forces of our nature in love, because the God whose action Bernard discerns within himself desires Bernard more than an act of Bernard's disembodied will. The concept of a formal object of love clarifying the nature of present experience would, indeed, have helped in the question regarding the possibility of perfect love before the general resurrection, but the metaphysical minimalism of *formal object* is not well suited to the needs of an experiential account such as Bernard wants to give.[342] This is not to disparage attention to metaphysical correctness, which means, in this instance, respect for reality. It is, rather, to observe that the weakness uncovered in Bernard's argument on the fourth degree does not invalidate his concept of love.[343] We know that under the press of life's necessities, he reflected upon the priority of *caritas in actu* over *caritas in affectu* and concluded that in this wisdom one sees things simply as they are.[344] Such a thinker was not altogether unaware of metaphysical distinctions regarding love's object. To say, as Delfgaauw does, that the abbot's opinion on the general resurrection reveals an imperfection in the bernardine concept of love is to claim too much.[345]

Bernard's second existential concern has to do with a recognition and acceptance of our embodiment as a dimension of what we inalienably are. If at the consummation of our development, the author believes, the body plays no role in the love and enjoyment of God, then there is no reason even in life to find any element of personal identity in the body. The abbot's sense of eschatological imagery gives him a prospective view of the end time, a vision of the fulfillment of present realities, rather than an involvement in mere anticipatory reporting of events that are to happen later.[346] This is made plain by the pocket lecture on the benefits received from the body (31–33) which follows upon his opinion about the resurrection. To become receptive of this value in the treatise is not to reject the ecclesiastical judgment that pronounced a delay before the full beatific vision to be contrary to the belief of the community of faith. What was so crucial to Saint Bernard in this matter that, to safeguard it, he should hazard publication of a doctrinal view that not even his most faithful disciples would share?

There were patristic precedents, but they were mere fragments. Rahner has said, 'Whenever the Fathers became "philosophers", . . . it is noticeable that they find it difficult to include the body in the victory of the "spirit".'[347] Ambrose, who had guided Bernard most on the issue, spoke of the body as the soul's prison. How instructive to observe that the abbot excised this theme from his source, omitting it completely![348] A similar modification of precedents occurs in Bernard's treatment of a New Testament image that weighed heavily in the question, especially with Ambrose— Rev 6:9–11, which speaks of the souls of the martyrs waiting 'underneath the altar'. In later sermons Bernard departs from his sources and declares that the altar in question is the very body of Christ.[349] In the matter of the general resurrection, therefore, Bernard could dredge up very little from the tradition to encourage him in the special inspiration he takes from the theme.

Today, when christian thinkers lament a broadly shared excessively 'other-worldly' conception of the Gospel (irreconcilable with the prophetic strain of biblical literature, in both testaments), Bernard's view that, even in eternity, we cannot be wholly present to God except as embodied beings is striking. The preoccupation behind it pushed the author into an uncharted area of eschatology and led him to accept the possibility of error. Despite Saint Bernard's sense of urgency, the area is still largely uncharted.[350]

The christian response to the hypothesis Bernard entertains is divided. Many theologians have a furtive recognition of the alternatives he faced: to relinquish the biblical image of the human being as essentially embodied or to delay the full joy of heaven until the general resurrection. They choose what seems the safer course, but fail to avoid a weakened conviction about the dignity of our physicality. Others consider the hypothesis of a divided human essence a metaphysical impossibility and, in consequence, relegate the biblical image of a general resurrection either to the category of ineffectual poeticizing or to that of a theologoumenon of only peripheral concern. To recognize, instead, that the eschatological

images of the Bible need to be reconciled with the biblical image
of a human person's integrity, or unity of body and soul, is to share
the concern which pushed Bernard to the position he espoused.

We may reconstruct his thinking in this way: the self cannot
love completely unless it is itself complete (30). Since God is the
guarantor of its essence (23), creating it and pledging through
the promise of God's own love to sustain it (25), every moment
of human consciousness should verify that God's promise is kept.
But, before the resurrection, the awareness that the self exists in
a denatured state, deprived of what is truly its *proprium*, its body,
throws it back upon itself (30), on what it was always tempted to
fear would have to be its own resources (23). Bernard is led to
think that even in the beatific vision, where faith and hope have
been left behind, the promise that death would be swallowed up
in victory (he alludes to 1 Cor 15:54) would not yet be kept;
the self, then, would be incapable of relinquishing its own self-
concern (30). The hypothesis was forced on him by the failure of
the theological tradition to move beyond a literal reading of the
eschatological symbols of the New Testament.

We must stop there for a moment. DeVregille's caution against
mollifying the character of Bernard's error may not be altogether
good advice. It is incumbent on readers to discern the meaning of
Bernard's teaching, and something of significance may lie under
the error itself. We must begin in the formal object of Bernard's
argument rather than in the formal object of love. He affirms,
first, that until the soul is again embodied after death, God's
promise is not yet kept; and, second, that until the self is again
complete in its nature (embodied), it cannot be complete in its
action (love). These are unexceptionable tenets. Their objective
is the safeguarding of a central biblical insight: the human being,
though matter and spirit, is one unit; the body constitutes the
person even as the soul does.[351] The abbot goes on to say that only
after the general resurrection will the saved fully love and enjoy
God only because received notions of death as the separation of
soul and body and of the general resurrection as the restoration of
the body made this an inevitable conclusion. Christian doctrine,
however, does not include a set of metaphysical definitions of
soul and body and death, any more than it prescribes a literal

reading of such eschatological symbols as the general resurrection. These are intellectually negotiable quantities, and in these we will find Bernard's error. Given his anthropological assumptions— which remain those of most Christians to this day—he had to choose either to affirm the dignity of the body, while tolerating in consequence an unfamiliar idea about the delay of the perfect love and enjoyment of God, or to profess a safer teaching about beatitude, while evading the fact that, at least in the popular mind, this compromised a biblical sense of the unity of the human being. He knew the harm that came from a spiritualistic concept of the self, and he thought he had a precedent for his choice in patristic authorities.

Rather than wince in embarrassment over the later condemnation of what Saint Bernard had proposed, admirers of the saint might take up, as others have not, his challenge to find, in the cultural substratum of their awareness of the bible's eschatological symbols, a religious anthropology that will enable them to affirm these symbols consistently. For example: will the self perhaps be embodied in some way after death before the Last Day—an idea possibly warranted by 1 Cor 35–49? In practice, this may mean affirming so close a connectedness of the soul to the earth and the human community—to the body—that even in death, before the Last Day, the soul's effectual relation to the body will allow the person to function completely, to love and enjoy God totally.[352]

Eschatological symbols have been low on the theological agenda, perhaps because they are deemed to have slight pastoral significance. And this contrast of evaluation is surely the remarkable feature of the issue. The abbot of Clairvaux, that most practical of spiritual guides, the writer who declined to entertain any reflection which was not immediately *ad nostram salutem,* believed it to be so important that, virtually alone in his time and without the protection of a solid body of authoritative opinion, he articulated a precise and explicit view and repeatedly set it forth.[353] In this, surely, he was not wrong.

In paragraphs 31–33 the author composes a lyrical reprise to his treatment of the question that has occupied him in his reflection upon the general resurrection: the necessity of the body's sharing

in the consummation of divine love. He continues preoccupied
with certain tendencies to conceive of human embodiment in
spiritualistic ways, to disown 'the body'. His evaluation of our
bodiliness enlarges upon his argument on the general resurrection: THE FLESH IS CLEARLY A GOOD AND FAITHFUL PARTNER FOR A
GOOD SPIRIT (31); it is beneficial in life, after death, and after its
resurrection.[354] The idea is illustrated in a lengthy moral and ana-
gogical interpretation of the Song of Songs 5.1: EAT, FRIENDS, AND
DRINK; BE INEBRIATED, DEAREST ONES (31). This is not intended
as scriptural 'proof'; the treatise has already made its case using
other texts.[355]

Bernard's development of the image from the Song is original.[356]
We must not remain insensitive to the weight he gives the reflection that there is no human wholeness apart from the body. Any
reader surprised by these paragraphs and inclined to consider
them the sudden and fanciful ballooning of a commonplace idea
should step back to set the treatise at some aesthetic distance
and consider the following: the 'body' theme is planted early,
developed variously—e.g., in the ubiquitous motif of *necessitas*, in
that of compassion, of the social character of human beings, of
the resurrection, and finally of an eternal revelry—and recapit-
ulated forcefully. Nothing but uncritically held preconceptions
concerning a 'platonic mind' can jam the signal of Saint Bernard's
consciousness here.[357] As he clothes his idea in biblical imagery—
the inebriation of the Song, reserved for the moment when the
body will be restored—he assumes a more lyrical manner.

Rousselot acknowledged a different kind of surprise. He found
in *De diligendo Deo* something approaching the non-dualistic relationship of body and soul which he had not expected to emerge
from theological literature until Aquinas a century later.[358] Indeed, Bernard's antiphonary manner of affirming that, until the
resurrection, there will be SOMETHING MISSING (31) in heaven
sends us to his works for further development of this strong sense
of the essential oneness of body and soul.[359] We are drawn to
make inferences from the logic of the following points: the soul
gives life and sentience to the body (besides Dil 29, above, SC
30.9; SBOp 1:215,30); the soul sees, hears, etc. in the senses of
the body (Csi 5, 12; SBOp 3:476,16–18); the body is the human

mode of presence (SC 4.5; SBOp 1:20,25); one must distinguish between the self and the soul, which is one with the body (SC 30.9; SBOp 1:215,21–216,16); between soul and body there is an *unitas naturalis* (Div 80.l; SBOp 6/1:320,5–6).

Bernard's discussions of body and soul contain no set of concepts to match the elegant simplicity of thomistic hylomorphism, which holds that the soul is the substantial form of the body. Bernard's distance from any notion of body and soul as metaphysical principles is evident in the problem he and those of his era find in situating the soul in *place*.[360] Nevertheless, he seems to have an intuition that operates as almost the functional equivalent. His opinion on the general resurrection forces attention to this possibility. His conclusion contradicts facile attributions of a platonic dualism to his work, or at least of the existential consequences of what is understood ordinarily and inaccurately as platonic dualism.[361]

Bernard's poetic style of treating the resurrection as entry into an eternal inebriation, uncovers an attitude more than an idea. We may not be easily satisfied with the many bernardine expressions on the body that seem negative and severe, even when we know they are biblical and traditional.[362] But we reach this ascetic's true sense of human life when we grant equal attention to his very frequent celebrations of the body. Early in the treatise, he claimed that natural law could be seen IN THE PERFECTION OF MAN'S MIND AND BODY (6).[363] The sentiment is found in other works as admiration for the way the body maintains a likeness to God lost by the soul (Div 12.1), for the upright posture of the body (SC 24.6; Sent 3.66; Mor 42.5), for the 'glory of the human condition' (Nat 2.1), for the way the body mirrors the mind and manifests the beauty of the soul (SC 85.11), by an exhortation to love the body (QH 10.3), and still others.

The abbot's most systematic valuation of our embodiment, however, is his imagistic treatment of three stages in the body's collaboration in divine love—eat, drink, and be innebriated. Only when the blessed in heaven again have bodies, A SECOND GARMENT . . . THEIR RESUMED AND GLORIFIED BODIES (31), will they be wholly free to love (and one must continue by inference), *because* they are inspirited bodies even as they are embodied spirits.[364] For the reader who would know Saint Bernard's mind, this *reason*, standing for a conviction of biblical faith, is the true content of his reflection on the resurrection. He calls attention to what he considers a corollary of the indivisibility of body and soul only to overcome possible spiritualistic, unbiblical attitudes toward the body in his readers.

This purpose is made plain by his careful development of the body's three stages, which begins, THE FLESH IS CLEARLY A GOOD AND FAITHFUL PARTNER FOR A GOOD SPIRIT (31).[365] WHILE IN THE FLESH, IT [the good spirit] MOVES BY FAITH, WHICH NECESSARILY ACTS THROUGH CHARITY (32).[366] Eating bread in this first phase means doing the will of God (cf Jn 4.34). AFTERWARDS, HAVING CAST OFF ITS FLESH, [the spirit can] DRINK MORE DEEPLY OF THE WINE OF LOVE . . . WINE MIXED WITH MILK (32).[367] Before the resurrection the departed soul's capacity for love is kept from full realization by the admixture of this milk of an *affectio naturalis* for the body. But, at the general resurrection INTOXICATION OVERTURNS THE MIND AND MAKES IT WHOLLY FORGETFUL OF ITSELF (32).[368] In this state it passes entirely into God, CEASING ALL THE MORE TO BE LIKE ITSELF AS IT BECOMES MORE AND MORE LIKE GOD (32).[369]

Bernard speaks of likeness to God in a different context from his classic treatment of the image and likeness of God in the soul. In our sentence, the soul, having received its glorified body, is not now, in its completion, pronounced more like *itself*, as we might expect. In the God-self polarity of the four degrees of love, the self is closely associated with its *proprium*, what one seeks for oneself, though the self will never be defined in such terms.[370] It is not the new glorified body, as distinguished from the body of earth, that accounts for our superior possibilities; it is the elimination of desire for what is our own. After the resurrection, in the absence of this self-seeking, we are less like that self. In the perfection of self-knowledge we have arrived at the perception which Bernard will later describe: 'You are an altogether unworthy object even of your own love, except for the sake of him without whom you are nothing'.[371]

Desire for what is one's own is a care, and care (we have seen) withdraws one's *affectio* from God. With the restoration of the body, we shall be finally FREE FROM THE GNAWING CARE ABOUT

WHAT IS ONE'S OWN (32).[372] Only then, for such care cannot be entirely eliminated from the earthly situation of human beings. *Cura* is a motif in Bernard's great *necessitas* theme.[373] It belongs to *caritas actualis*, which involves itself ordinarily with things of lesser sublimity: 'The actual [charity] prefers more lowly things; the affective, those that are higher'.[374] In the instance of the soul's desire for its body, the continued involvement with creaturely necessity is more than a preference.

In a transitional sentence the place of the great revelry is given, WITH CHRIST IN HIS FATHER'S HOUSE (32). To conclude his exposition of four degrees of divine love, Bernard expands this image poetically. The three phases of the body-soul relationship are spoken of as a TRIPLE BANQUET OF CHARITY (33) over which Wisdom presides.[375] Wisdom stands for the experiential dimension in which love has been discussed, but it denotes the eternal Word as well, the Bridegroom of the Canticle, whose words we have been reflecting upon. This last paragraph is pointedly Christological. The feast is THE NUPTIALS OF THE LAMB, who TAKES HIS CHURCH TO HIM IN HER GLORY (33).[376]

Only at this final moment in the discussion of the four degrees (and, indeed, of most of the treatise) does the author set Christ in the foreground. Some commentators have fitted a carnal love for Christ into the first degree of love.[377] But Bernard himself omitted this. With reflections on religious experience dealing self-consciously and explicitly in the *memoria Christi*, would he not have had to forgo his chosen point of view, that of human beings as such, exemplified in the *infideles*? True, Christ-centered arguments for loving God are eloquently offered in paragraphs one and seven-to-thirteen; but, in a declared comparative approach, they do not form that part of the study from which the four degrees-of-love pericope is constructed. And yet, here in the end it is revealed that the One who waits on all those who partake of the eternal banquet of charity—that triple banquet which includes those in the body nourishing themselves laboriously on earth—is the Son of God. The author's affirmation of the necessity of the body is very affectingly illustrated in this meeting with Christ in his resurrected body.

This beautiful image serves Bernard well. In his Christology, devotion to the earthly Jesus is enjoined on the faithful as a beginning in the love of God. Christ is 'a spirit before our face' and must now be discerned as eternally in the bosom of the Father.[378] The tender vignette of the end, in which the Son of God, IN HIS FATHER'S HOUSE (32), serves divine love to all humanity—those in labor, in rest, and in glory—presents an image in which the divine Word and the earthly Jesus are now eternally one. At the same time, Bernard remains within his chosen perspective: at the end (even as in the last judgment of Mt 25:31–40) the 'infidels' who have loved *God*, without the benefit of christian faith, will identify their Lord.

The TRIPLE BANQUET (33) which Bernard depicts makes no explicit reference to the Eucharist. The bread which we eat while in our earthly bodies is the laborious action by which we do God's will; he cites Jn 4:34: 'My food is to do the will of my Father' (32).[379] In the abbot's monastic theology, as we have suggested earlier, the sacraments are elementary and earthly means of moving to divine union; the contemplative monk must not stop in these.[380] In monastic writings of the period, less emphasis is placed on the Eucharist as a means of union with God, or of making oneself present to God, than is found toward the end of the twelfth century.[381] This sacramental theology is consistent with Bernard's Christology and with the character of his devotion to Christ's humanity: the Christian must not rest in that humanity which is but the sacrament of the eternal Word.

Here at the end of the four degrees of loving God we may ask what, in essence, this process is. The structural symmetries provoke the question: a love-of-self forms bookends at either side of a love-of-God, for oneself in the second degree and for God in the third. We come full-circle from self to self. Is this not, in one important aspect, a discovery of the true self? Although the quest has been for God, not for the self, the questions the author accepted has established the perspective, a self-preoccupied one; and he has striven to produce a new beginning. The highest degree of love reveals who we truly are. The center of wonderment here is the mystery of self, a progress from a self that had been seen as the one known reality, assumed to be in tension with God, to a self seen as unfathomable in its ties to the reality of God.

Despite its rational refinement, the process may seem to be elementary, just as the author labeled it in his introduction. Those experienced in the spirit seek the God known to be within, rather than inquire how God relates to the self—why and how God should be loved. They see their need in the guise of the radical biblical image of conversion and do not require an account of the rationality of this. When Bernard addresses a discourse on divine love explicitly to his monks, as in the *Super Cantica*, he begins with the kiss—a triple kiss. The first kiss, to the feet of the divine Word, represents conversion.[382] But, again, the abbot is pleased to pay his debt to the 'unwise', aware that even advanced souls, occasionally falling out of wisdom, will find support in his argument.

In his finale on the four degrees, Bernard mentions the Church: HE TAKES HIS CHURCH TO HIM IN HER GLORY WITHOUT A BLEMISH, WRINKLE, OR ANY DEFECT OF THE SORT (33).[383] It is not incidental that the author chooses this setting in ultimate glory to identify the Church. The Church he addresses is always the Church of the perfect (*ecclesia perfectorum*, as in SC 14.5), those intent on being, collectively, the spouse of Christ the Bridegroom—*nos qui simul ecclesia sumus* (SC 57.3). The tradition extends from Origen.[384] This Church, which Congar observes is 'very spiritual, very monastic', recognizes itself at the great wedding banquet.[385]

Bernard seems to be composing an ending. The *affectio* which he has traced from its beginnings in nature remains as THAT ETERNAL, INEXPLICABLE DESIRE KNOWING NO WANT (33).[386] He eloquently collates many eschatological images, and closes the paragraph grandly with a variation on the double thesis of the treatise, that the way, or measure, of loving God is beyond measure and that the reason for loving God is God: now finally, with this fourth degree, he writes, GOD ALONE IS LOVED IN THE HIGHEST WAY . . . THAT HE MAY BE THE REWARD OF THOSE WHO LOVE HIM (33).[387] Then his text continues.

PART THREE

ON LOVING GOD: COMPLEMENTARY ARGUMENTS (34–40)

The third part of *De diligendo Deo* is, as Bernard declares, simply his earlier letter to the Carthusians, minus its introduction and conclusion.[388] We shall refer to it simply as the letter. PERHAPS I MADE SOME OTHER REMARKS IN IT ABOUT CHARITY, he writes, BUT NOT DIFFERENT FROM WHAT I SAY HERE (34).[389] Are we to expect from these 'other remarks . . . about charity' no organic contribution to the treatise? Readers become accustomed to this skillful and highly organized writer's disarming protestations of in-difference to formal organization, but this is a special case. To the body of thought the letter affixes three units: first, a reflection on three ways of relating to God (34–37), a construct which Bernard in no way attempts to connect to the four degrees of love, and in which he ignores the spousal relationship developed in the text so far; second, an exposition of the law of love (35–38), an idea which offers fine possibilities for organizing the pervasive themes of rationality and justice which have preceded, but which Bernard allows to remain, in point of form, unrealized; and, third, a final two paragraphs (39–40) which are an appropriate conclusion to what we have read so far but which seem, strangely, to be loosely connected to the letter in which they occur.

Jean Leclercq, in studying the art of composition in Bernard's treatises, declared *De diligendo Deo* 'un cas surprenant'.[390] It is the only instance we know where Bernard published an extended earlier work joined to his principal effort. The letter itself seems to be a composite work, if we consider the disjunction of those final two paragraphs, where, incidentally, even the vocabulary of love changes, seemingly to accomodate that of the treatise.[391] Leclercq speculates on the sequence of the composition—(a) Ep 11.1–7, (b) Dil 1–33, (c) a recapitulation of the thought of *De diligendo Deo* in Ep 11.8–9, (d) the addition of Ep 11.1–9 to *De diligendo Deo*. Another possibility, he allows, is that the two summary paragraphs (Ep 11.8–9) were the abstract from which Bernard formed his later work. This we find more plausible. But all this must remain conjecture; no trace of it is found in the manuscript tradition.[392]

What is most surprising is that Bernard, who was adept at revising and seamlessly integrating adjustments to his texts, should have left this popular treatise in an unpolished, unintegrated condition. May we surmise that a rapid propagation of the manuscript removed it from his control?[393] Some awareness of these conditions can assist interpreters, discouraging desperate attempts at uncovering linkages which the author seems never to have formed. For once we may take the busy abbot at his word without suspecting him of that high art which conceals art: Dil 34–38 is an add-on, SOME OTHER REMARKS . . . ABOUT CHARITY (34), left without a well-worked bonding of parts because this was EASIER (*non inutile. . . facilius*).

And yet, despite some formal untidiness, we easily perceive this added material as complementary rather than supplementary, to the central thrust of the text. To this point we have read of love as desire (an *affectio*) and state of spirit (*affectus*). It now assumes the guise of relationship (34), law (35–38), and substance (35). This bernardine triad of love in God (substance), in the totality of beings (law), and in humans (*affectus*) recurs in authors of the Renaissance.[394] The letter to the Carthusians conceives of love very broadly, while the later treatise delves into that one dimension of the subject, *affectio naturalis*, which seems most to engage Saint Bernard. Given this relationship between the two works, joining the letter to the treatise provides a metaphysical context for the author's deliberately restricted experiential focus on love as *affectio naturalis*.[395] Beyond that, we must recall what we said earlier about the influence of Guy, whose presence is first sensed in the letter addressed to him: the philosophical perspective which his *Meditationes* encouraged extends to most parts of Bernard's treatise.

The study of a more specific sense for *caritas* in the letter can be placed in continuity with the treatise's reflections on *amor*. Bernard reviews the relationships to God symbolized by a slave (fear), a hireling (desire for gain), and A SON WHO HONORS HIS FATHER (34), in order to argue that only in the last model is there charity.[396] What each of these figures finds in God determines the relationship: A MAN CAN ACKNOWLEDGE THAT THE LORD IS POWERFUL, THAT THE LORD IS GOOD TO HIM, AND THAT THE LORD IS

SIMPLY GOOD (34).[397] Although faith recognizes THE LORD under
any guise (Bernard does not say this), only CHARITY CONVERTS
SOULS BECAUSE IT MAKES THEM ACT WILLINGLY (34).[398] What we
read earlier leads us to interpret this way: charity, which is God's
love, moves our natural affections, making it possible for us to
love God 'spontaneously'—*sponte afficit, et spontaneum facit* (17).
But we pause, finding ourselves working now with a different
vocabulary. The rich connotations that built up around *amor* as
*affectio naturalis* seem absent from these sentences; and the *spontaneus* of paragraph 17, suggesting the movement of the whole
psyche, has become *voluntarius*. Though the two manners do not
diverge from one another, we may gain an inkling here of why
Bernard determined to move from the more general concepts of
metaphysical psychology in his earlier letter to the more concrete
phenomenological method of the treatise. He was not preoccupied with reconciling the claim that the love of God exists only
in the highest and purest relationship to God, with his preceding
development of four *degrees* of love for God. Nor does he hesitate
to define love for God as not seeking what is one's own, after
having argued that this state of love will be possible to us only
after the general resurrection. We must, then, read Bernard's new
assertions about the *caritas* he is describing—he speaks of it even
in the treatise as *verus amor* (17)—not as divine love simply, but
as the perfection of that divine love towards which he encourages
all persons to strive.[399]

This typology of love, comprising slave, hireling, and son, fits
awkwardly into a text which has often and at length spoken of
the highest form of love as that between spouses (7, 9–10, 12–13,
33). In his letter Bernard follows a tradition that interprets the
prodigal son in the parable as passing through three conditions
and experiencing three states of soul, the *affectus* of fear, cupidity,
and love.[400] In the *Super Cantica* (SC 7.2; 83.5) he will accept the
necessity of choosing one type, finally rejecting filial love's claim
to preeminence because of ambiguities in a son's mentality, and
declaring the love of spouses to be superior on the grounds they
hold all things in common.[401] What Bernard admired in spousal
love is not different, however, from what the tradition found in

the love of father and son—the implications of 'all that is mine is yours' (Lk 15:31).[402]

## Love as Universal Law (35–38)

Bernard now moves to the central topic of this part of the treatise, love as the eternal law. IT IS CALLED THE LAW OF THE LORD, he writes, EITHER BECAUSE HE LIVES BY IT OR BECAUSE NOBODY POSSESSES IT EXCEPT AS A GIFT FROM HIM (35).[403] He is bemused that one can say, GOD LIVES BY A LAW (34). But, this law is not something outside of God. He explains that the law he speaks of is THAT CHARITY WHICH SOMEHOW HOLDS AND BRINGS TOGETHER THE TRINITY IN THE BOND OF PEACE (35).[404] CHARITY IS THE DIVINE SUBSTANCE. . . . GOD IS LOVE (35).[405] This same charity *gives* charity, so that ALL THINGS WERE MADE ACCORDING TO THIS LAW IN WEIGHT, MEASURE, AND NUMBER (cf Wis 11:21) (35).[406] In this we have a vision of the entire universe made and sustained by one creative energy which is love, the love which flows from that substantial love which is God: SUCH IS THE ETERNAL LAW WHICH CREATES AND GOVERNS THE UNIVERSE (35).[407]

It is curious that, although Bernard emphasizes the substantial character of the love by which God lives—LET NOBODY THINK I HOLD CHARITY TO BE A QUALITY OR A KIND OF ACCIDENT IN GOD (35)—he does not identify this love as the Holy Spirit.[408] It is as if, at this juncture, the aesthetic character of the argument would not be bolstered by a recognition of love as Person, the love of the Father and Son, taking the foreground from the utter oneness of love as the universal law. Von Balthasar speaks of a 'sacral monism' in the era, and traces it from the Fathers through Boethius and Eriugena and 'Bernard and his school' to the Victorines. This 'monism' regards the unity of *eros*, taken by the Fathers from the classical world: '*Amor* [*eros*] is, . . . the vital-subjective side of the harmony of the world, which is rooted in God and therefore must necessarily (in the sense of the *Symposium*) be universal'.[409] What Christian thought accepted from the classical world in this instance was not a blurring of the distinction between Creator and creation or a concept of divine immanence that would detract from the reality of God's transcendence; it was instead what Bernard wished to reaffirm in his generation against the gathering force of a new profane philosophy—'the world-view of an unbroken sacrality'.[410] In this we discern the impetus of his meditation upon a single universal law.

The author has described three relationships with God (34) and one law which embraces all reality (35). He now shows how these relationships come under the eternal law, how the fear of the slave and the cupidity of the hireling are themselves laws (36), and how the love of a son exemplifies the law of the Lord (37).

THE SLAVE AND THE MERCENARY HAVE A LAW OF THEIR OWN, we read, WHICH IS NOT FROM THE LORD. . . . WHICH IS SUBJECT ALL THE SAME TO THE LORD'S LAW (36).[411] The first thought, that there are other laws, sets up a contrast to the point of exclusivity between real love and the condition of those FORCED ON BY SLAVISH FEAR OR DRAWN ON BY A HIRELING'S CUPIDITY (36).[412] A person makes his own law WHEN HE PREFERS HIS OWN WILL TO THE COMMON, ETERNAL LAW (36).[413] To establish one's will as one's law, Bernard continues, is a perverse imitation of the Creator. Though he does not say so here, it is the essence of sin. THIS HEAVY AND UNBEARABLE YOKE WEIGHS ON ALL ADAM'S SONS (36).[414] The biblical reminiscences are of interest: Sir 40:1 enumerates the disorders of human sinfulness; and in Acts 15:10 Peter rejects the idea that the faithful are subject to the law of Moses. The references to the Epistle to the Romans are numerous in these paragraphs (36–39), with five links to Rom 7 and 8, highlighting Paul's contrast between 'the law of sin which dwells in my members' (Rom 7:23) and 'the law of the Spirit of life in Christ Jesus' (Rom 8:2). The laws of fear and of cupidity belong to THIS BODY OF DEATH (36); they are antagonistic to the law of the Lord.[415]

In the Rule (Chapter 7), 'the perfect love of God which casts out fear'[416] comes at the top of the ladder of humility. But Bernard does not intend a gradual displacement of the imperfect; his antithesis is between contradictory values.

Of special significance for *De diligendo Deo* in the contrast Bernard has set up is the clear meaning of concupiscence on which this contrast rests. We spoke earlier of two senses which christian tradition found in the notion of concupiscence. So far in his reflection upon the law of love the abbot has assumed the one which bonds concupiscence more tightly to sin. The slave and the hireling become ideal types, and their fear and cupidity (as specifications of concupiscence) are abstractions which derive their meaning from the polarity in which they occur: they are *not* love, they are hostile to love, they displace love. It suits the author's purpose at the moment to look at this side of the human condition: he is arguing for the exclusivity of charity as the universal and eternal law.

But even within the paragraph where this is established, a seed is planted for future growth: Bernard wants to speak of connections between the law of love and what he has labeled the laws of fear and of cupidity. EACH ONE CAN MAKE A LAW FOR HIMSELF, he writes, BUT HE CANNOT WITHDRAW IT FROM THE UNCHANGEABLE ORDER OF THE ETERNAL LAW (36).[417] And later: HE HAS NOT ESCAPED FROM GOD'S LAW (36).[418] Finally, addressing God: THERE IS JUST ONE LAW FOR BOTH OF US (36).[419] How, precisely, are those who contradict God's law of love found nevertheless contained within it? Bernard says that the fugitive from God cannot escape the law of *justice*; and, more to the point, that the hell which sinners endure is not God's doing but their own. HE WHO CASTS AWAY THE PLEASANT YOKE AND LIGHT LOAD OF CHARITY, he writes, WILL HAVE TO BEAR UNWILLINGLY THE UNBEARABLE BURDEN OF HIS OWN WILL(36).[420] The justice of which Bernard speaks must be seen as the truth, as simple reality asserting itself. As counter-reality, the law of self is an unbearable burden. Our punishment is that we are allowed to obey the fictive law of self-will. Merton called the contrast between this and more conventional views of God's justice: ' . . . an extremely subtle and deeply spiritual analysis. . . . one of the most astute pieces of spiritual psychology ever written'.[421]

Bernard seems to say that even sinners pursue the good to which their wills are ordained, and in that exhibit a perversion of what is nonetheless the law of love. He has, in fact, put it that way earlier in the treatise: EVERY RATIONAL BEING NATURALLY DESIRES ALWAYS WHAT SATISFIES MORE ITS MIND AND WILL. . . . HE CANNOT FIND PEACE THIS SIDE OF WHAT IS HIGHEST OR BEST (18).[422] It is unusual to have to surmise what this powerful rhetorician *seems* to be saying. Within a passage that develops the contrast between charity and the natural drives of a fallen human nature, the author is in no position to illustrate the great theme we have referred to as the unity of a universal *eros*. For this he needs a different context, the one from which he argued for a natural desire for 'what is highest or best'. In this context concupiscence assumes its other meaning as simply the not-yet regulated energies of the psyche. Merton sensed the tension. He remarks that Bernard here 'seems to be caught in the apparent contradiction of an "exterior" law that is no longer exterior'.[423]

The third relationship with God, that of a son who loves, also comes within the universal law of the Lord. The only challenge the abbot finds here is in reconciling the idea of law with the freedom of those who love. He reads in 1 Tim 1:9: LAWS ARE NOT MADE FOR THOSE WHO ARE GOOD (37).[424] This means, Bernard believes, they are not imposed by God but freely accepted by the good. And yet, one follows the universal law of the Lord when one lives by charity.

To this point in his discussion of law, the author has seen the love of God abstractly, as an exclusion of fear and cupidity. Now he considers how the law of charity is actually borne by human beings—GAILY AND EASILY (38).[425] Charity is indeed the universal law, but how, concretely, does it accomplish its purposes within the human being? The change of perspective brings about a striking reassessment of the fear and cupidity the author finds in the slave's and the hireling's love of God. In fact, these one-dimensional types seem to lose their serviceability, and fear and cupidity become merely parts of the *affectus* of love, for the begining of all love is in the flesh. Suddenly this is a more familiar Saint Bernard.

When the abbot describes the experience of sin it is always part of that larger experience in which a divine force draws us *out* of sin. Bernard presents not a simple antagonism of the two laws, but rather the victory of the law of the spirit over the law of sin.[426] The abstractness of our passage (34–37) differentiates it from this ordinary manner. Paragraph 38 is a transition to the experiential point of view from which Bernard will envision the four degrees of love (39).

Of the laws of the slave and the hireling, Bernard says the law of charity DOES NOT DESTROY THEM BUT FULFILLS THEM. . . . IT TEMPERS THE SLAVE'S LAW AND SETS THE HIRELING'S IN ORDER,

MAKING BOTH LIGHTER (38).[427] With the presuppositions of the last few paragraphs, it would be impossible to say this. Here we speak of a fear that will always accompay charity and of a cupidity which charity will put in order but not destroy. In fact, CHARITY OBEYS the laws of the slave and the hireling. This remark, in its paradoxical form, brings to mind Bernard's abiding sense of the force of *necessitas* in things of the spirit. Obviously, the underlying sense of concupiscence has shifted, for charity does not obey sin.

As to the mutual exclusiveness of charity and our imperfect human *affectus*, Bernard tests the maxim of 1 Jn 4:18: PERFECT CHARITY DRIVES AWAY FEAR (38). IT IS A FIGURE OF SPEECH (38), he says: charity drives out only the effects of fear.[428] CUPIDITY IN TURN IS SET IN RIGHT ORDER BY THE ARRIVAL OF CHARITY (38), but cupidity remains. Now, however, IT PREFERS WHAT IS BETTER TO WHAT IS GOOD (38).[429] We have already seen the author's expansion of this statement (18). From our new standpoint, the fragility of the arguments which affirm that even sinners are encompassed within the law of charity (36) is easily firmed up.

We are witnessing an opening onto that bernardine vision of an *agape* which works its redeeming will within our fallen nature, softly guiding, transforming, but respecting the *eros* of its creation. The greatest triumph of this *agape*, this eternal law which all reality obeys, is its gentle and welcomed possession of the freedom it creates. Bernard can here begin to project such a vision because of the new position he has taken up.

## Recapitulation (39–40)

The last two paragraphs (39–40) summarize the treatise. (The operative term, we remember, is *amor*, replacing the *caritas* of which the author has spoken in his letter until now, and linking with the rest of the work.) On the other hand, within the confines of the letter, the thought is a magnificent development, which Bernard's meditation upon the cold discontinuity between charity and the condition of a fallen creature (its fear and cupidity) has prepared us to appreciate. We may surmise, especially from the weakness of the argument in paragraph 36, that the abbot did not set out to build this contrast, but that he found a way out in the shift of perspective we have just witnessed. In closing his letter to the Carthusians, he said he felt himself at that point driven to compose a long discourse but his duties did not permit it.[430] What he suddenly had to compose, it seems, was *On Loving God.*

The entire process of the growth in divine love, its beginning in the flesh and its consummation in the spirit, is envisioned in one sentence:

> SINCE WE ARE CARNAL (ROM 7:14) AND BORN OF CONCUPISCENCE OF THE FLESH, OUR CUPIDITY OR LOVE MUST BEGIN WITH THE FLESH, AND WHEN THIS IS SET IN ORDER, OUR LOVE ADVANCES BY FIXED DEGREES, LED ON BY GRACE, UNTIL IT IS CONSUMMATED IN THE SPIRIT (Gal 3:3), FOR NOT WHAT IS SPIRITUAL COMES FIRST, BUT WHAT IS ANIMAL, THEN WHAT IS SPIRITUAL [1 Cor 15:46] (39).[431]

Clearly the concupiscence of which the author speaks is not sin, for it is to be judged by its effects, in the flesh which grace can set in order. Then, it is parallelled by WHAT IS ANIMAL (39), which (in 1 Cor 15:46) means belonging to the creature. And, the cupidity OR LOVE he mentions is the *affectio naturalis* of the treatise, to be LED ON BY GRACE (39). It is not appropriate, then, to return for clarification to Bernard's discussion of the *affectiones* of fear and cupidity (34–37) which, in the perspective of a different understanding of concupiscence, locked out or excluded charity. The 'law of cupidity' in that context cannot render Bernard's meaning of cupidity in this new setting. One must not, therefore, interpret the abbot to mean that the cupidity, or *amor carnalis,* of the first two degrees of love excludes the condition of justification before God.[432]

Of the two ways of looking at concupiscence, the one which places in the foreground an absolute discontinuity between *agape* and *eros* renders any talk of human progress toward God dangerously ambiguous when not wholly meaningless. Concepts of progressive growth can be based only on the other view of the same reality, the one which rests on the equally biblical truth that the *eros* of our fallen nature is not *in itself* sin, but (in its lack of order) the effect of sin.

That these are different perspectives on the same reality is signalled in our treatise by the use of *cupiditas* to bear both meanings. Consider *cupiditas mercenaria* (36): it is tied to the law of the mercenary, which Bernard describes in the following terms:

> I MEAN EACH ONE WANTS TO MAKE HIS OWN LAW WHEN HE PREFERS HIS OWN WILL TO THE COMMON, ETERNAL LAW. HE SEEKS TO IMITATE HIS CREATOR IN A PERVERSE WAY, SO THAT AS GOD IS FOR HIMSELF HIS OWN LAW AND DEPENDS ON HIMSELF ALONE, SO DOES MAN WANT TO GOVERN HIMSELF AND MAKE HIS OWN WILL HIS LAW (36).[433]

It is difficult to read in this law of bad *will* merely the residue of human weakness after sin.

Then consider *cupiditas vel amor noster*, that which is CONSUMMATED IN THE SPIRIT (39).[434] The text moves from one to the other as it approaches the development of four degrees of love. Readers accustomed to Saint Augustine's more ordinary use of *cupiditas* as the self-love (*amor sui*) or pride which is the root of all sin must take special note of this. Bernard is more optimistic than Augustine in the manner in which he emphasizes and dwells upon that side of concupiscence which opens onto grace.[435]

In the light of this interpretive difficulty, how effectively clarifying is that religious anthropology which keeps an eye on both sides of the human condition, expressed in the traditional double meaning of concupiscence, by stating that sin has not deprived us of God's image but that our lost likeness to God can be restored only by redeeming grace working progressively within us! The theme comes into its own only in works after *De diligendo Deo*.

Since Bernard, following Gregory the Great and the monastic tradition before him, is committed to a gradualism in the life of the spirit, he focuses upon fallen human nature's capacity to be moved from within by grace.[436] OUR LOVE (*cupiditas vel amor noster*) ADVANCES BY FIXED DEGREES, he says, LED ON BY GRACE (39). In his first work, he wrote, 'No one becomes perfect suddenly; everyone ascends by degrees'.[437] The theological foundation of this classic Christian idea is what Bernard presents in the sweeping sentence that introduces his schema of four degrees of divine love (39). An awareness of how the ground shifts in his sense of concupiscence should allow us to follow him without difficulty.

The four degrees of love are outlined in one paragraph. MAN FIRST LOVES HIMSELF FOR HIMSELF BECAUSE HE IS CARNAL AND SENSITIVE TO NOTHING ELSE BUT HIMSELF (39).[438] The author moves immediately to the second degree: THEN WHEN HE SEES HE CANNOT SUBSIST BY HIMSELF, HE BEGINS TO SEEK FOR GOD BY FAITH AND TO LOVE HIM AS NECESSARY TO HIMSELF (39).[439] The love of neighbor is omitted from this brief sketch, though we have seen what weight the abbot will place on it in the development of the first two degrees (23–25). Convinced of their need, human beings begin to pursue God in prayer and meditation, and God is revealed to them gradually. WHEN MAN TASTES HOW SWEET GOD IS HE PASSES TO THE THIRD DEGREE OF LOVE IN WHICH MAN LOVES GOD NOT NOW BECAUSE OF HIMSELF BUT BECAUSE OF GOD (39).[440] The abbot believes the human being remains a long time at this level. I DOUBT IF HE EVER PERFECTLY ATTAINS THE FOURTH DEGREE DURING THIS LIFE, THAT IS, IF HE EVER LOVES HIMSELF ONLY FOR GOD'S SAKE (39).[441]

The author completes his exposition of the fourth degree, lightly touching on a few topics he will expand when this letter is joined to the treatise. The perfect love of God seems impossible in this life, but, LET THOSE WHO HAVE HAD THE EXPERIENCE MAKE A STATEMENT (39).[442] The blessed one in God's dwelling forgets himself: HE PASSES ENTIRELY INTO GOD (39).[443] He is inebriated. Several statements dwell on transcending the flesh. Wholly in the spirit, the blessed one is MINDFUL OF GOD'S JUSTICE ALONE (39).[444] (God's justice, instead of simply God, suggests a tie to the large theme of this letter, the universal *law* of love.) Just as we no longer know Christ according to the flesh (cf 2 Cor 5.16), NOBODY THERE KNOWS HIMSELF ACCORDING TO THE FLESH (40).[445] The substance of the flesh, however, remains.

Bernard draws a curtain over his picture of heaven with a final affirmation of two architectonic themes: First, ALL CARNAL NECESSITY WILL DISAPPEAR (39).[446] This lays to rest the incessant lament over the bondage of *necessitas*. Second, OUR PRESENT WEAK, HUMAN AFFECTIONS WILL BE CHANGED INTO DIVINE (39).[447] We have followed the long, laborious career of *affectio naturalis*; this, finally, is its happy ending. In the last reflection of *De diligendo Deo,* Saint Bernard in his best fashion joins several motifs in his picture of charity's great cosmic net:

> THEN CHARITY'S NET WHICH IS NOW BEING DRAGGED ACROSS THE BROAD AND MIGHTY OCEAN OF TIME, CATCHING ALL KINDS OF FISH, WILL BE PULLED ASHORE; THERE THE BAD WILL BE THROWN AWAY AND ONLY THE GOOD WILL BE KEPT (40).[448]

The metaphor is an allusion to Mt 13:47–50. The comprehensive enclosure of the net suggests the author's insistence that no one escapes the embrace of the law of God's love. The net of charity is drawn (*tracta*), just as God's lovableness has been spoken of as drawing our affections, as necessity pushes them. Onto the eternal shore of the resurrection and of judgment all are gathered, for the process of human history is consummated only there. Only in that resurrection, according to Bernard, are all tensions of human duality and ambivalence resolved.

Other images follow, of a somewhat anticlimactic quality. Charity's net is an effective coda to *De diligendo Deo.* While not the final unit in Bernard's letter to the Carthusians, it functions powerfully here in the treatise. In the sentences which he adds to this great image, he makes oblique references to the possibility of damnation and dwells on the soul's absolute absorption in God: WHERE THERE IS NO PLACE FOR MISERY (*miseriae*) OR TIME FOR MERCY (*misericordiae*), THERE WILL SURELY BE NO FEELING OF COMPASSION (*miserationis*) (40).[449] He has not dealt here with the question of souls awaiting the resurrection, but the same preoccupation is present: Bernard envisions a state in which nothing can hinder a total absorption of our *affectus* in God. Only in that complete presence to God is our love perfected. Therefore, there cannot be even a FEELING OF COMPASSION (40)—*nullus profecto esse poterit miserationis affectus.* The author does not flinch from accepting, with respect to the saved, the implication of a total absorption in God; or for the lost, their total alienation in self. The human solidarity which now prompts the reflection would moderate one's joy in God; it cannot survive the solidarity in God of those possessed by divine love. Nevertheless, in the interim, this final reflection provides *De diligendo Deo* with a consummation of strangely muted triumph.

This treatise has studied the love of God from the perspective of *affectio/affectus*. *Affectio* in which love was first observed is, in the end, fully transformed, but it remains forever. The last word is *affectus*.

The two concluding paragraphs are a recapitulation, not so much of the treatise in its entirety, as of the four degrees of loving God, contributing to the general, if imprecise, impression that in this lay the content of the work. But the author himself, it seems, would not have altogether objected to this view, since none of his reflections—including the poetry of the *memoria Christi*—altogether eludes the sweeping envelopment of this composition at the center of the work. The four degrees are a graphic intellectualization of the character of love in its metamorphosis within human awareness. They form an abstract schema drawn up to assist in the understanding of a mysteriously simple and paradoxically difficult truth: love, as a movement from within, is the very action of God drawing us out of ourselves toward God, in whom all are loved; this movement is given, unexacted, to the free creature made in God's image. In its organization of ideas, its balance and its comprehensiveness, the schema is an intellectualization; in its inspiration and justification, it is a reading of Scripture. Against this grid of concepts, the experiences which Saint Bernard insightfully traces are revealed to be stages in the growth of that divine love which is the only possible human fulfillment. In the manner of Johannine dualism (light-darkness, life-death, Word-world, truth-falsehood), Bernard penetrates the opaqueness of human motivation and organizes its complexity into the bipolar directionality of God and self. Human existence moves either to its eternally intended consummation in God or to its own arbitrarily chosen frustration in self. We follow the law of love and become our true selves, or we move centripetally toward the idol of the illusory self.

In the strength of its fidelity to the most elemental truths of consciousness this interpretation of the data of experience is justly prized by the philosopher, who is satisfied in the unity of its vision, and by the theologian, who discovers in it, not applications of doctrine, but a source of doctrinal clarification. The philosopher and theologian in everyone who reads Saint Bernard has succumbed to him. What wins attention is not so much his personality—though history agrees he was a charmer—or his style—though his craft was finely honed—but a powerful simplicity in his perception of the human struggle. Breaking through the successive barriers left by cultural evolution to reappropriate this vision is a richly rewarding task. What the man or woman of the spirit, or the student of spirituality, finds in it is the reassurance and guidance of a clear witness to God's presence in human life.

# NOTES

1. In Hum 3 (SBOp 3:18,24–26) Bernard says that at the top of the ladder of humility is *ipsa caritas*, alluding to Saint Benedict's remark in Chapter 7 of the Rule: *Ergo his omnibus humilitatis gradibus ascensis, monachus mox ad caritatem Dei perueniet. The Rule of Saint Benedict: The Abingdon Copy*, ed. from Cambridge, Corpus Christi College MS 57 by John Chamberlin (Toronto: Pontifical Institute of Mediaeval Studies, 1982) 7,67; p. 32.23–24. Our references to Saint Bernard's text are to J. Leclercq, OSB, C. H. Talbot, and H. M. Rochais, OSB, *Sancti Bernardi Opera* [SBOp], 8 Vols (Rome: Editiones Cistercienses, 1957–77). The earlier standard was Johannes Mabillon's edition, *De diligendo Deo liber seu tractatus ad Haimericum S.R.E. Cardinalem et Cancellarium*, in *S. Bernardi, Clarae-Vallensis abbatis primi, opera omnia*, Vol. 1, PL 182 (Paris, 1892) Introduction, 971–74, Text, 973–1000.

2. Gra 1 (SBOp 3:165,15–19).

3. *Itaque divinitus inspiratus, Christi et ecclesiae laudes, et sacri amoris gratiam, et aeterni connubii cecinit sacramenta.* SC 1.8 (SBOp 1:6,13–14).

4. Jean Leclercq, 'Saint Bernard Docteur', in *Recueil d'études sur saint Bernard et ses ecrits*, 3 Vols (Rome: Edizioni di storia e letteratura, 1962–69) 2:387.

5. 'Conference Notes by Thomas Merton: The Cistercian Fathers and Their Monastic Theology. Part One: Saint Bernard, 2. *De diligendo Deo*', ed. Chrysogonus Waddell, OCSO, in *Liturgy*: OCSO, Vol. 27, No. 1 (1993) 15–53, at p. 15. Taken from the schematized notes Merton Prepared for his weekly monastic-orientation conferences (1963) at the Abbey of Gethsemani. Father Waddell explains his editorial procedure in *Liturgy*: OCSO, Vol. 24, No. 1 (1990) 41–42. Reproduction of this text is by kind permission of the Merton Legacy Trust, which holds the copyright.

6. See bibliography at end of commentary.

7. Etienne Gilson, La théologie mystique de s. Bernard (Paris: Vrin, 1934). References will be to *The Mystical Theology of Saint Bernard*, trans. A. H. C. Downes (London, New York: Sheed and Ward, 1940; rpt Kalamazoo, 1990). More than others, Delfgaauw has focused attention upon *On Loving God*, following Gilson's lead in exploring Bernard's spirituality comprehensively through the medium of this treatise. See Pacifique Delfgaauw, OCSO, 'Saint Bernard mâitre de l'amour divin', diss. [unpublished], Rome, 1952; and 'La nature et les dégrès de l'amour

selon saint Bernard', *Saint Bernard théologien*, Actes du congrès de Dijon 15–19 septembre, *Analecta SOC* 9 (1953) 234–252.

8. The zeal of Gilson, in *The Mystical Theology*, to demonstrate to a neo-scholastic generation the cohesiveness and orthodoxy of Bernard's thought pushed him at times to argue from that point of view—as in his extended explanation of *cupiditas* (pp. 85–90). Delfgaauw, 'La nature et les degrès de l'amour', in searching for Bernard's 'contexte doctrinale' p. 234), concludes that the first two degrees of *love for God* are not truly love for God (p. 238).

9. We shall discuss the instance of image and likeness, below, under 'The Place of the Treatise in Bernard's Works'.

10. Sebastian Moore, *The Fire and the Rose Are One* (New York: The Seabury Press, 1980) 26. The sense in which involvement with God is 'emotional', in Bernard's thought, will be discussed in our comments on paragraphs 17 and 23.

11. Damien Van Den Eynde, OFM, 'Les premiers écrits de saint Bernard', *Antonianum* 41 (1966) 189–259, reprinted in Jean Leclercq, *Recueil*, 3:325–422 at p. 356.

12. Ep 11 is in SBOp 7:52,1–60,24. It is Letter 12 in *The Letters of Saint Bernard of Clairvaux*, trans. Bruno Scott James (London: Burns Oates, 1953) 41–48.

~~13. Van Den Eynde 387. The author sees Ep 11 as 'un véritable traité sur l'amour~~ de Dieu'.

14. *Nec tamen ad omnia spondeo me responsurum: ad id solum quod de diligendo Deo quaeritis, repondebo quod epse dabit. . . . Reliqua diligentioribus reservate.* Dil *Prologus* (SBOp 3:119,14–17) The translation of the treatise will generally be that of Robert Walton, OSB, in this volume. The numbers set in parentheses after quotations excerpted from the text will refer to the numbered paragraphs of the Latin. The manuscripts divide the work into fifteen chapters as well; we omit chapter numbers.

15. For a contrary view, see Ermenegildo Bertola, 'Introduzione', *Liber de diligendo Deo (Sul Dovere di Amare Dio)*, in *Opere di San Bernardo 4: Trattati*, ed. Ferruccio Gastaldelli (Milano: Scriptorium Claravallense, 1987) 221: the author would dissuade readers from looking for doctrine in the work because of what he believes to be its 'occasional' character.

16. Jean Leclercq, *Otia monastica: Études sur le vocabulaire de la contemplation du Moyen âge* (Rome, 1963). Among the author's examples is the 'visit' (Dil 7 and 10) which the bride awaits from the Bridegroom, p. 124.

17. 'Introduction', SBOp 3:112.

18. A manuscript from Anchin (Douai 372), copied around 1165, fuses the three books under the title of *De amore*. Jean Leclercq, 'Études sur S. Bernard et le texte de ses écrits', *Analecta SOC* 9 (1953), fasc. 1–2, Jan.-June, 124–132, discusses the history of the text. Jacques Hourlier, 'S. Bernard et Guillaume de Saint-Thierry dans le "Liber de Amore"', *Saint Bernard théologien*, 223–233, compares the content of the three books.

19. Jacques Guy Bougerol, 'Saint Bonaventure et Saint Bernard', *Antonianum* 46 (Rome, 1971), reprinted in Jacques Guy Bougerol, *Saint Bonaventure: Études sur les sources de sa pensée* (Northampton: Variorum, 1989) art. 4, 3–79, at p. 5, on quotations in the work of Alexander of Hales. For Bernard's influence among

thirteenth-century Franciscans, see O. Lottin, *Psychologie et morale au XIIe4 et XIIIe siècles, 1 (Louvain, 1942) esp. 280–281; J. Chatillon,* 'Influence de S. Bernard sur la scholastique', *Saint Bernard théologien,* 281–282.

20. Bougerol, 22.

21. See Saint Francis de Sales, *Treatise on the Love of God,* trans. Henry Benedict Mackey, OSB, with Introduction [1884] by the translator (Westport, Connecticut: Greenwood Press, 1971 [1942]). In cataloging past writers on his subject, the saint omits Bernard (p. 5). Yet, much of this huge and ponderous treatise is in close accord with *On Loving God*—e.g., a concept of gradual progress in the love of God (e.g., p. 128), of 'natural affections' which is not contrasted to the supernatural (p. ix), of 'cupidity' as a love for God in so far as he is good for us (p. xii), and of a primitive love for God in which faith is already assumed (pp. xvi-xvii). It is instructive to observe that, just as *On Loving God* has frequently been ill served by interpreters, so Saint Francis' masterpiece—principally because of the controversy it stirred between Bossuet and Fénélon, both of whom read it poorly—was soon neglected.

22. Philippe Delhaye, 'La conscience morale dans la doctrine de S. Bernard', *Saint Bernard théologien,* 219–221, finds in Bernard a sense of moral conscience, in the tradition of Origen, enlarged to consciousness, with a mystic dimension— the presence of God in the soul. Michael Casey, Monk of Tarrawarra, *Athirst for God: Spiritual Desire in Bernard of Clairvaux's Sermons on the Song of Songs,* CS 77 (Kalamazoo: Cistercian Publications, 1988) 319, forcefully affirms the necessity of seeing in Bernard an exploration of more than consciousness: 'There is a zone of being which is beyond consciousness, which is pre-conscious'. Casey links the unconscious to Bernard's concept of 'the human heart', where God dwells and acts.

23. Note the several instances below (par. 23–29) in which the author points to the experience of need as the motivating force behind the soul's progress. The classic statement of this bernardine manner is in SC 1.9 (SBOp 1:6, 22–24), where the abbot asks: 'Furthermore, if you look back on your own experience [*si verstram experientiam advertatis*], is it not in that victory by which your faith overcomes the world . . . that you yourself sing a new song to the Lord . . . ?' See also, Conv 3.4 (SBOp 4:74, 9): 'You find in your own awareness what is to be done [*proprio disces experimento quid agatur*]'.

24. A strong precedent was set in Augustine—e.g., *Noverim me, noverim te* . . . . *Soliloquia* 2,1: 1.885, 17; see also In evangelium Joannis 12, 13:26; Enarrationes in Psalmo 44, 18:19.

25. Étienne Gilson in *Vie Spirituelle* (September 1934) p. 163. Guy's *Meditationes* (PL 153), written for his personal use around 1110–1116, received almost no attention until the sixteenth century. See the editions of Dom Wilmart, *Le Recueil des pensées du B. Guigue* (Paris: J. Vrin, 1936) and of John J. Jolin, *Meditations of Guigo, Prior of the Charterhouse* (Milwaukee: Marqueette University Press, 1951), and A. Gordon Mursell, *The Meditations of Guigo I, Prior of the Charterhouse,* CS 155 (Kalamazoo, 1995).

26. Merton, 'Conference Notes', 33.

27. *Inest omni utenti ratione . . . appetere potiora.* Dil 18 (SBOp 3:134,16–17) *Justitia siquidem ratione utentis spiritus cibus est vitalis et ventus.* Dil 21 (SBOp 3:137,7–8).

28. S. Vanni Rovighi, 'S. Bernardo e la filosofia', *Revista di filosofia neo-scholastica,* 46 (1954) 33.

29. *Contra quodplane fideles norunt, quam omnino necessarium habeant Iesum, et hunc crucifixum.* Dil 7 (SBOp 3:124, 12–13.

30. *Iustitia siquidem ratione utentis spiritus cibus est vitalis et naturalis.* Dil 21 (SBOp 3:137,7–8).

31. *Illum ratio urget et iustitia naturalis totum se tradere illi, a quo se totum habet.* Dil 15 (SBOp 3:131,12–13).

32. *Ipsis ergo dulcis et rectus Dominus legem dat viam humilitatis, per quam redeant ad cognitionem veritatis.* Hum 2 (SBOp 3:185–187), developed in Hum 3–4.

33. Luke Anderson, O.Cist., 'The Appeal to Reason in Saint Bernard's *De diligendo Deo*', in E. Rozanne Elder and John R. Sommerfeldt, eds., *The Chimaera of His Age: Studies on Bernard of Clairvaux,* Studies in Medieval Cistercian History 5, CS 63 (Kalamazoo: Cistercian Publications, 1980) 135, calls attention to these expressions.

34. In Saint Bonaventure's typology of theologian, preacher, and mystic, Bernard is named the great preacher, one who finds in Scripture the rule of life; he succeeds Gregory the Great in the role. *De reductione artium ad theologiam* n.5 (5:321), cited by Bougerol, art. 4,4.

35. For example, Gianni Dotto, 'La "caritas" come principio di vita e di dottrina in S. Bernard', *Studi su S. Bernardo di Chiaravalle nell' ottavo centenario della canonizzazione,* Convegno internazionale Certosa de Firenze: 6–9 Novembre 1974 (Rome: Editiones cistercienses, 1975) 351–354, speaks of Bernard's 'antropologia esistenziale'.

36. Vanni Rovighi, 20–35.

37. *Porro voluntas est motus rationalis, et sensui praesidens, et appetitui. Habet sane, quocumque se volverit, rationem semper comitem et quodammodo pedissequam: non quod semper ex ratione, sed quod numquam absque ratione moveatur. . . . Neque enim prudentia seu sapientia inesse creaturae potest, vel in malo, nisi utique per rationem.* Gra 3 (SBOp 3:168.1–9) E. Rozanne Elder,'William of Saint Thierry: Rational and Affective Spirituality', in *The Spirituality of Western Christendom* , ed. E. Rozanne Elder, CS 30 (Kalamazoo: Cistercian Publications, 1976) 85–105, observes that, unlike William, Saint Bernard never allowed the rationalism against which he struggled to threaten his acceptance of the place of reason in the spiritual life.

38. Joseph Maréchal, sj, *Studies in the Psychology of the Mystics,* trans. with an Introduction and Foreword by Algar Thorold (Albany, N.Y.: Maji Books, 1964) 166–167, concludes, 'Metaphysics and Psychology teach the same lesson of fundamental humility as does Christianity'. Bernard's manner of arguing assumes this is so. A Christian sense of the self's relation to God can, then, be shown to have a rational and psychological validity.

39. *scienter nescius et sapienter indoctus.* Gregory the Great, *Dialogi* 2, prol; 2:1226–1227, ed. A. deVogüé in SCh. 251 (Paris, 1978).

40. Jean-Marie Déchanet, osb, 'Aux sources de la pensée philosophique de S. Bernard', *Saint Bernard théologien,* 56–77, surveys the philosophical content of

Bernard's thought. Here we claim only what is rather obvious; in Dechanet's words: 'D'abord il y a chez lui une manière bien rationelle et toute humaine d'envisager la Création et même le monde de vérités connues par la Révélation' (p. 56). Jacques Hourlier, 'S. Bernard et Guillaume de Saint-Thierry', 233, is struck by Bernard's need for logic, desire for classification, and spirit of analysis in this work.

41. See Hans Urs Von Balthasar, *Herrlichkeit: Eine theologische Ästhetik*, 3 vols. (Freiburg im Bresgau, 1961–1969). Much of this is translated as *The Glory of the Lord: A Theological Aesthetics* (New York: Crossroad; San Francisco: Ignatius Press, 1982, 1984, 1986, 1989); in *Vol 4: The Realm of Metaphysics in Antiquity*, trans. Brian McNeil *et al.* (San Francisco: Ignatius Press, 1989) 324, 356, the author finds an aesthetics in the Middle Ages identical with that of classical times; he includes within it all twelfth-century writings on love, and specifically Bernard's. See E. Von Ivanka, *Plato Christianus: Übernahme und Umgestaltung des Platonismus durch die Väter* (Munich: Johannesverlag, 1964), for patristic and medieval links to classical antiquity. Irving Singer, *The Nature of Love*, 3 Vols (Chicago: The University of Chicago Press, 1984) 1:147–150, discusses 'the eros tradition'. See esp. 'Eros: The Mystical Ascent', 1:162–97.

42. See M.C. D'Arcy, sj, *The Mind and Heart of Love: Lion and Unicorn, A Study in Eros and Agape* (New York: Meridian Books, 1956 [1947]) 74. Although the *desiderium* of christian tradition rests largely on a platonic *eros*, one detects in this *eros*, beyond Augustine's baptizing of it, elements of Aristotle and of the Neo-Platonists, who incorporate Indo-European influences (pp. 72–73).

43. Claude Bodard, ocso, 'La bible, expression d'une expérience religieuse chez S. Bernard', *Saint Bernard théologien* 27, n.1: 'Dans l'expérience du péché, l'essentiel n'est donc pas de découvrir en nous l'existence de forces mauvaises, mais de découvrir que, par la grace du Christ, le péché, sans être détruit, a cessé de regner en nous'. Jacques Hourlier, 'S. Bernard et Guillaume de Saint-Thierry', 230, finds in this type of optimism the chief distinction between Bernard and William. Though, in some respects, Bernard's evaluation of the effect of sin is more confident than Augustine's, Irving Singer, 1:172, is correct in tracing the joyful, comfortable manner of medieval mystics in general to Augustine.

44. Maurice Blondel, *L'Action: Essai d'une critique de la vie et d'une science de la pratique*, 2 vol. (Paris, 1893). The author, who is not well known in English, sets out to formulate a philosophy which will be recognizably open to biblical revelation. The first of his works to be translated into English can be found in A. Dru and I. Trethowan, *M. Blondel, The Letter on Apologetics, and History and Dogma* (London, 1964). For a study of *L'Action*, see James M. Somerville, *Total Commitment* (Washington, D.C., 1968). See also Henry Bouillard, *Blondel and Christianity*, trans. James M. Somerville (Washington, D.C.: Copus Books, 1969), where the translator offers the significant comment that, though Blondel remained a controversial figure throughout the Modernist period, 'an entire generation of French Catholic intellectuals, many of them theologians, was nourished on his thought' (p. vii). On the link between Blondel's *L'Action* and Bernard's *De diligendo Deo*, see Chrysologue Mahamé, sj, 'Les auteurs spirituels dans l'élaboration de la philosophie blondelienne (1883–1893)', *Recherches de science religieuse* 56.2 (1968) 231–234. The author finds Bernard is the source which Blondel quotes most frequently, never

except once with references. (The philosopher did not wish to appear medieval or tendentiously Christian.) The extensive borrowings are traced in his student-notebooks, where pages at a time are copied from Bernard, the most significant being from *De diligendo Deo*. The indirect influence seems even greater, for it was not until late in the preparation of his thesis that Blondel went to the *opera* of Bernard to copy these texts and spread them through his own work. Bouillard, *Blondel and Christianity*, 168–169, notices that his subject, while determined to do the work of a philosopher, declared several times 'that he owed much to the reading of St. Bernard [his compatriot from Dijon] and to the practice of the New Testament'. The 'nouvelle théologie', laying the groundworks for the Vatican II era, was more indebted to *On Loving God* than most of its practitioners realized.

45. For an account tracing the Blondelian influence, see Gregory Baum, *Man Becoming: God in Secular Experience* (New York: Herder and Herder, 1970) 1–36. Baum labels the trend away from 'extrinsicism' in twentieth-century Roman Catholic thinking 'The Blondelian Shift'. Bougerol, art. 4, 221, finds in Blondel also a revival of Bonaventure, the spirit most akin to Bernard in the thirteenth century. Denis Farkasfalvy, O.Cist., 'La conoscensa di Dio nel pensiero di san Bernardo', *Studi su S. Bernardo di Chiaravalle*, 214, asks perceptively for greater attention to the philosophical merit of Bernard's work: 'Il pensiero filosofico di San Bernardo ha bisogno di una valutazione nuova'.

46. Though this thought is, in the end, a theology, it is bonded to continuous psychological and philosophical analysis. Its principal exponents are Rahner and Lonergan. We make several references in this commentary to the work of Karl Rahner and to the Lonerganian spiritual writer Sebastian Moore. Bernard J. F. Lonergan, *Method in Theology* (New York: Herder and Herder, 1972) 27–55, on 'The Human Good', gives an account of our psychological operations which, while being at variance with modern conventional thinking, could be appealed to at many turns to explain Bernard's text.

47. SBOp 3:111–112. The editors keep the terminal date of 1141 because the possibility 'cannot be excluded' that Bernard directed certain considerations in Dil against Abelard's *Commentaria in epistolam ad Romanos*, written between 1136 and 1140. What opens this possibility is a long invective (written between 1140 and 1150) against *De diligendo Deo* by the disciple of Abelard, Peter Berengarius (*Apologeticus*, PL 178; 1867A). Watkin W. Williams, in *Select Treatises of St Bernard of Clairvaux: De diligendo Deo*, ed. Watkin W. Williams, and *De gradibus humilitatis et superbiae*, ed. Barton R. V. Mills (Cambridge: Cambridge University Press, 1926) 5, is inclined to see our treatise as a response to Abelard, on the basis of the opposition between the two doctrines. Gilson, *The Mystical Theology*, 166, 169, and 244, n.228, discounts this, arguing that it is more probable that Abelard was responding to Bernard's treatise. Irving Singer, *The Nature of Love*, regularly contrasts Bernard's selfless love with Abelard's—e.g. 'Unlike Bernard, Abelard had argued that a pure love of God would renounce even an interest in beatitude' (2:195). This 'possibility' of an Abelard connection, explainable also in Gilson's terms, will have to be measured against other evidence. Bertola, 'Introduzione', 222, n.2, with good documentation, corrects the date of Haimeric's appointment as Chancellor, given in SBOp 3:111 as 1126, to 1123.

48. Ep 18.5 (SBOp 7:69). The letter is no. 19 in *The Letters of St. Bernard of Clairvaux*, trans. Bruno Scott James. On the date of Ep 18, see Damien Van den Eynde, 'Les premiers écrits de S. Bernard', 356, 394. Proposals of a date earlier than 1126 have to reckon with letter 18. See J. Hourlier, 'S. Bernard et Guillaume de Saint-Thierry', 225. The author opts for 'assez proche de 1125'. He would have *De diligendo Deo* close to the time of William of St. Thierry's two works, *De contemplando Deo* and *De natura et dignitate amoris*, dated between 1119 and 1124.

49. In letter 16 to Haimeric, Bernard refers to the fame their friendship enjoyed. But, if one compares Bernard's Haimeric correspondence with his letters to another high ranking ecclesiastic, a certain 'Lord Peter, Cardinal Deacon and Legate of the Roman Church', one observes an intimacy and an easy presumption of affection in the latter that is missing in the letters to Haimeric. See Ep 17, 18, and 19 to Peter, in SBOp 7:65–70; these are numbers 18, 19, 20 in James, *The Letters*, 51–55.

50. On Haimeric's role in the papal succession and on Saint Bernard's collaboration with the chancellor, see Hans Georg Beck, *et al.*, *From the High Middle Ages to the Eve of the Reformation*, vol. 4 of Hubert Jedin and John Dolan, edd. *History of the Church* (London, 1980) 3–10.

51. See n.18, above.

52. Hourlier, 'S. Bernard et Guillaume de Saint-Thierry', 225.

53. A. Wilmart, 'La série et la date des ouvrages de Guillaume de Saint-Thierry', *Revue Mabillon* 14 (1924) 156–167. Jean-Marie Déchanet, *William of St-Thierry: The Man and his Work*, CS 10 (Spencer, Mass.: Cistercian Publications, 1972) 24, arrives at 1118 as a date for William's first visit to Clairvaux. Stanislaus Ceglar, *William of Saint Thierry: The Chronology of his Life with a Study of his Treatise* On the Nature of Love, *His authorship of the* Brevis commentatio, *the* In Lacu, *and the* Reply to Cardinal Matthew (Ann Arbor, Mich.: University Microfilms, 1971) 40, would bring William's dates forward to 1124–1126, and date Bernard's treatise 1120. M. Basil Pennington, ocso, 'Two Treatises on Love', in *Saint Bernard of Clairvaux: Studies Commemorating the Eighth Centennary of his Canonization*, ed. the author (Kalamazoo: Cistercian Publications, 1977) 137–139, 148, pursuing mutual influences, finds that in Bernard's tenth sermon *De diversis*, which may antedate William's *De natura et dignitate amoris*, a series of ideas is entertained similar to those in William's work; but he declines to derive dates from the comparison.

54. William of Saint Thierry tells of these day-long conversations in the Clairvaux infirmary in his biography of Bernard, *Vita prima* xii and 59; PL 185: 259a–260a. Gilson, *The Mystical Theology*, 236, n.121, comparing the work of Bernard and William, notes 'the remarkable coincidence of the standpoints adopted', but concludes: 'In the absence of all certain chronological data . . . no hypothesis on their probable filiations can be put forward. . . . I have been unable to detect the least trace of influence of either on the other'.

55. Bertola, 'Introduzione', 223.

56. *Orationes a me, et non quaestiones, poscere solebatis: et verum fatear, ea mihi deesse video, quae maxime necessaria viderentur, diligentiam et ingenium.* Dil *Prologus* (SBOp 3:119.5–8).

57. *Ego ad neutrum idoneum me esse confido. Verum illud [orationes] indicit professio, etsi non ita conversatio.* Dil *Prologus* (SBOp 3:119, 6–7).

58. Bernard McGinn, 'Introduction', *Bernard of Clairvaux: Treatises 3, On Grace and Free Choice* and *In Praise of the New Knighthood*, CF 19 (Kalamazoo: Cistercian Publications, 1977) 4, 31. See SBOp 3:xi and 157. Watkin Williams, *Saint Bernard of Clairvaux* (Manchester: Manchester University Press, 1935) xv and 221, also gives 'shortly before 1128' as the date of *On Grace and Free Choice*, accepting this from Mabillon's edition (PL). See also SBOp 3:xi and 157; and Elphege Vacandard, *Vie de Saint Bernard, abbé de Clairvaux*, 2 Vols (Paris, 1927) 1:227.

59. Vacandard, 1:227.

60. Bernard plays variations on the theme from one work to the next, significantly changing his vocabulary late in life, in SC 80 through 82. See esp. SC 81.6 (SBOp 2:287.17–18). The most thorough study is Maur Standaert, 'La doctrine de l'image chez saint Bernard', *Ephemerides Theologicae Lovaniensis*, 23 (1947) 70–129. On development within Bernard's doctrine, see pp. 100–101. See also R. Javelet, *Image et ressemblance au douzieme siècle. De saint Anselme à Alain de Lille*, 2 Vols. (Paris, 1967) 1:189–197. Bernard had several doctrines on image-likeness, thinks Javelet (pp. 100–101). Standaert (pp. 102–104), however, finds nothing deeply inconsistent in the difference. More briefly, S. Otto, *Die Funktion des Bildbegriffes in der Theologie der 12. Jahrhunderts*. Beiträge zur Geschichte der Philosophie und Theologie des Mittelalters, 40.1 (Münster/w., 1963) 283–284. The traditional character of cistercian image-and-likeness anthropology is set forth in David Bell, *The Image and Likeness: The Augustinian Spirituality of William of Saint Thierry*, CS 78 (Kalamazoo: Cistercian Publications, 1984) e.g., 34–37.

61. Gra 28–35 (SBOp 3:185–191).

62. *Quis item vel impius putet alium eius, quae in anima splendet humanae dignitatis autorem, praeter illum ipsum, qui in Genesi loquitur: Faciamus hominem ad imaginem et similitudinem nostram?* (Gen 1.26) Dil 6 (SBOp 3:123,24–27).

63. Standaert, 'La doctrine', p. 75, believes it probable that Bernard, by explicitly citing Genesis, means to leave image and likeness undifferentiated in this instance. But, Standaert finds nothing to remark upon concerning an absence of the image-likeness construct until Bernard's *De gratia*. It is worth noting that Bernard does not present his case in terms of image and likeness despite the fact that a probable patristic source of the treatise describes the *excessus* about which the abbot writes in his discussion of the fourth degree of love, explicitly and emphatically in these terms: Gilson, *The Mystical Theology*, 25–27, makes a strong case for Bernard's acquaintance with a passage of the *Ambigua* of Maximus the Confessor (PL 122:1202 A,B, and D), in Erigena's translation from the Greek, and for the use of it in Dil 28 (see n.281, below). Bernard would have known the image-and-likeness anthropology, among other sources, principally from Augustine. The image-and-likeness dialectic forms the structure of the soul's ascent in William of Saint Thierry's *De natura et dignitate amoris*, written most probably before Bernard's treatise. Javelet, *Image et ressemblance* 1:196–197, speaks of an influence of Willialm on Bernard's doctrine. Javelet illustrates the widespread adherence to an image-and-likeness anthropology in the twelfth century.

64. On the date of Ep 11 to the Carthusians, see n.76, below.

65. *quid iam impedit a se ipsa quodammodo abire et ire totam in Deum, eoque penitus sibi dissimilimam fieri, quo Deo simillimam effici donatur?* Dil 32 (SBOp 3:146,21).

66. Notice also the following: *Et prius necesse est portemus imaginem terrestris, deinde caelestis.* Dil 39 (SBOp 3:152,12–13). This allusion to 1 Cor 15:49 is not of the same nature as the patristic use of Gen 1:26.

67. 'Once I had set aside the image of the earthly being, I began wishing to bear the image of the heavenly being'. *Deposita imagine terrestris hominis, imaginem caelestis velle portare coepi.* Div 3, 2 (SBOp 6–1:87,12).

68. 'Man is made in the image and likeness of God, possessing free choice in the image and virtues in the likeness. The likeness perishes, but the image in man endures'. *Ad imaginem nempe et similitudinem Dei factus est homo, in imagine arbitrii libertatem, virtutes habens in similitudine. Et similitudo quidem perriit, verumtamen in imagine pertransit homo.* 1 Ann 7 (SBOp 5:19,11–13).

69. In Gra 11.36 (SBOp 3:19,5–7) Bernard writes of free choice as a 'prerogative of the divine dignity': *Hac sane dignitatis divinae, ut dictum est, praerogativa rationalem singulariter creaturam Conditor insignavit.* The usage has changed. It is generic in Bernard's remark about the soul's dignity in SC 81.5 (SBOp 3:287,12–13): *Nec mediocris tamen animae dignitas praesenti disputatione comperta est. . . .*

70. *Non capit eum* [Deum] *nisi imago sua. Anima capax illius est. . . .* Ded 2.2 (SBOp 5:376,19–20).

71. One might pause, however, over Div 103 (SBOp 6/1:371–374), where Bernard's subject, contained in his opening sentence, is the following: *Quattuor gradibus distinguitur omnis electorum profectus.* Despite a few similarities to Dil, this scheme is not that of four degrees of divine love.

72. See n.1, above.

73. For variants on *amor carnalis, rationalis, et spiritualis,* see Div 59 (SBOp 6/1:290,6) and Sent 3.74 (SBOp 6/2:114,17).

74. Jean Leclercq, 'Introduzzione Generale', in Gastaldelli, ed., *Opere di San Bernardo 4: Trattati*, p. L, says that image-and-likeness is, without doubt, the most frequently studied theme in Saint Bernard, from Gilson to the present. Delfgaauw, '*Saint Bernard maître de l'amour divin*' 146, calls image and likeness 'la clé de son enseignement spirituel'. This author, in 'La nature' 235, begins his exposition of our treatise by underlining the centrality of image and likeness in Bernard's thought. He is representative, however, in not noticing that the interaction of which he speaks is never mentioned in this work.

75. Gilson, *The Mystical Theology*, 27–28, 89; Edgar DeBruyne, *Études D'Esthétique Médiévale*, 3 Vols (Bruges: De Tempel, 1946) 3:41; Delfgaauw, 'La nature', 235, 247–248, 251; Aimé Forest, 'S. Bernard et Nôtre Temps', *Saint Bernard Théologien*, 290; Hourlier, 227; Rowan Williams, *Christian Spirituality: A Theological History from the New Testament to Luther and Saint John of the Cross* (Atlanta: John Knox Press, 1979) 112; Robert M. Dresser, 'Gradation: Rhetoric and Substance in Saint Bernard', in E. Rozanne Elder, ed., *Goad and Nail*, CS 84 (Kalamazoo: 1985) 79.

76. 'Les premiers écrits de S. Bernard', 386–388. The author, p. 387, cites Mabillon (ca. 1125), Vacandard (no firm conclusion), A. Wilmart (1120–1123),

L. Grill (1117). He rejects the view that Ep 11 is the saint's earliest letter, as proposed by L. Grill, 'Epistola de Charitate: der älteste Saint Bernhards-Brief', *Cîteaux*, 15 (1964) 26–51.

77. See n.116 below, on the assumptions behind *fulfillment.*

78. Gra 9.28–10.35 (SBOp 3:185,21–191,4).

79. G. R. Evans, *The Thought of Gregory the Great* (Cambridge: Cambridge University Press, 1986) vii, on Gregory.

80. *Causa diligendi Deum, Deus est; modus, sine modo diligere.* Dil 1 (SBOp 3:119.19). William of Saint Thierry used a similar expression in *De natura et dignitate amoris*, 3; PL 184:382. in Saint Augustine: *Praemium Dei ipse Deus est* (Enarr. in Ps. 72.32; PL 36:928; and 104.40; PL 36A:1404). In a letter to Augustine from his friend Severus, bishop of Milevis (PL 33:419), one reads that God is to be loved *sine modo.* Bernard McGinn, 'St. Bernard and Meister Eckhart', *Cîteaux, commentarii cistercienses*, 31 (1980) 378 and n.24, observes that Eckhart quotes Bernard's sentence five times.

81. *Dixi supra: causa diligendi Deum, Deus est. Verum dixi, nam et efficiens, et finalis.* Dil 22 (SBOp 3:137,17–18).

82. Leclercq, 'Introduction' to Dil (SBOp 3:111), observes that the title given in the manuscripts reproduces a phrase from the introductory paragraph: *de diligendo Deo quaeritis.* Dil, Prologus (SBOp 3:119,15).

83. *sive quia nihil iustius, sive quia nil diligi fructuosius potest.* Dil 1 (SBOp 3:120,2–3).

84. *Dedit seipsum nobis.* Dil 1 (SBOp 3:120,10).

85. Anderson, 135, on the appeal to reason.

86. *Dignitatem in homine liberum dico arbitrium . . . ; scientiam vero, qua eamdem in se dignitatem agnoscat, non a se tamen; porro virtutem, qua subinde ipsum a quo est, et inquirat non segniter. . . .* Dil 2 (SBOp 3:121.15–19). In other words a reader may notice that, while Bernard will accept the conventional designation of the human being as *animal rationale*—see Csi 2,4.7 (SBOp 3:415,10)—he will claim *voluntas* as that which distinguishes humans from trees and beasts, in Gra 2.4 (SBOp 3:168,27–169,2).

87. *Frustra glorietur de libertate arbitrii, quae in mente est; captivus ducitur in legem peccati, quae in carne est.* Mart 3 (SBOp 5:401, 17–19).

88. E.g., in *De Genesi ad litteram*, 3.20.30; PL 34:294.

89. McGinn, 'Introduction' to *On Grace and Free Choice*, 35. Earlier (p. 18) the writer charted the disagreement among scholars as to whether Bernard's *liberum arbitrium* is to be ascribed primarily to the will or to the intellect.

90. *Ut liberum ad voluntatem, arbitrium referatur ad rationem.* Gra 3.6 (SBOp 3:170,11–12). See SC 81.6 (SBOp 2:287,22–23): *Is animae oculus, diiudicat et discernit, sicut arbiter in discernendo, ita in eligendo liber.* G. Venuta, *Libero Arbitrio e Liberta della Grazia nel Pensiero di San Bernardo* (Rome, 1953) 132–137, points out the rationality as well as the liberty in Bernard's *liberum arbitrium.*

91. McGinn, 'The Human Person, II. Western Christendom' in *Christian Spirituality: Origins to the Twelfth Century*, eds. Bernard McGinn and John Meyendorff, in collaboration with Jean Leclercq (New York: Crossroad, 1986) 325.

92. Gilson, *The Mystical Theology*, 243, n.222, thinks the idea of a *dignitas*, as in Dil 2, is probably of Stoic origin. In this vein, Williams, *Select Treatises of Saint Bernard*,

11, n.15, cites Cicero (*De natura deorum* 2:11) on the preeminence conferred upon human beings by *dignitas*. Perhaps another suggestion of familiarity with Stoic ideas may be found below in Bernard's concept of a universal law which includes even God (Dil 35–38); but, that this law is love is not Stoic. Late in life, in SC 80 and 81, Bernard spoke of *liberum arbitrium*, or *libertas* (together with *simplicitas* and *immortalitas*) as pertaining, not to the soul's *dignitas*, but to its *magnitudo*, a closely comparable term. See, e.g., SC 81.11 (SBOp 2:291,17–18).

93. *Itaque geminum unumquodque trium horum apparet.* Dil 3 (SBOp 3:121,20).

94. *Habet gloriam, sed non apud Deum.* Dil 3 (SBOp 3:121,29–30).

95. *Poro virtus et ipsa aeque bifaria cognoscetur, si auctorem consequenter inquirimus, inventoque inseparabiliter inhaeremus.* Dil 3 (SBOp 3:121,25–26).

96. *Opus virtute habes, et non quaecumque, sed qua induratis ex alto. Ipsa enim, si perfecta sit, facile facit animum victorem sui, et sic invictum reddit ad omnia. Est quippe vigor animi cedere nescius pro tuenda ratione; aut, se magis probas, vigor animi immobiliter stantis cum ratione vel pro ratione; vel sic: vigor animi, quod in se est, omnia ad rationem cogens vel dirigens.* SC 85.4 (SBOp 2:310,111–116).

97. *Utrumque ergo scias necesse est, et quid sis, et quod a teipso non sis, ne aut omnino videlicet non glorieris, aut inaniter glorieris.* Dil 4 (SBOp 3:122,8–9).

98. *Dignitas ergo sine scientia non prodest.* Dil 3 (SBOp 3:121,26–27).

99. *Quis item vel impius putet alium eius, quae in anima splendet, humanae dignitatis auctorem, praeter illum ipsum, qui in Genesi loquitur: Faciamus hominem ad imaginem et similitudinem nostram?* (SBOp 3:123,24–27). This associating of *dignitas* with the image of God falls short of the forthright claim, which Bernard makes in Gra 19 (SBOp 3:180,16), that human dignity is situated in the image.

100. *Clamat nempe intus ei innata, et non ignota rationi, iustitia, quia ex toto se illum deligere debeat, cui totum se debere non ignorat.* Dil 6 (SBOp 3:124,5–7).

101. Our translation. *Verum id difficile, immo impossibile est, suis scilicet quempiam liberive arbitrii viribus semel accepta a Deo, ad Dei ex toto convertere voluntatem, et non magis ad propriam retorquere, eaque sibi tamquam propria retinere.* Dil 6 (SBOp 3:124,7–10).

102. *Quod si infideles haec latent, Deo tamen in promptu est ingratos confundere super innumeris beneficiis suis*, etc. Dil 2 (SBOp 3:121,7–8). In the expression *Si infideles haec latent*, the verb *latere* (with accusative) means, in late latin usage, 'to remain concealed from'. This will affect the sense of both *ingratos* and *confundere*. Cf. Walton translation; also, Anderson, 'The Appeal to Reason', 132.

103. Rom 2:15: 'Their conflicting thoughts accuse, or perhaps excuse, them (*inter se cogitationibus accusantibus aut etiam defendentibus*)'.

104. *Proinde inexcusabilis est omnis etiam infidelis, si non diligit Dominum Deum suum toto corde, tota anima, tota virtute sua.* Dil 6 (SBOp 3:124,3–5).

105. *dum demonstrare satagimus, eos quoque qui Christum nesciunt, satis per legem naturalem ex perceptis bonis corporis animaeque moneri, quatenus Deum propter Deum et ipsi diligere debeant.* Dil 6 (SBOp 3:123,17–20).

106. *quatenus Deum propter Deum et ipsi diligere debeant.* Dil 6 (SBOp 3:123.19–20) *Meretur ergo amari propter seipsum Deus, et ab infideli.* Dil 6 (SBOp 3:124,2–3).

107. *quia ex toto se illum diligere debeat, cui totum se debere non ignorat.* Dil 6 (SBOp 3:124,6–7).

108. *quatenus deum propter Deum et ipsi diligere debeant.* Dil 6 (SBOp 3:123,19–20).

109. Denis Farkasfalvy, O.Cist., 'La conoscenza di Dio', 207–208. In the author's well documented study, there are no examples from *De diligendo Deo.* J. M. Déchanet, 'Aux sources de la pensée philosophique de saint Bernard', *Saint Bernard théologien,* 59–60, gathers texts from Bernard on the idea that the only true knowledge of God is that which takes place in religious experience. See especially SC 33.8 (SBOp 1:239,8–22).

110. *Contra quod plane fideles norunt, quam omnino necessarium habeant Iesum, et hunc crucifixum.* Dil 7 (SBOp 3:124,12–13).

111. *Fulcite me floribus, stipate me malis, quia amore langueo.* (Cant 2.5) Dil 7 (SBOp 3;124,19).

112. . . . *impii . . . propinquent fini: fini dico, non consumptioni, sed consummationi. Quamobrem non beato fine consummari, sed consumi vacuo labore accelerant.* Dil 19 (SBOp 3:135,17–19).

113. *Ipse dat occasionem, ipse creat affectionem, desiderium ipse consummat.* Dil 22 (SBOp 3:137,18–19).

114. *Dicendum iam unde inchoet amore noster, quoniam ubi consummetur dictum est.* Dil 22 (SBOp 3:138,4–5).

115. ~~*Necesse est cupiditas vel amor noster a carne incipiat,*~~ . . . *duce gratia proficiens, spiritu tandem consummabitur.* Dil 39 (SBOp 3:152, 19–21).

116. Connotations have accumulated around the English *consummation* which tend to cloud its identification with *fulfillment.* The two terms represent different metaphors, but to the same effect. The metaphor in each word stands for the bringing into reality of the true possibilities of a nature. In this light, the current vogue of self fulfillment as the ultimate criterion of a proper orientation in spirituality will be seen to rest, in many instances, on shallow assumptions. (Nevertheless, it is promising, to the extent that something of it is shared in an authentic christian tradition.) Bernard's vision of the self's *consummatio* may be viewed as self-fulfillment through self-transcendence. In later works, when he begins to explain this as a dialectic of image and likeness, the abiguity in *self* emerges strongly: though made in God's image and likeness, we take on in sin the false self of an unlikeness to God. This is a self that must not be fulfilled.

117. *quorum fructum generalis futura resurrectio in fine parturiet sine fine mansurum.* Dil 8 (SBOp 3:126,22–3). *Christo utique moriente . . . et quandoque redituro ad consummationem nostram.* Dil 9 (SBOp 3:126, 19–22).

118. *Gaudet sponsus caelestis talibus odoramentis, et cordis thalamum frequenter libenterque ingreditur, quod istiusmodi refertum fructibus, floribus respersum invenerit.* Dil 8 (SBOp 3:125,18–20).

119. On the marriage chamber, see esp. SC 23.15–16 (SBOp 1:148,17–150.10).

120. *Memoria ergo in generatione saeculorum, prasentia in regno caelorum.* Dil 10 (SBOp 3:127,11–12).

121. Dil 11 (SBOp 3:127,21–22). Memory here is not Augustine's *memoria* (the mind's knowledge of itself); there is no suggestion of a psychological trinity. Cf. *De Trinitate* 15.3.5; PL 42:1060. Von Ivanka, 'La structure de l'âme selon S. Bernard', in *Saint Bernard théologien* 203–204, seizes upon the term *recordatio* in this text in order to point out the character of Bernard's *memoria.*

122. *Dei ergo quaerentibus et suspirantibus praesentiam, praesto interim et dulcis memoria est.* Dil 10 (SBOp 3:127,23–24). From these remarks on 'memory', one may discern the bernardine meaning in the hymn once attributed to the abbot, *Iesu dulcis memoria,* referred to as the *Jubilus Rhythmicus de Nomine Jesu*: what is invoked is not merely past memory of the earthly Jesus, but an expectant 'remembering' of the resurrected Lord as he will be encountered.

123. *Laeva eius sub capite meo, et dextera eius amplexata est me.* (Cant 2:6). Dil 10 (SBOp 3:126,28–29).

124. On the stooped soul, see *anima curva* in SC 24.7 (SBOp 1:159,5), SC 36.5 (SBOp 2:7,14).

125. *Spiritus paraclitus, . . . ille vos docebit omnia, et suggeret vobis omnia quaecumque dixero vobis* (cf Jn 14:26). Dil 13 (SBOp 3:130,10–11). The joining of past and future in *memoria* remained with Saint Bernard. Saint Augustine speaks of memory as holding also the future, e.g. in Conf 10. In Csi 5.32 (SBOp 3:493.13–20) Bernard speaks of four types of contemplation (*contemplationis species quattuor*), where the last two spring from the remembrance of blessings and the expectation of what has been promised. In William of Saint Thierry we find *Memoria quippe habet et continet quo tendendum sit.* Nat am 382 C (Davy 5), cited in David Bell, *The Image and Likeness* 97, n.37. On how memory makes the earthly Jesus present, see Augustine's opinion that the chief cause of the Incarnation was an incitement to love through the manifestation of love, in *De catechizandis rudibus* 4,7; PL 40:314.

126. *Qui manducat carnem meam et bibit sanguinem meum, habet vitam aeternam* [Vulgate: *meam carnem, meum sanguinem*]. *Hoc est: qui recolit mortem meam, et exemplo meo mortificat membra sua quae sunt super terram, habet vitam aeternam.* (SBOp 3:128,8–10).

127. For Bernard's conception of the relation of the Eucharist to contemplation of the Word, see SC 33.2–3 (SBOp 2:235,6–25). For a survey of all the eucharistic pasages in Bernard's works, see René-Jean Hesbert, 'Saint Bernard et L'Eucharistie', in *Mélanges Saint Bernard* (Dijon, 1953) 156–176.

128. Jean Leclercq, 'The Imitation of Christ and the Sacraments in the Teaching of St. Bernard', *Cistercian Studies*, vol. 9 (1974) 36–54, at 44–45.

129. *non enim de suis meritis, sed de floribus agri, cui benedixit Dominus.* Dil 8 (SBOp 3:125,16).

130. *Quo, inquam, merito suo: nam quanto, cui sane appareat? Quis dicat? Quis sapiat?* Dil 16 (SBOp 3:133,10–11).

131. *Nunc quo nostro commodo diligendus sit, videamus.* Dil 17 (SBOp 3:133,12).

132. In *On Grace and Free Choice,* where he will distinguish 'free counsel' and 'free pleasure' from 'free choice', Bernard will explain that with sin human beings have, in large measure, lost free counsel (the ability to ascertain what is expedient for salvation) and free pleasure (Joy in choosing the good). See Gra 4.11 (SBOp 3:173,19–174,14). Again: *Sola interim plena integraque manet in hominibus libertas arbitrii. Nam libertas consilii ex parte tantum, et hoc in paucis spiritualibus.* Gra 12 (SBOp 3:174,23–25).

133. *Non enim sine praemio diligitur Deus, etsi absque praemii sit intuitu diligendus.* Dil 17 (SBOp 3:133,21–22). See Bougerol 23: Saint Bonaventure uses this statement from *De diligendo Deo* in order to entertain a question: Can charity seek a reward

(*Ergo motus caritatis non potest esse mercenarius*)? He answers that there is a double movement in charity, *motus amicitiae et motus concupiscientiae*. He continues: *Motus amicitiae est ille quo quis desiderat Deo placere et servire; motus concupiscientiae est quo desiderat Deum habere et videre. Cum ergo Bernardus quod Deo sine intuitu praemii est serviendum itelligit de amore amicitiae. . . . sed per hoc non excluditur quin caritatis amore concupiscientiae exoptet et desideret illam summam mercedem apprehendere, ad quam finaliter intendit pervenire.* (3 Sent., 606s, d.27, a.2, q.2, arg.2 et ad 2) Bonaventure's distinction reconciles his more comprehensive view of *caritas* to Bernard's *amor*—a strategy made possible, I would say, by substituting Bernard's *sine praemio* diligitur *Deus* with *sine intuitu praemii est* serviendum. Without this benign misrepresentation of Bernard, it would not be possible to say that he speaks of an *amor amicitiae* in Bonaventure's sense.

134. We have noted that this is the common usage of our treatise; but, in the letter to the Carthusians (34–40), *caritas* replaces *amor*. Casey, *Athirst for God*, 88–94, studies Bernard's uses of *amor, dilectio, caritas*, especially the 'overlap between the concepts of love and desire' (p. 94). After tracing varying connotations, he rightly concludes: 'The distinctions between *amor, dilectio*, and *caritas*, represent tendencies or preferences in language rather than an inflexible semantic rule. In a writer like Bernard they are not to be pressed vigorously' (p. 91). Merton, 'Conference Notes', p. 18, suggests the following broad bernardine meanings: *amor* =love as *affectus; dilectio* =love as *consensus; caritas* =love as *amplexus*. Bell, 147–165, observes discriminations in William of Saint Thierry's usage of *voluntas, amor, dilectio, caritas, sapientia*, and *unitas spiritus*—with a tabulation at p. 153. While there are differences, the author notes William's comment in his *Exposition on the Song of Songs* (6), that divisions here are not important. Bell explains that William is delineating a progression of love: 'Progression is a continuous and not a discreet phenomenon' (p. 152).

135. [*Caritas*] *Affectus est, non contractus: nec acquiritur pacto, nec acquirit. Sponte afficit, et spontaneum facit. Verus amor seipso contentus est. Habet praemium, sed id quod amatur. Nam quidquid propter aliud amare videaris, id plane amas, quo amoris finis pertendit, non per quod tendit.* Dil 17 (SBOp 3:133.23–134.1–4) Regarding the spontaneity of love (*spontaneum facit*), Gilson's *The Mystical Theology* 221, n.24, finds sources in Augustine, *Enarrationes in Psalmam* 53.10; PL 36:626, and *Enarr. in Ps* 55.17, PL 36:658. He cites as well, *Quod non propter se amatur, non amatur. Soliloq.* 13.22; PL 32:881. We may add *De doctrina christiana* 1.35.39; PL 34:34. Bernard's *amor* is not equated to will or to freedom, but as it develops it becomes always more free. Note his definition of the will's consent: *Nutus est voluntatis spontaneus.* Gra 3 (SBOp 3:167,29–30) McGinn, 'Introduction' (to Gra) 15, remarks on the originality of the definition.

136. For an example of a present-day interpretation of christian tradition which finds 'attraction' to be the beginning of a human being's growth in the love of God, see Sebastian Moore, *The Fire and the Rose Are One*, 11: 'In sum: the universal human need in its fully adult form is the need 'to be myself for another'', with the word 'for' referring both to my attraction to the other and to the other's attraction to me. . . . everyone wants to be attractive to someone whom they find attractive'.

137. Robert M. Doran, *The Theology and Dialectics of History* (Toronto: University of Toronto Press, 1990) 27–29, can assist our understanding of the 'feeling' dimension of this *affectus*, with his discussion of the intentionality of feeling in Bernard Lonergan.

138. For a complete account of *affectio* and *affectus* in Saint Bernard's usage (e.g., *affectio* is active in form and *affectus* passive, but they are usually used interchangeably), see Casey, *Athirst for God*, 94–110.

139. Irving Singer, 1:194–96, finding an 'internal tension within Christian eros' (p. 196), questions whether the medieval mystics' concept of a selfless love of God escapes self-contradiction. But Bernard's statement short-circuits this style of reasoning; all his subsequent analysis must be encapsulated in the statement, 'The reason for loving God is God'. Pierre Rousselot, *Pour l'histoire du problème de l'amour au moyen âge*, Beiträge zur Geschichte der Philosophie des Mittelalters, Texte und Untersuchungen 4/6 (Münster i.W, 1908) 1, opens his work with the question whether love as conceived in medieval authors can be selfless.

140. 'Conference Notes', 46–47.

141. The philosopher Maurice Blondell copied paragraphs 19 and 20 verbatim into his student ledger. Mahamé, 234–235.

142. *Inest omni utenti ratione naturaliter pro sua semper aestimatione atque intentione appetere potiora, et nulla re esse contentum, cui quod deest, iudicet praeferendum.* Dil 18 (SBOp 3:134,16–18).

143. *Et namque suae cupiditatis lege, qua in rebus ceteris non habita prae habitis esurire, et pro non habitis habita fastidire solebat, . . . tandem ad ipsum procul dubio curreret, qui solus deesset omnium Deus* (Dil 29 (SBOp 3:135,24–28). Some have been led to ask whether, in this conception of love as following the *lex cupiditatis*, there can be a love of God which is not egotistic (for example, see n.47, above, on Abelard). This was the heart of Rousselot's inquiry (n.139, above). Delfgaauw addresses the issue in his study of *amor-desiderium*, in 'Saint Bernard, maître de l'amour divine', 84–92. Casey, *Athirst for God*, 65–75, surveys Bernard's use of *desiderium*, and finds it rather regularly (though not invariably) associated with the life of the spirit—as in the usage of Augustine (*Sermo* 369.29; PL 39:1633a) and Gregory the Great (*In Evangelia homilia* 36.2; PL 76:1267a). This will explain Bernard's recourse in this section of *De diligendo Deo*, where he speaks of an elemental *cupiditas*. And, the difference confirms Casey's observation (p. 108) that in Bernard 'the conjunction of the two themes [*affectio/affectus* and *desiderium*] is . . . relatively rare'. In J. Blanpain, 'Langage mystique, expression du désir', *Collectanea cisterciensia* 36 (1974) 66, *affectio* is, for Bernard, a movement toward the object of one's *desiderium.*

144. *Sic ergo ut dictum est, ad id quod optimum est, quivis cupidus perveniret, si quidem ante, quod citra cupit, assequi posset.* Dil 19 (SBOp 3:136,2–3). See Bertola, *San Bernardo e la teologia speculativa* (Padua: CEDAM, 1959) 51–54, for a comparison between Bernard's *Quo nihil melius cogitari potest*, etc. (Csi 5, 15; SBOp 3:479,3–7) and Anselm's ontological argument.

145. *Distortum iter et circuitus infinitus, cuncta primitus attentare velle.* Dil 20 (SBOp 3:136,26–27). An entry from Blondell's notes reflecting upon this entire pericope

(19–20) reads as follows: 'L'esprit devance le coeur dans l'ordre de la conaissance, le coeur devance et eclaire l'esprit dans l'ordre réel de l'amour et de l'action'. Mahamé, 234–35.

146. *Quid enim animae et Verbo?. . . . naturarum tanta cognatio est, ut hoc imago, illa ad imaginem sit.* SC 80.2 (SBOp 2:277,21–23).

147. *Hi sunt, qui salubri compendio cauti sunt molestum hunc et infructuosum vitare circuitum, verbum abbreviatum et abbrevians eligents.* Dil 21 (SBOp 3:136,25–137,1). In Rom 9:28 Paul quotes Is 10:22, *Verbum breviatum faciet Dominus super terram*; and, playing on the words, Bernard refers to Christ as *verbum abbreviatum et abbrevians*, the eternal Word cut short in the Incarnation, but creating a short-cut for the faithful. See SC 59.9 (SBOp 2:140,25) and SC 79.2 (SBOp 2:273,9).

148. *Iustitia siquidem ratione utentis spiritus cibus est vitalis et naturalis.* Dil 21 (SBOp 3:137,7–8). Also, Dil 21 (SBOp 3:136,27–137,1): *Non cupere quaecumque vident, sed vendere magis quae possident et dare pauperibus.*

149. *Ipse facit ut desideres, ipse est quod desideras.* Dil 21 (SBOp 3:137,16). See Augustine, *Soliloq.* I.1,2; PL 32:869: *Deus quem amat omne quod potest amare, sive sciens, sive nesciens.* Bernard's conclusion states the meaning (regarding God's action beyond the Godhead) of the Johannine metaphor for God, 'God is love'. In this sense of the meaning, both God's loving (*agape*) and the human's desiring (*eros*) play well illustrated roles. In *Athirst for God*, Casey studies desire in Bernard's SC; see, e.g., pp. 244–314, 'Desire as Dialectic'. A stimulating opinion of David Tracy, *Blessed Rage for Order: The New Pluralism in Theology* (New York: Crossroad, 1975) 189, is that neither a Catholic 'caritas synthesis' of *agape* and *eros* nor a Lutheran view of purely agapic love has seemed able to render the central metaphor (God is love) 'both conceptually coherent and existentially meaningful'. Tracy finds satisfaction in process metaphysics as exemplified in Daniel Day Williams, *The Spirit and the Forms of Love* (New York: Harper and Row, 1968) 111–20.

150. The same organization in which an extended unit on spiritual progress is prefaced by an exposition on prevenient grace is found in the *Super cantica*: SC 84, on grace, precedes SC 85 on spiritual progress.

151. *Ipse dat occasionem, ipse creat affectionem, desiderium ipse consummat.* Dil 22 (SBOp 3:137,18–19) Compare: 'In loving, one is anticipated and *conquered*'. *Prorsus et praevenitur amando, et vincitur.* SC 83.6 (SBOp 2:302,14–15).

152. *Ipse fecit, vel potius factus est, ut amaretur.* Dil 22 (SBOp 3:137,19) The Walton rendering of this untranslatable sentence is, 'He makes, or rather is made himself lovable'. This may be linguistically desperate, but in reading Bernard's *Ipse fecit . . . ut amaretur* (he makes himself loved) as 'he makes himself lovable', the translator tries to communicate the context: Bernard claims that it is in bringing about the human perception of God's lovableness (he speaks, for example, of *affectio* and *desiderium*) that God makes God loved.

153. *Eius amor nostrum et praeparat, et remunerat. Praecedit benignior, rependitur iustior, exspectatur suavior.* Dil 22 (SBOp 3:137,20–21).

154. *Bonus es, Domine, animae quaerenti te. Quid ergo invenienti?* (SBOp 3:137,24–25). One will notice, again, the language of the traditional hymn, *Iesu dulcis memoria.*

155. *Sed enim in hoc est mirum, quod nemo quaerere te valet, nisi qui prius invenerit. Vis igitur inveniri ut quaeraris, quaeri ut inveniaris. Potes quidem quaeri et inveniri, non tamen preveniri.* Dil 22 (SBOp 3:137,25–138,2).

156. *Non dubium tamen quod tepida sit omnis oratio, quam non praevenerit inspiratio.* Dil 22 (SBOp 3:138,3–4).

157. D. Farkasfalvy, 'L'inspiration de l'Ecriture Sainte dans la théologie de S. Bernard', *Studia Anselmiana* 53 (1964) 7–146, at 45–46, speaks of the essentially internal character of *inspiratio* in Bernard.

158. The *Sententiae* are in SBOp 6/2.

159. *Recueil d'études,* 3:158–159.

160. By contrast, some of Bernard's enumerations seem to be in the order of wit, a form of decorous monastic humor—e.g., *Duo sunt novissima, mors, et vita. Ad haec volamus duabus alis, timore et spe. Duabus velamus pedes, paenitentia cordis et confessione oris,.... Duabus velamus caput, dilectione Dei et proximi....* Sent 1.33 (SBOp 6/2:18,15–19).

161. Dil 23 (SBOp 3:138,6). 'Passion' translates *affectio* here, not because it is an adequate equivalent (see the remarks on the impossibility of any such equivalent, re *affectus* in paragraph 17, above), but because it is common to the four disparate dispositions referred in the sentence. Von Balthasar, *The Glory of the Lord*—e.g., at 4:356–57—finds this meaning of *amor* ('the classical, Boethian *eros* without a break into christian *agape*') common to the era and in continuity with a broad patristic tradition, as we have noted (n.41, above). He cites (p. 357, n.173) Hugh of Saint Victor: *amor est dilectio cordis, . . . desiderium in appetendo. . . Ordinate ergo caritatem* (*De arrha animae* 2; PL 176:15D–16A).

162. *Sane etiam contra se innitens invalescet, et facta seipsa validior, coget pro ratione universa: iram, metum, cupiditatem et gaudium, veluti quemdam animi currum, bonus auriga reget, et in captivitatem rediget omnem carnalem affectum, et carnis sensum ad nutum rationis in obsequium virtutis.* SC 85.5 (SBOp 2:310,23–26).

163. Concerning the traditional concept of four affective states, which is traced through the Fathers to the Stoics, see Pacifique Delfgaauw, 'Saint Bernard maître de l'amour divin', 70–78; also 'La lumière de la charité chez Saint Bernard', *Collectanea OCR* 18 (1956) 61. In Div 50.2 (SBOp 6/2:271,16–17) Bernard lists the four *affectiones* as love, joy, fear, and sorrow. Bertola, 'Introduzione' 246, n.1, cites other works of Saint Bernard in which this notion is found: Div 72.4:QH 14.9; SC 85.5; Csi 5.9; Quad 11.3. The Walton translation adds Quad 2.3 (SBOp 4:361,11–13) and finds the concept to be simply 'classical', citing Juvenal, *Satires,* 1:85–86, as example.

164. *Soila quae in filio est caritas, non quaerit quae sua sunt.* Dil 34 (SBOp 3:148,21).

165. *Sed est affectio quam caro gignit, et est quam ratio regit, et est quam condit sapientia. . . . Nam prima quidem dulcis, sed turpis; secunda sicca, sed fortis; ultima pinguis et suavis est.* SC 50.4 (SBOp 2:80,11–18). A quite different reading of the typology *amor carnalis, rationalis, spiritualis* is found at SC 20.9 (SBOp 1:120,22–23), where the carnal love of Christ is good. Von Ivanka, 'La structure' 205–207, studies this terminology in Bernard and finds it takes on different meanings. He suspects

the abbot's version in Gra 3–4 (comparable to the one in SC 50.4, above)—'une curieuse variation du schema'—was derived from Cassian, *Collationes* 4.19.

166. *Prima [affectio quam caro gignit] est, quam Apostolus legi Dei dicit non esse subiectam, nec esse posse.* SC 50.4 (SBOp 2:80,12). For two meanings given to *concupiscentia* by Augustine, see Wolfhart Pannenberg, *Anthropology in Theological Perspective*, trans. matthew J. O'Connell (Philadelphia: Westminster Press, 1985) 87: 'Latin Scholasticism distinguished between sin and concupiscence, regarding the latter as simply the material element in sin (*materiale peccati*); the Reformers and the Jansenists, on the contrary, identified concupiscence and sin. Each interpretation is one-sided and fails to do justice to the complex thought of Augustine. . . . for his analysis of the concupiscence that Paul considers to be the very essence of all that is forbidden by the divine law shows it to be both sin and a consequence of sin'. The author refers to Augustine's *concupiscentia laudabilis* (p. 91). On the two-sided character of concupiscence in the tradition generally, see Karl Rahner, 'The Theological Concept of *concupiscentia*', *Theological Investigations* (Baltimore, 1961) 1:347–382—e.g., 'If from the first point of view *concupiscentia* appears as a power oppressing man in his very depths and driving him on to moral transgression, from the second point of view it presents itself as something immediately given with human nature' (p. 348).

167. *Bonus tamen amor iste carnalis, per quem vita carnalis excluditur, contemnitur et vincitur mundus.* SC 20.9 (SBOp 1:120,22–23).

168. Gilson, who does not remark upon two points of view for Bernard's *cupiditas*, speaks of it, when it operates in our second and more positive perspective, as something which functions 'under the guise of cupidity'. *The Mystical Theology* 87. This is a benevolent, if condescending, revision of Bernard's perception of the human condition.

169. *Necesse est cupiditas vel amor noster a carne incipiat.* Dil 39 (SBOp 3:152,19).

170. For the ordering of the *anima concupiscibilis* in Bernard, see Maur Standaert, 'Le principe de l'ordination dans la théologie de saint Bernard', *Collectanea OCR* 8 (1946) 176–216.

171. Juan Alfar, 'Nature: B. The Theological Concept', in Karl Rahner *et al*, eds. *Sacramentum Mundi*, 6 vols. (New York: Herder and Herder) 4:172–75. The writer gives these references for the historical sense of nature in Augustine: PL 13, col 352; 32, col 597, 1203; 33, col 767 f; 37, col 173; 41, col 357; 44, cols 272–76, 744, 896; 45, cols 51, 53, 59, etc. A concept of 'pure nature' arose in sixteenth and seventeenth century debates concerning Baius and Jansenius.

172. *In primo opere me mihi dedit, in secundo se; et ubi se dedit, me mihi reddidit.* Dil 15 (SBOp 3:132,10–11). Gra 11 ff (SBOp 3:173,19–74), explains the weakening of human nature through sin: we continue to enjoy freedom of choice, but we have lost both freedom of counsel and freedom of pleasure. See SC 83.2 (SBOp 2:299,15–16): . . . *quae tamen dissimilitudo, non naturae abolitio, sed vitium est* ('Our unlikeness [through sin] is not the destruction of our nature but a vice'). Pannenberg, 107, understands the sinfulness of fallen human nature as 'the natural conditions of our existence', laiden with the results of sin—as against 'the essence', which is not sinful.

173. *Porro ipsum ut esset, creans gratia fecit; ut proficiat, salvans gratia facit; . . . et aliud amare, aliud amare Deum.* Gra 16 (SBOp 3:178,2–6) McGinn, 'Introduction' (to Gra) 25, n.71, suspects that this distinction, from Augustine, was made popular by Bernard. See also Sent 1.28 (SBOp 6/2:17,1–2): *Gratia quadripartita: gratia creans, gratia redimens sive miserans, gratia donans, gratia remunerans.* William of Saint Thierry (*Expositio super Cntica Canticorum* 22 and 174) distinguishes a *gratia creans* from other levels of grace.

174. *In desideriis uero carnis ita nobis Deum credamus semper esse praesentem.* The Rule of Saint Benedict, 7,29; p. 31,20–21.

175. *Lex autem Domini dicitur, sive quod ipse ex ea [caritas] vivat, sive quod eam nullus, nisi eius dono possideat.* Dil 35 (SBOp 3:149,17–18). In the context, *caritas* is simply love, not the more specified theological virtue. Bernard accorded such a role to grace that in *On Grace and Free Choice*, his next treatise, he had to face the question, 'What part do *you* play, then'? *Quid tu ergo?* Gra 1 (SBOp 3:165,17).

176. *Quod tamen utrumque dixerim de gratia praesumendum, non de natura, sed ne de industria quidem.* SC 82.7 (SBOp 2:297,8–9).

177. *Simplices namque affectiones insunt naturaliter nobis, tamquam ex nobis, additamenta ex gratia. Nec aliud profecto est, nisi quod gratia ordinat, quas donavit creatio, ut nil aliud sint virtutes nisi ordinatae affectiones.* Gra 17 (SBOp 3:178,9–11).

178. *Dicendum iam unde inchoet amor noster, quoniam ubi consummetur dictum est.* Dil 22 (SBOp 3:138,4–5).

179. *Itaque liberum arbitrium nos facit volentes, gratia benevolos.* Gra 16 (SBOp 3:178,3–4).

180. Pacifique Delfgaauw, 'La lumière de la charité chez saint Bernard', p. 44, observes that Bernard explains our approach to God in knowledge and love with the remark, *De ratione naturae similis similem quaerit* (SC 82.7; SBOp 2:297,13–14).

181. E. von Ivanka, 'La structure de l'âme', 207.

182. Delfgaauw, 'Saint Bernard, mâitre de l'amour divin', 71–72. See Div 32.2 (SBOp 6/1:219,20–21): *Nam cogitatio in memoria est, affectio in voluntate, intentio in ratione consistit.*

183. [*Sponsa*] *animam suam sponsum diligere dicit, monstrans perinde spiritum esse sponsum, et a se non carnali, sed spirituali amore diligi.* SC 75.9 (SBOp 2:252,18–20). In SC 83.2 (SBOp 2:299,13–14), when the soul moves away from God it is *cum suis affectibus, immo defectibus.*

184. *Instructio doctos reddit, affectio sapientes.* SC 23.14 (SBOp 1:147,24).

185. Bell, 128, interprets William (Nat am 382D–383A; Davy 6): 'It is only when will cooperates with grace that it becomes love'. But there are exceptions to this usage (pp. 127–129). William too, at times, speaks of love as an *affectio*, or a *vis naturalis* (e.g., nat am 381B; Davy 3).

186. *Cum secundum carnem diligit vel potius appetit anima.* SC 75.9 (SBOp 2:252,15–16). Cited in Delfgaauw, 'La nature', 238, n.6.

187. *Verumtamen, quia carnales sumus et de carnis concupiscentia nascimur, necesse est cupiditas vel amor noster a carne incipiat.* Dil 39 (SBOp 3:152,18–19).

188. *Numquid erit caritas . . . sine cupiditate, sed ordinata.* Dil 38 (SBOp 3:152,5–6).

189. SBOp 4:474,16–20.

190. *Anima vero in triplici vi subsistit. Est enim rationalis, concupiscibilis, irascibilis.* Div 74 (SBOp 6/1:312,11–12). Cited in Delfgaauw, *Saint Bernard,* 70.

191. *Operatur, non ut ipse Deo placeat, sed quia placet ei Deus.* Div 103.4 (SBOp 6/1:373,17–18). The context is of four degrees of spiritual progress in which this is the highest; wishing to please God has preceded, as a less advanced stage.

192. Pierre Rousselot, *Pour l'histoire du problème de l'amour au moyen âge,* 49–58, announces his findings: In De *diligendo Deo,* love is physical (the Greek *physis,* nature), in the sense later developed by the Scholastics, while in Bernard's sermons it is ecstatic and self-annihilating. This author errs in his stated assumption that Bernard is simply an early Scholastic. P. Pourrat, *La spiritualité chrétienne* (Paris, 1928) 2:29–116, was in the same camp: he reproached Bernard for beginning the ascent to God from nature (pp. 47–48).

193. Anders Nygren, *Agape and Eros,* trans. Philip S. Wetson (Philadelphia, 1953) 645–648. The author fails to consider the possibility that *agape* might exercise its agency through *eros.* D'Arcy, p. 80, summarizes Nygren's position as 'a superficially clear and sharp distinction between Eros and Agape, egocentric and theocentric love'. 'In his system', where Christian love (Agape) eliminates Eros, 'there is no man left'(p. 245). 'If the Agape in man is truly the divine nature itself', asks D'Arcy, 'how can man himself escape being divine or else in no relation with the love which he seems to exercise?' (pp. 374–375). In Bernard, by contrast, *affectio* pertains to a self which is never lost, even in the final union with God.

194. *The Mystical Theology,* 86.

195. 'La nature', 238: 'L'amour charnel qui constitue le premier degré n'est donc pas un amour authentique, mais l'amour diminué d'une âme inflechie sur elle même'. 'Si, aux premiers degrès, c'est encore l'*affectus carnalis* qui domine la volonté c'est pourtant là un stade prèparatoire et nécessarire pour aboutir à la 'conversion' du troisieme degré. . . .' (237). Delfgaauw and Gilson seem not to notice how Bernard's thoughts on *affectus* (or *affectio*) *carnalis* are offered from two points of view, two understandings of *concupiscentia,* and how one set of reflections cannot, therefore, be used as explanation of the other. This should become clear in our discussion of paragraphs 36–38 below.

196. The OED defines *chiasmus* as a diagonal arrangement, especially of clauses in a sentence. A grammatical figure by which the order of words in one of two parallel clauses is inverted in the other.

197. Karl Rahner, 'Concerning the Relationship between Nature and Grace', *Theological Investigations,* 1:312.

198. Our translation. *Sed quoniam natura fragillior atque infirmior est, ipsi primum, imperante necessitate, compellitur inservire.* Dil 23 (SBOp 3:138,12–13).

199. *Et est amor carnalis, quo ante omnia homo diligit seipsum propter seipsum.* Dil 23 (SBOp 3:138,13–14). Bernard's development of the idea will show this love of self to be different from Augustine's self-love, that *amor sui* equated with *superbia* as the root of all sin, as in *Serm* 96.2, and in *De Gen.ad lit.* 11.15 (19). H. M. Delsart, 'Introduction' to *Traité de l'amour de Dieu par saint Bernard* (Paris: Desclée, 1929) 5, n.1, finds a text In Augustine: *Ergo dilectio unicuique a se incipit et non potest nisi a se incipere, ut nemo monetur ut se diligat* (*Serm.* 368.4.4; PL 34:1654). Gilson, *The*

*Mystical Theology*, 221, n.24, believes the sermon to be not by Augustine, though it would have been taken as such in Bernard's day.

200. In Div 103.1 (SBOp 6/1:371,19–372,2) Bernard conceives the love of self as a kindness and a forgiveness which is to precede the love of neighbor as its model: *Miserere animae tuae, placens Deo* (cf Sir 30:23). *Primum igitur est diligere se, deinde proximum* etc.

201. *Prius quod animale, deinde quod spirituale.* Dil 23 (SBOp 3:138,15). An allusion to 1 Cor 15:46, not a quotation. Walton translates *quod animale* as 'what was animal'. Instead, to clarify, we accept *animale* as pertaining to the *anima* or animating principle. Paul contrasts to the life of the Spirit, not the life of animals, but that of humans; in his terminology *animale* is of the same order as *carnale*. Bernard repeats the allusion later in paragraph 39, taken from Ep 11.8 (SBOp 7:58,18). For other references to this text, see Apo 14 (SBOp 3:94,6); SC 60.2 (SBOp 3:143,2); Palm 1,1 (SBOp 5:42,18); Div 8,2 (SBOp 5:112,1); Div 16,1 (SBOp 5:145,11).

202. *Nec praecepto indicitur, sed naturae inseritur* (SBZOp 3:138,15–16). Saint Bonaventure (3 Sent. 556, d.26, a.1, q.1, arg.5) associated Bernard with Augustine, for whom the seeds of virtue, in relation to the *habitus*, are planted in the nature of the rational spirit. Cited in Bougerol 73. Gilson, *The Mystical Theology*, 221, n.24, refers to a parallel in Augustine: *Ut se quisque diligat, praecepto non opus est. De doctrina christ.* 1.35.39; PL 34:34.

203. *The Mystical Theology*, 222, n.34.

204. This instructive paradox is from Sebastian Moore, *The Fire and the Rose Are One*, 8–11, 32.

205. *'Conference Notes'*,49.

206. 'S. Bernard et nôtre temps', *Saint Bernard théologien*, 289: 'Il [la philosophie rèflexive] ne s'agit pas de saisir l'essence du moi; mais plutôt de rèflèchir l'acte par lequel il se pose. Le problème devient ainsi celui de nôtre genèse spirituelle'.

207. Michael Casey, 'In Pursuit of Ecstasy: Reflections on Bernard of clairvaux's *De diligendo Deo'*, *Monastic Studies*, 16 (Christmas, 1985)149, proposes distinctions among four phases in Bernard's first degree of love: moving from self-hatred to a love of the superficial self, a love of others for self, and love of Christ for self. The proposal, it seems, is more an aid to appreciating gradations within this first degree than a precise restatement of Bernard's text. See n.238, below.

208. *Inest ergo naturae, si peccato non obsolescat, . . . ut molliorem magis ad compatiendum peccantibus quam ad indignamdam asperiorem se sentiat.* SC 44.4 (SBOp 2:47,1–4).

209. 'Conference Notes', 49–50.

210. Bernard's concept of the self-destructiveness of a love of self not yet set in order by grace is discussed in Bernhard Stoeckle, 'Amor carnis—*abusus amoris*: Das Verstãndnis von der Konkupiszenz bei Bernhard von Clarivaux und Aelred von Rival', *Studia Anselmiana* 53 (1964) 173–174). The concupiscence of this love is more than nature's incapacity to achieve its destiny; it is a nihilistic tendency, in Stoeckle's view; and he likens Bernard's and Aelred's grasp of it—'erstaunlich gegenwartsnãhe'—to the perceptions of present-day depth psychology (documentation at p. 174, n.52), which sees such self-absorption in numerous forms of human regression. No one will fail to be impressed by how close to our present-day

understanding this bernardine insight is. But, that Bernard, in this context, sees concupiscence as simply bad (Stoeckle, 173: 'Die Begierlichkeit ist in sich wirklich "böse" ') is imprecise. See the discussion, below, of Dil 38–39. The abbot accepts the traditional teaching on the soul: *Sapientes mundi huius animam humanam rationalem, irascibilem, concupiscibilem esse tradiderunt;* and he does not demure from describing the eternal satisfaction of the soul in heaven as the satisfaction of all three drives— e.g., *'Implebit concupiscibile nostrum fonte iustitiae'* (OS 4.5; SBOp 5:358,18–359,2).

211. *At vero si coeperit amor idem, ut assolet, esse profusior sive procliior et, necessitatis alveo minime contentus, campos etiam voluptatis exundans latius visus fuerit occupare, statim superfluitas obviante mandato cohibetur, cum dicitur: Diliges proximum tuum sicut teipsum.* Dil 23 (SBOp 3:138,16–20). The *voluptas-necessitas* contrast is found in Chapter 7 of the Rule.

212. Pannenberg, *Anthropology,* 108, represents a strong current of contemporary anthropology: ' "According to their nature", that is, in respect to their destination to humanity, human beings are exocentric beings'.

213. Our translation. *Ex intimis sane humanis affectibus primordia ducit sui ortus fraterna dilectio, et de insita homini ad seipsum naturali quadam dulcedine, tamquam de humore terreno, sumit procul dubio vegetationem et vim, per quam, spirante quidem gratia desuper, fructus parturit pietatis.* SC 44.4 (SBOp 2:46,25–29).

214. *Iustissime quidem, ut consors naturae non sit exsors et gratiae, illius praesertim gratiae, quae naturae insita est.* Dil 23 (SBOp 3:138, 20–23).

215. *Iustissime quidem, ut consors naturae non sit exsors et gratiae, illius praesertim gratiae, quae naturae insita est.* Dil 23 (SBOp 3:138,20–23).

216. This is a different meaning from the one given to nature as the absence of grace. The *natural* necessity Bernard speaks of here is in contrast to what he elsewhere refers to as *libera necessitas:* we suffer *a libera necessitate* (SC 81.9; SBOp 2:288,19) when sin takes liberty captive and we are constrained by our own will, not by nature: *Corpus quod corrumpitur aggravat animam* [Wis 9:15], *sed amore, non mole. . . . Voluntas in causa est* (SC 81.7; SBOp 2:288,10 and 12).

217. Gra 6 (SBOp 3:170,25–28). On the originality of *libertas a necessitate,* see McGinn, 'Introduction', 19. Saint Bernard situates the divine image in the soul's *liberum arbitrium* in Gra 28 (SBOp 3:185,24).

218. *Item dicit Scriptura, 'Uoluptas habe penam, et necessitas parat coronam'. The Rule of Saint Benedict,* 7.33; 30:3–4. From *Vita S. Anastasiae',* 1.9 in the *Acta sanctorum, Aprilis* 3, p. 249.

219. 'Celle-ci [connaissance de soi] lui revele que l'homme est avant tout acte libre. L'action libre jallit, toutefois, d'un acte nécessaire qui est l'amour de soi: *amor sui, amor carnalis'.* Edgar DeBruyne, *Études D'Esthétique Médiévale* 3:40.

220. Bernard regularly uses the verb *urgere* with *necessitas,* and *trahere* with *caritas* (or also with *cupiditas*), as in the following examples: *alliciat gustata suavitas quam urgeat nostra necessitas.* Dil 26 (SBOp 3:141,6). *Quod videmur magis urgeri necessitate, trahi cupiditate.* QH 11.3 (SBOp 4:450,4). For the coupling of *necessitas* with *caritas,* see the following: Ep 41 (SBOp 7:99,16); Gra 14 (SBOp 3:17,21); QH 7, 11 (SBOp 4:421,3); Miss (SBOp 4:13,11); Csi 3,18 (SBOp 3:445,25).

221. 'This does not mean that the substance of the flesh will not be present, but that all carnal necessity will disappear. . . . *Non quod carnis illic substantia futura non sit, sed quod carnalis omnis necessitudo sit defutura.* Dil 40 (SBOp 3:153,18–19).

222. See Dil 32, below, in regard to *cura.*

223. *Necessitas non habet legem.* SC 50.5 (SBOp 2:81,18–19). *Dirige actus nostros, prout nostra temporalis necessitas poscit.* SC 50.8 (SBOp 2:83,14–15).

224. Charles Taylor, *Hegel and Modern Society* (Cambridge: Cambridge University Press, 1979) 113, traces to Hegel the idea of the freedom of the developing self as absolute value.

225. DeBruyne, 2:139, describes the architecture overseen by Bernard as 'l'architecture du necessaire'. And, of special interest to our concerns in *De diligendo Deo*, he studies Bernard's influence upon 'le rationalisme de l'art du necessaire' (2:140).

226. The key text is Apo 7 (SBOp 3:87,22–26). Bernard explains his sense of vocation, not according to theoretical possibilities, but according to what his self-knowledge declares concretely necessary. His criterion: 'All things are lawful, but not everything is to be recommended' [cf 1 Cor 10:22].

227. Regarding conformity, see Gra 33 (SBOp 3:189,9–11, and *passim*) and, among the many texts in the *Super Cantica*, these two: *Transformamur cum comformamur* (SC 62.5; SBOp 2:158,20) and *Conformitas maritat animam verbo* (SC 83.3; SBOp 2:299,21). For the language of *forma* in Bernard, see Standaert, 'La doctrine de l'image', 118.

228. E. Gilson, *The Spirit of Mediaeval Philosophy* (New York: Scribner's, 1948) 210–213, notes the deviation. In Augustine the image is the *mens*—as in *De Trinitate*, 9.2,2 (PL 42:962) and 14.16,22 (PL 42:1053) cited by E. Gilson, *The Christian Philosophy of Saint Augustine* (New York, 1960) 219, 254, n.10. Bernard states his position best in Gra 30 (SBOp 3:187,9–16): 'You may properly conclude that the other freedoms [freedom of council and freedom of pleasure] correspond to God's likeness, but this one [freedom of choice] corresponds to his image' (our translation). *Merito illae [duae istae libertates, consilii scilicet atque complaciti] similitudini, haec [libertas arbitrii] imagini deputantur.*

229. . . . *non gravaris amorem tuum a carnalibus desideriis, quae militant adversus animam* [cf 1 Peter 2:10]. dIL 23 (SBOp 139,17–18).

230. *Quod subtrahis hosti animae tuae consorti naturae puto non gravaberis impertiri.* Dil 23 (SBOp 3:139,8–9).

231. Our translation. *Quantum vult, sibi indulgeat, dum aeque et proximo tantumdem meminerit exhibendum.* Dil 23 (SBOp 3:139,1–2).

232. 'Remove that [*discretio*], and . . . natural affection itself is changed to utter disorder—or rather, nature is destroyed'. *Tolle hanc, . . . ipsaque affectio naturalis in perturbationem magis convertetur exterminiumque naturae.* SC 49.5 (SBOp 2:76,10–12). Bernard develops the same theme under the rubric *Qui diligit iniquitatem, odit animam suam* (Ps 10:6), Conv 4.5 (SBOp 4:76, 5–6).

233. *Frenum tibi temperantiae imponitur, O homo, ex lege vitae et disciplinae, ne post concupiscentias tuas eas et pereas, ne de bonis naturae hosti servias animae, hoc est libidini.* Dil 23 (SBOp 3:139,2–4).

234. *Discretio quippe omni virtuti ponit ordinem . . . . Est ergo discretio non tam virtus, quam quaedam moderatrix et auriga virtutum, ordinatrixque affectuum et morum doctrix.* SC 49.5 (SBOp 2:76,4–10).

235. *Simplices affectiones insunt naturaliter nobis tamquam ex nobis . . . , gratia ordinat quas donavit creatio'.* Gra 17 (SBOp 3:178,9–12). Note also: *Deus sic inest ut afficiat.* Csi 5.12 (SBOp 3:476,12).

236. *Dubitari solet, utrum dilectio Dei praecedat tempore dilectionem proximi. . . . Sic ergo dilectio Dei praecedit ut incipiens, et praeditur a dilectione proximi, ut illa nutrienda.* Sent 1.21 (SBOp 6/2:14,17–15,2). Cited in Delfgaauw 'La nature', 241.

237. Volney P. Gay, 'Kohut on Narcissism: Psychoanalytic Revolution from Within', *Religious Studies Review*, 7.3 (July, 1981) 199–203. Also, Peter Homans, 'Introducing the Psychology of the Self and Narcissism into the Study of Religion', *Religious Studies Review*, 7.3 (July, 1981) 193–199.

238. In Dedic. 5.2 (SBOp 5:390,3–4), Bernard speaks of the success of loving himself: *Oderam ergo eam [animam meam], et odissem adhuc nisi hoc mihi quodcumque amoris eius initium is, qui prior eam dilexerat, contulisset.* Delfgaauw, 'La nature', 239, cites this. Casey, 'In Pursuit of Ecstasy', 149–150, seems to claim that Bernard's perspective is wider than the saint's explicit reflections will give us to understand. Self-hatred, says Casey, is the point of departure for the growth of love, with the *love* of self a positive advance: 'There are darker and more destructive mechanisms at work within human reality than the love of self and the pursuit of human gratification' (150). While accepting that some sinners may have to begin in self-hatred, we must nevertheless observe that *On Loving God* restricts itself, in its philosophic manner, to a human condition where the most destructive consequences of sin have not been realized—where God, then, is loved (though unidentified) in the love of self.

239. Casey, 'In Pursuit of Ecstasy', 149.

240. *Porro autem et hoc iustitiae est, cum quo tibi est natura communis, naturae quoque cum eo munus non habere divisum.* Dil 24 (SBOp 3:139,22–24).

241. *. . . ab eo qui dat omnibus affluenter et non improperat, qui aperit manum suam et implet omne animal benedictione* [Ps 144:16]? Dil 24 (SBOp 3:139,13–16).

242. *Nam et ita condita fuit* [natura] *ut habeat iugiter necessarium protectorem, quem habuit et conditorem.* Dil 25 (SBOp 3:140,2–3).

243. Delfgaauw, 'La nature', 239, remembers that Luther and Baius condemned as bad will the attitudes which he traces in Bernard's first and second degrees of love. His response is that what precedes the third degree of loving God is 'un acte préparatoire à la justification'. Gilson, in *The Mystical Theology*, would have it both ways: he understands and defends Bernard's *cupiditas* in the four degrees (p. 87), speaks of 'the apprenticeship of charity' (pp. 90, 97), yet annuls this as he applies the critique of Bernard's other sense of *cupiditas* (34–36) to Bernard's outline of the ascent, concluding inevitably that the first degree is not love (p. 86).

244. W. Grundmann, 'Verständnis und Bewegung des Glaubens im Johannes-Evangelium', *Kerygma und Dogma*, 6 (1960) 131–154. F.-M. Braun, 'L'accueil de la foi selon S. Jean', *La Vie Spirituelle*, 92 (1955) 344–363. Wilfred Cantwell Smith, *Faith and Belief* (Princeton: Princeton University Press, 1979) 69–104, traces the

meaning of faith in the history of Roman Catholicism: in the early Church, through Augustine, *credo* designates 'an act of self-commitment in which the will is predominant' (p. 79). Saint Thomas represents a development in which the mind (never disengaged from the will) is seen to play a predominant role. Smith locates Saint Bernard, instead, in the Augustinian tradition (pp. 79–80). The author finds in Bernard's discussion of *fides* and *opinio* in Csi 5.3.6, precisely the distinction he wishes to make between faith and its intellectualization in belief. Nevertheless, let us add, while holding this integrative view of faith, Bernard will speak of growth in the spirit as the progress of love. The great Reformers took a different tack, as Irving Singer (1:212) observes: 'In his *Commentary on Galatians* Luther explicates the verse from St. Paul by saying: "Faith connects you so intimately with Christ, that He and you become as it were one person". But note that *faith* connects, not the love of God or a spiritual marriage'. Terence Penelhum, ed. *Faith* (New York: Macmillan, 1989) 43–44, shows how Luther developed even the Song of Songs theme from the point of view of faith rather than love.

245. For a brief, comprehensive historical account of a sequence, from the theology of charity to that of faith and, currently, to that of hope, see Mary Daly, 'Faith, Hope, and Charity', in Philip P. Wiener, ed *Dictionary of the History of Ideas: Studies of Selected Pivotal Ideas*, 5 vols. (New York: Charles Scribner's, 1973) 2:209–216.

246. *In carne quippe manens adhuc ambulat per fidem, quam sane operari per dilectionem necesse est, quia, si non operatur, mortua est* [cf. Jas 2:20]'. Dil 32 (SBOp 3:146,7–8).

247. For reference to 1 Cor 13:7, see SBOp 1:206,2; 5:245,18; 5:260,7; 6/2:20,2; 7:60,18; 7:168,13; 8:98,17. Reference to 1 Cor 13:10, at SBOp 2:18,3; 2:229,12; 2:297,27; 3:175,1; 3:292,5; 4:215,7; 5:225,24; 5:276,22; 6/1:38,25; 6/1:77,24; 8:280,3. See Hans Urs Von Balthasar, *Love Alone* (New York: Herder and Herder, 1969), Ch. 7: 'Love as Justification and Fatih', 81–86. Regarding Paul's 'I live by faith' (Gal 2:20): 'Faith here means my response to the love that has sacrificed itself for me' (p. 82).

248. McGinn, 'Introduction' (to Gra), 45–49, finding some recent treatments of the relation of the Reformers to Bernard unsatisfactory, calls attention to pivotal agreements with Bernard on the part of both Luther and Calvin. While underlining their differences with the abbot (some of which he suggests may be misreadings), McGinn notes that 'after St Augustine, Bernard was Luther's most admired theologian' (p. 45); and that 'Calvin's attitude towards Bernard is a remarkably positive one'—e.g., Calvin 'couples Bernard with Augustine in recognizing that men are made righteous by the free acceptance of God' (p. 49). The reference is to *Institutes*, 3.11.22.

249. He describes the process: *Ex intimis sane humanis affectibus primordia ducit sui ortus fraterna dilectio, et de insita homini ad seipsum naturali quadam dulcedine . . . summit procul dubio vegetationem et vim, per quam, spirante quidem gratia desuper, frutus parturit pietatis.* SC 44.4 (SBOp 2:46,25–29).

250. Bernard speaks of loving others 'in God': *Proximum pure diligere quomodo potest, qui in Deo non diligit?* Dil 25 (SBOp 3:139,26–27). The human being as destined spouse of the Word is the dwelling of God—*Sanctuarium Dei . . . aula*

*regia . . . templum lucis,* etc. SC 27.14 (SBOp 1:191,16–18). We are made in God's image. SC, *passim,* but esp. SC 80–82 (SBOp 2:277–298). On *caritas in affectu,* which can be *carnis, rationis, vel sapientiae,* see SC 50.4 (SBOp 2:80,11–22).

251. *Proficitur autem in eo* [amor], *cum sit et rationalis . . . Porro rationalis tunc est, cum in omnibus quae oportet de Christo sentire, fidei ratio ita firma tenetur, ut ab ecclesiatici sensus puritate nulla veri similitudine, nulla haeretica seu diabolica circumventione aliquatenus devietur.* SC 20.9 (SBOp 1:120,23–27).

252. In carnal love of Christ, the devout soul contemplates the humanity of Christ: *Adstat oranti Hominis Dei sacra imago, aut nascentis, aut lactentis, aut docentis,* etc. SC 20.6 (SBOp 1:118,18–19). Through this carnal love, a carnal life is excluded: *Bonus tamen amor iste carnalis, per quem vita carnalis excluditur.* SC 20.9 (SBOp 1:120,22). For ecclesiastical orthodoxy, see SC 20.9 in preceding note.

253. Henri DeLubac, *Exegèse médiévales: Les Quatre sens de l'Ecriture,* 4 Vols (Paris, 1959–64) 2:408, notices in other medieval writers an intermediate sense which is merely a sort of parenthesis. J. Schuck, *Das religiöse Erlebnis beim hl. Bernhard von Clairvaux* (Würzburg, 1922) 42, sees this *amor rationalis* as merely a dogmatically correct *amor carnalis.* Delfgaauw, 'La nature', 243, n.3, calls it, not truly a different degree of love, but *amor carnalis* 'informé par la science'.

254. Anders Nygren, *Agape and Eros,* 127.

255. SBOp 4:69–70.

256. *Fugite de medio Babylonis, fugite et salvate animas vestras. Convolate ad urbes refugii.* Conv 11.37 (SBOp 4:113,16–17).

257. Jean Leclercq, 'Introduction', [to *Ad clericos de conversione*] SBOp 4:61, n.4.

258. 'It is wisdom to know things truly for what they are'. *Est enim sapientia, per quam utique quaeque res sapiunt prout sunt.* SC 50.6 (SBOp 2:81,22–23; also 83,6–7).

259. *Quamobrem puto de illa dictum: Lex Domini immaculata, convertens animas, quod sola videlicet sit, quae ab amore sui et mundi avertere possit animum et in Deum dirigere. Nec timor quippe, nec amor privatus convertunt animam.* Dil 34 (SBOp 3:148,21–149,3).

260. Delfgaauw, 'Saint Bernard, maître de l'amour divin', 73, 81, n.43, cites Z. Alszeghy, *Gründformen der Liebe: Die Theorie der Gottesliebe bei dem hl. Bonaventura* (Rome, 1946) 133–136, wehre the tradition from Saint Augustine to Saint Bernard is traced.

261. *Cumque se videt per se non posse subsistere, Deum quasi sibi necessarium incipit per fidem inquirere et diligere.* Dil 39 (SBOp 3:152,24–25).

262. In Div 103, where Bernard presents a four-degree schema of spiritual progress, he conceives of a beginner as *amicus suae animae,* somewhat similar to one who loves self for the sake of self in the first degree of Dil. The Faith of this beginner, however, is evident: *Hoc modo fit amator animae suae per Spiritum Sanctum, quem ex fide accepit.* Div 103.1 (SBOp 6/1:372,2).

263. 'Neither fear nor love of self changes the soul'. *Nec timor quippe, nec amor privatus convertunt animam.* Dil 34 (SBOp 3:149,3).

264. *Si timor est initium caritatis, perfectum sequatur etiam plenitudo dilectionis.* Div 56.2 (SBOp 6/1:285,14–15).

265. *De illa* [*caritas in actu*] *quidem quae operis est . . .* SC 50.2 (SBOp 2:79,5). *Nolite, ait, diligere verbo neque lingua, sed opere et veritate* (CF 1 Jn 3:18). SC 50.4

(SBOp 2.80,22). [*Est*] *secunda* [*affectio quam ratio regnit*], *quam perhibet, e regione, consentientem legi Dei.* SC 50.4 (SBOp 2:80,13–14).

266. *Tunc amor tuus et temperans erit, et iustus, si quod propriis subtrahitur voluptatibus, fratris necessitatibus non negetur.* Dil 23 (SBOp 3:139,9–11).

267. *Mihi profecto fides tanto plus indicit amandum, quanto et eum me ipso pluris aestimandum intelligo, quippe qui illum non solum mei, sed sui quoque ipsius teneo largitorem.* Dil 15 (SBOp 3:131,14–15).

268. *Denique nondum tempus fidei advenerat. . . . nondum, inquam, commendaverat in nobis suam multam dilectionem, illam de qua iam multa locuti sumus.* Dil 15 (SBOp 3:131,16–19).

269. *Et ubi se dedit, me mihi reddidit.* Dil 15 (OB 3:132,10–11).

270. Representative of this conviction is the secular humanist Eric Fromm, *The Art of Loving* (New York: Harper & Row, 1956; 1962) 121, speaking of 'rational faith'.

271. Some authors integrate Bernard's discussion of the carnal love of Christ into the four degrees of love. See Delfgaauw, 'La nature', 242–243; Casey, 'In Pursuit of Ecstasy', 149, 151. Although this serves a purpose, one must not fail to inquire why Bernard himself did not formally incorporate the *memoria Christi*, so extensively treated in Dil (1,7,8,11,14, and 15), into his construciton of four degrees of divine love.

272. Some would read this as loving, not one's neighbor, but God. Irving Singer, *The Nature of Love*, 1:187–188, is representative. He writes that Bernard 'never admits to any justifiable love other than the love of God'. Instead, Bernard seeks to safeguard the inviolable otherness of the neighbor from our self-interest by pointing to God as the source of each human being's autonomy. God and others, then, are not competing alternative objects of one's love.

273. *Oportet ergo Deum diligi prius, ut in Deo diligi possit et proximus* [cf. Mk 12:30]. Dil 25 (SBOp 3:139,28).

274. *Facit ergo etiam se diligi Deus, qui et cetera bona facit.* Dil 25 (SBOp 3:130,28–131,1).

275. *Ut . . . Deus ab homine, ut dignum est, honoretur.* Dil 25 (SBOp 3:140,7–8).

276. *Vult hominem idem conditor, alto quidem salubrique consilio, tribulationibus exerceri.* Dil 25 (SBOp 3:140,6–7).

277. *Fit itaque hoc tali modo, ut homo . . . etiam Deum vel propter se amare incipiat, quod in ipso nimirum, ut saepe expertus est, omnia possit, quae posse tamen prosit, et sine ipso possit nihil.* Dil 25 (SBOp 3:140,10–13).

278. *Amat ergo iam Deum, sed propter se interim, adhuc non propter ipsum.* Dil 26 (SBOp 3:140,16–17).

279. There is an ambiguity to be overcome, in the succession of negatives, in order to reach this conclusion. Does the 'nevertheless' with which Bernard begins the discussion (*tamen* in the quotation of the following note) signal an objection to the position of those in the second degree, and thus start a move toward the third degree? If so, the sense of 'however' (*at*) in the next sentence would have to leap-frog back to this same position, opposing it. Or, is this 'nevertheless' a compassionate elaboration on the beginner's position, where love is 'not *yet* for

God's sake'? The first option is correct. The critical edition of the text shows no discrepancies among the manuscripts.

280. *Est tamen quaedam prudentia scire quid ex te, quid ex Dei adiutorio possis, et ipsi te servare infensum, qui te tibi servat illaesum.* Dil 26 (SBOp 3:140,17–18).

281. *Etsi fuerit ferreum pectus vel cor lapideum . . . emolliri necesse est ad gratiam liberantis.* Dil 26 (SBOp 3:140,20–22).

282. Dil 7 (SBOp 3:124,12). In a later text, God again is lovable as liberator: *Hi . . . vacant, considerantes quid sit Deus . . . contemplantes quia Deus est mundi rector et gubernator, hominum liberator et adiutor, angelorum sapor et decor . . . in creaturis mirabilis, in hominibus amabilis, in angelis desiderabilis . . .* Div 48 (SBOp 6/1:9–14).

283. *Deum homo diligat, non propter se tantum, sed et propter ipsum.* Dil 26 (SBOp 3:140,22–23).

284. *Ex occasione quippe frequentium necessitatum crebris necesse est interpellationibus. Deum ab homine frequentari, frequentando gustari, gustando probari quam suavis est Dominus.* Dil 26 (SBOp 3:141, 3–5).

285. *Et sic, gustato quam suavis est Dominus, transit ad tertium gradum.* Dil 39 (SBOp 3:153,2). See also: *iam operatur, non ut ipse Deo placeat . . . sed quia placet ei Deus ei.* Div 103.4 (SBOp 6/1:373, 17–18). Near the end of his life Bernard wrote: 'This is the final reason for which the soul seeks the Word, namely that it may find delight through enjoying him'. *Hoc est quod supra, post alia, memini me dixisse, quaerere utique animam Verbum, quo fruatur ad iucunditatem.* SC 85.13 (SBOp 2:216,9–10).

286. *Ita fit, ut ad diligendum pure Deum plus iam ipsius alliciat gustata suavitas quam urgeat nostra necessitas.* Dil 26 (SBOp 3:141, 5–6).

287. *At vero cum ipsum coeperit occasione propriae necessitatis colere et frequentare, cogitando legendo, orando, oboediendo quadam huiuscemodo familiaritate paulatim sensimque Deus innotescit, consequenter et dulcescit.* Dil 39 (SBOp 3:152,27–153,2).

288. *Est enim carnis quaedam loquela necessitas, et beneficia quae experiendo probat, gestiendo renuntiat.* Dil 26 (SBOp 3:141,12–13).

289. Delfgaauw, 'La lumière de la charité', 306ff, treats of desire as an aspect of love. Casey, *Athirst for God*, 92–94, speaks of the 'overlap' of love and desire in Saint Bernard.

290. *Qui Domino confitetur, non quoniam sibi bonus est, sed quoniam bonus est, hic vere diligit Deum propter Deum, et non propter seipsum.* Dil 26 (SBOp 3:141,23–24).

291. *Justus est, quoniam qualis suscipitur, talis et redditur. Qui enim sic amat, haud secus profecto quam amatus est, amat, quaerens et ipse vicissim non quae sua sunt, sed quae Iesu Christi, quemadmodum ille nostra, vel potius nos, et non sua quaesivit.* (SBOp 3:141,19–22).

292. *Dulce nempe dixerim, quod carnem induit.* SC 20.3 (SBOp 1:115,19–20).

293. See Sebastian Moore, *The Fire and the Rose Are One*, 26: 'Religion is the believed-in answer of the unknown other, to the question: "Am I valuable in your eyes?" '

294. *Amat caste, et casto non gravatur oboedire mandato, castifican magis cor suum, ut scriptum est, in oboedientia caritatis* (CF. 1 Pet 1:22). Dil 26 (SBOp 3:141,15–16).

295. *Sponte afficit, et spontaneum facit.* Dil 17 (SBOp 3:134,1).

296. *Qui enim sic amat, haud secus profecto quam amatus est, amat, quaerens et ipse vicissim non quae sua sunt, sed quae Iesu Christi, quemadmodum ille nostra, vel potius nos, et non sua quaesivit.* Dil 26 (SBOp 3:141,20–23).

297. Of special interest is SC 23.15, where, comparing the rooms of the Bridegroom, Bernard prefers the bedroom: *Sed est locus ubi vere quiescens et quietus cernitur Deus: locus omnino, non iudicis, non magistri, sed sponsi, et qui mihi quidem—nam de aliis nescio—plane cubiculum sit, si quando in illum contigerit introduci.* (SBOp 1:148,17–19). On the speculative character of Augustine's contemplation, see Emero Stiegman, 'Metaphysics in the Prayer of Saint Augustine', '*Atti del Congresso internazionale su s. Agostino nel XVI centenario della conversione.* Roma, 15–20 settembre 1986, Vol 2, Studia Ephemeridis '*Augustinian*', 25 (Rome, 1987) 59–77: Augustine, after his conversion to faith, prayerfully and playfully *returns* to metaphysical reflection to replay the miracle of this conversion.

298. *Felix qui meruit ad quartum usque pertingere, quatenus nec seimpsum diligat homo nisi propter deum.* Dil 27 (SBOp 3:142,3–4). See also SC 50.6–7 (SBOp 2:81,29–82,25). Perhaps a remark of Augustine can be taken as precedent: *Oportet ut oderis in te opus tuum et ames in te opus Dei.* In Jo. 12.13.26; also Enar.in Ps. 44.18.19.

299. *Te enim quodammodo perdere, tamquam qui non sis* Dil 27. (SBOp 2:142,16). *Mihi, fateor, impossibile videtur.* Dil 39 (SBOp 3:153,6). *Quando huiuscemodi experitur affectum?* Dil 27 (SBOp 3:142, 9–10). *Alioquin quomodo omnia in omnibus erit Deus?* Dil 28 (SBOp 3:143,22–23). That the perfection of this condition is reserved for the next life, see SC 50.2 (SBOp 2:79,9–10): *Plane consummationem defendimus futurae felicitati.*

300. Bernard, nevertheless, demured this way, not only to Cardinal Haimeric, but in his letter to the Carthusians (see Dil 39). He has a clear concept and a 'standard', one might say, for the state he speaks of; and his aspiration has not been satisfied. Such statements can offer little information to those who ask whether he has enjoyed 'mystical experience'.

301. *Heu! Redire in se, recidere in sua compellitur.* Dil 27 (SBOp 3:142,22).

302. *Quando huiuscemodi experitur affectum, ut . . . oblitus sui, . . . unus cum eo spiritus fiat.* Dil 27 (SBOp 3:142,9–12).

303. The theme is a confluence of several motifs, such as finding God in self-knowledge (SC 23.17; 46,5), the dynamism of desire (SC 32.2), the vocation of all people to contemplation (SC 62.6; 83,1), and faith as seeing (SC 70.2). This is studied in Emero Stiegman, 'Action and Contemplation in Saint Bernard's Sermons on the Song of Songs', Introduction to *Bernard of Clairvaux* On the Song of Songs III, trans. Kilian Walsh, OCSO, and Irene M. Edmonds, CF 31 (Kalamazoo: Cistercian Publications, 1979) xiii-xviii. Bernard speaks of freedom from misery in Gra 6 (SBOp 3:170,20–24).

304. *The Mystical Theology*, 220, n.23.

305. Delfgaauw, 'La lumière de la charité', 43–45, identifies the patristic tradition. Bell, 217–249, uncovers the heritage of Augustine in William of Saint Thierry's *amor ipse intellectus est.* On a meaning of mysticism consistent with the larger christian tradition, see Bernard McGinn, *The Foundations of Mysticism*, Vol 1

of *The Presence of God: A History of Western Christian Mysticism* (New York: Crossroad, 1991) xii-xx.

306. Bertola, *Introduzione*, 257.

307. *Caelestis est conversationis, non humanae affectionis.* Dil 27 (SBOp 3:142,17–18). *O dulcis et suavis affectio!* Dil 28 (SBOp 3:143,12).

308. *Manebit quidem substantia, sed in alia forma.* Dil 28 (SBOp 3:143,23–24). Bell, 174–175, notes that, for William of Saint Thierry, in the wake of Augustine (*De natura et gratia*, 37; PL 44:265; *De Trinitate* 15.26; PL 42:1079; *Enar. in ps.* 62.16; PL 36:758, and 61.2; PL 36:730) union with God is, not identity, but *unitas similitudinis* (*Exp Rm* 638 D; *Ep frat* 352 SCh 389; *Aenig* 399 C-D); he finds that in SC 71.7 (SBOp 2:218–220) Bernard too follows Augustine closely on this theme.

309. *Delectabit sane non tam nostra vel sopita necessitas, vel sortita felicitas, quam quod eius in nobis et de nobis voluntas adimpleta videbitur.* Dil 28 (SBOp 3:143,8–10). Elsewhere Bernard offers this account of the love of self for God: 'Then you will experience as well your own true self, since you perceive that you possess nothing at all for which you love yourself, except insofar as you belong to God [*cum te senseris nil habere prorsus unde te ames, nisi in quantum Dei es*]: you pour out upon him your whole power of loving. I repeat: you experience yourself as you are [*sapies, inquam, tibi prout es*], when by that experience of love of yourself and of the feeling that you feel toward him, you discover that you are an altogether unworthy object even of your own love, except for the sake of him without whom you are nothing'. SC 50.6 (SBOp 2:82,4–9).

310. *Erit profecto ut factura sese quandoque conformet et concordet Auctori.* Dil 28 (SBOp 3:143,4–5). One may trace a *transformatio ut conformatio* theme in the *Super Cantica*— e.g., SC 36.6 (SBOp 2:8,1–7), SC 62.7 (SBOp 2:160,5–7), SC 67.8 (SBOp 2:194,1–3), as suggested by Farkasfalvy, 'La conoscenza di Dio', 209. The highest union, the kiss of the lips, is thus described: *Conformitas maritat animam Verbo.* SC 83.3 (SBOp 2:299,21). See also SC 7.2 (SBOp 1:31,16–32,14) on the common will of spouses—esp.*nil proprium, nil a se divisum habentibus.*

311. *O pura et defaecata intentio voluntatis, eo certe defaecatior et purior, quo in ea de proprio nil iam admixtum relinquitur.* Dil 28 (SBOp 3:143,12–14). Bernard seems to contrast this *defaecatio* with *deificatio:* pure love requires a purging, or 'defecation', of self-will. Michael Casey has called the rough language to my attention.

312. *Sic affici deificari est.* Dil 28 (SBOp 3:143,15). My reflection, above, upon the effect of this love in the self owes much to conversations with Paul Quenon, OCSO, of the Abbey of Gethsemani. Rowan Williams, *Christian Spirituality*, 112–113, collates passages in which Bernard distinguishes our oneness with God from Jesus' oneness with the Father—esp. in SC 62.5–10 and SC 67.8. See also Bernard's excursus on union with God in SC 71.6–11 (SBOp 2:218–222): it is not a *confusio naturarum* but a *voluntatum consensio.*

313. Gilson, *The Mystical Theology*, 25–27, compares Maximus' *Ambigua* translation of Scotus Eriugena), cap.2; PL 122:1202A, with Dil 28. Bertola, *Introduzione*, 238, observes that Bernard could have found the *deificatio* theme in Augustine (where it is, however, rare), in the introduction to the Rule (*deificum lumen*), or in the office of Saint Martin. But, Gilson's parallels make a considerable case. The three

similes of union, on the other hand, are found together outside of Maximus, who uses only the last two. Bertola concludes, then, that they are taken from one of these other sources.

314. See *San Bernardo di Chiaravalle, Il dovere di amare Dio,* Introduzione e note di Ambrogio M. Piazzone, Traduzione di Ettore Paratore (Torino: Edizioni Paoline, 1990). The Introduction proposes this view. Note the objections of Edmund Mikkers in *Cîteaux,* 41, fasc.3–4 (1990) 506–507: such a reading contradicts the anthropology set forth early in the treatise. Jean-Baptiste Auberger, OFM, *L'Unanimité cistercienne primitive: mythe ou realité?* (Achel: Administration de Cîteaux, 1986) 267, holds that, for Bernard (but not for William of Saint Thierry), union with God could be only by juxtaposition until the beatific vision. One infers, then, that what our text describes as the fourth degree is reserved for heaven.

315. *In hac mortali vita raro interdum.* . . . Dil 27 (SBOp 3:142,14). *Et si quidem e mortalibus quispian ad illud* . . . *et ad momentum admittitur, subito* . . . *sollicitat carnis necessitas* . . . *fraterna revocat caritas.* Dil 27 (SBOp 3:142,18–22).

316. *Si quis in nobis est ita desiderii vir, ut cupiat dissolvi et cum Christo esse* [Phil 1:23], *cupiat autem vehementer* . . . *is profecto non secus quam in forma sponsi suscipiet Verbum* . . . *etsi adhuc peregrinanti in corpore* [2 Cor 5:6], *ex parte tamen, idque ad tempus et tempus modicum.* SC 32.2 (SBOp 1:227,7–13). See also SC 1.1 (SBOp 1:3,10–15), where Bernard, reversing the symbols of bread and milk in our treatise, announces he will break the bread of the Song of Songs for advanced souls (*inter perfectos*). Also SC 3.1 (SBOp 1:14,10–16) and SC 82.8 (SBOp 2:297,21–29): *Caritas illa visio, illa similitudo est* . . . *eritque ad alterutrum casta et consummata dilectio.* . . .

317. McGinn, *The Foundations of Mysticism,* 412, n.53, points to Augustine's *Enarr. in Pss.* 43.4, 48.1.5; *Tr. in Jo.* 124.5.

318. *Te enim quodammodo perdere, tamquam qui non sis, et omnino non sentire teipsum, et a temetipso exinanire, et paene annullari, caelestis est conversationis non humanae affectionis.* Dil 27 (SBOp 3:142,16–18). Note also, *In hoc ultimo genere interdum exceditur et seceditur etiam a corporeis sensibus, ut sese non sentiat quae Verbum sentit. Hoc fit, cum mens* . . . *rapitur atque elabitur a seipsa, ut Verbo fruatur.* SC 85.13 (SBOp 2:315,28–316,3). Ecstasy in Bernard, then, is a deeply meaningful objective, even as it is pure gift. McGinn, *The Foundations of Mysticism,* 253–254, traces *ecstasis* and *excessus* in Augustine's works. A concordance to Augustine, he notes, shows 87 uses of *ecstasis.*

319. E.g., Nygren 650: the mysticism of Agusutine, Bernard, and Aquinas 'attacks not only selfishness but selfhood'. To the contrary, in the *Super Cantica,* the soul's union with God is, not a fusion of natures, but a conformity of wills. SC 83.3 (SBOp 2:299,21–23). See Dil 28, below.

320. Andrew Louth, 'Bernard and Affective Mysticism', in Sister Benedicta Ward, SLG, ed. *The Influence of Saint Bernard: Anglican Essays* (Oxford: Fairacres, 1976) 5. But, Louth sees Bernard's *affectio/affectus,* in our view erroneously, as outside the patristic tradition's unity of faculties. In Bernard, he thinks, it is reduced to 'feeling'.

321. Bernard does not write of the human 'individual'. We use the term here, encouraged by his conviction regarding the indivisibility of the human being, to

signify the inviolable 'self' (*Homo diligit se propter Deum*) of whom he speaks. But, notice the expressions *individuus comes*, SC 32.7 (SBOp 1:231,4), and *individuus amor*, SC 8.2 (SBOp 1:37,17).

322. Gilson, *The Mystical Theology*, 26–28, suspects Bernard's proximate source for *excessus* and *deificatio* is Maximus the Confessor, a seventh-century heir to the Eastern tradition (See n.63, above). Ben Drewery, 'Deification', in Peter Brooks, ed., *Christian Spirituality: Essays in Honour of Gordon Rupp* (London: SCM Press, 1975) 33–62, finds that Eastern theologians criticize Augustine as the start of a Western departure from the theme of *deificatio*, also with its psychological implications for the end-time. Drewery traces the tradition from Theophilus of Antioch, in the second century, to Irenaeus. Then, 'the Alexandrian school, from Clement and Origen through Athanasius to Cyril, with the allied Cappadocian Fathers, bring the doctrine to its theological consolidation in John of Damascus; and alongside this is the 'mystical' elaboration from Pseudo-Dionysius to Gregory Palamas' (p. 38). In speaking of the consciousness of the blessed, Saint Bonaventure refers to our treatise. He singles out the same Pauline concept as starting point and the same effect of love: *Item, in patria Deus erit omnia in omnibus, et effectus beatorum sic erit dilectione inebriatus, secundum quod dicit Bernardus in libro De diligendo Deo, ut sui obliviscatur.* 3 Sent d.31, a.3, q.fund.3 (3.692). Cited by Bougerol, 40.

323. *quousque ipsum cor cogitare iam non cogatur de corpore, et anima eidem in hoc statu vivificando et sensificando intendere desinat.* Dil 29 (SBOp 3:144,1–3). Hourlier, 227, finds that William of Saint Thierry is different from Bernard in posing no limits to the restoration of the image of God. But for William too (Aenig 407 A-B; Davy 23) love is perfected only in heaven, as Bell, 173 and n.25, observes. The difference is more apparent than real.

324. The Walton translation omits 'integral body'. *Itaque in corpore spirituali et immortali, in corpore integro, placido placitoque, et per omnia subiecto spiritui, speret se anima quartum apprehendere amoris gradum . . .* Dil 29 (SBOp 3:144,6–8).

325. *Putamusne tamen hanc gratiam vel ex parte sanctos Martyres assecutos, in illis adhuc victoriosis corporibus constitutos?* Dil 29 (SBOp 3:144,12–13).

326. *Quid autem iam solutas corporibus?* Dil 30 (SBOp 3:144,16–17).

327. *Immersas ex toto credimus immenso illi pelago aeterni luminis et luminosae aeternitatis.* Dil 30 (SBOp 3:144,17.18).

328. *Itaque ante restaurationem corporum non erit ille defectus animorum, qui perfectus et summus est ipsorum status.* Dil 30 (SBOp 3:145,5–6).

329. *Christo utique moriente . . . et quandoque redituro ad consummationem nostram.* Dil 9 (SBOp 3:126,19–22).

330. See, e.g., Gra 9 (SBOp 3:172,15–16): *Nam sanctis animabus, etsi necdum corpora receperunt, deest quidem de gloria, sed nihil prorsus inest de miseria.* OS 3.1 (SBOp 5:350,1–2): *Neque enim praestari decet integram beatitudinem, donec sit homo integer cui detur, nec perfectione donari Ecclesiam imperfectam.* Div 78 (SBOp 6/1:318,11–13): *Animae quae in amore Dei sunt . . . non habent tectum, adhuc expectantes augmentum, quod non erit nisi in resurrectione corporum suorum.* Adv A 6.5 (SBOp 4:194,12–20): *Ipse Dominus Sabaoth . . . descendet ad reformanda corpora nostra et configuranda corpori claritatis suae. . . . praecurrentibus angelis et tubae concentu excitantibus de pulvere corpus inops et rapientibus illud obviam Christo in aera?*

331. Bernard McGinn, 'Saint Bernard and Eschatology', in *Bernard of Clairvaux: Studies Presented to Dom Jean Leclercq*, CS 23 (Washington, D.C.: Cistercian Publications, 1973) 161–185, reviews the content of the saint's eschatology. The abbot's views were quite in accord with those of his generation (p. 184).

332. Bernard DeVrégille, sj, 'L'attente des saints d'après saint Bernard', *Nouvelle revue théologique*, No. 3 (March, 1948) 225.

333. Bertola, 'Introduzione', 233–235.

334. X. Le Bachelet, 'Benôit XII' in *Dictionnaire de théologie catholique*, 2, 659–961, discusses the episode, especially the connection between John XXII's opinion and Saint Bernard.

335. Delfgaauw, 'La nature', 250, answers: 'It is without doubt because of something in the way of a metaphysical inadequacy in the experiential thought of Saint Bernard [par un certain deficit metaphysique de la pensée 'expérimental' de S. Bernard]. He does not yet have a preicse theory on the formal object of vision nor on that of charity. The one and the other are for him, above all, experiences, unions [des adhésions], which therefore require the presence (let us say, material) of their object'. See also Delgaauw, *Saint Bernard, mâitre de l'amour divin*, 71–73,81, n.41.

336. *per omnia subiecto spiritui*. Dil 29 (3:114,7).

337. *Enimvero absque profectu animae nec ponitur corpus, nec resumitur*. Dil 30 (SBOp 3:145,7–8).

338. *Ego puto non ante sane perfecte impletum iri: diliges Dominum Deum tuum ex toto corde tuo, et ex tota anima tua, et ex tota virtute tua, quousque ipsum cor cogitare iam non cogatur de corpore, et anima eidem in hoc statu vivificando et sensificando intendere desinat, et virtus eiusdem relevata molestiis, in Dei potentia roboretur*. Dil 29 (SBOp 3:143,28–144,3).

339. . . . *quamdiu ea hic fragili et aerumnoso corpori intenta et distenta necesse est subservire*. Dil 29 (SBOp 3:144,4–5). *In eo autem minus Deum amare convincitur, quod carnis adhuc necessitatibus occupatur. Illa vero circa corpus occupatio quid est, nisi a Deo quaedam absentatio?* Pre 60 (SBOp 3:293,5–7). Note also the following: *Duas ad intelligendum se condidit universitatis Auctor creaturas, hominem et angelum. Hominem iustificant fides et memoria, angelum beatificant intellectus et praesentia . . . nam fide mundatur cor, ut intellectus videat Deum. . . . hic merebitur quandoque, ut eius quoque videat praesentiam. Habeant igitur intellectum et praesentiam angeli Dei in caelo; habeamus et nos eius fidem et memoriam in mundo.* Sent 1.12 (SBOp 6/1:10,13–22). Here, as in Dil 29–33, the 'absence' from God is not explained in the existence of the body, but in the necessity for purity of heart.

340. *Et sunt carissimi, qui recepta iam secundo stola, in corporibus utique cum gloria resumptis* . . . Dil 31 (SBOp 3:145,29–146,1).

341. Delfgaauw, 'Saint Bernard, mâitre de l'amour divin', 81 n.48, remarks that not until Philip the Chancellor (d.1230) do we find a metaphysical distinction between nature and grace elaborated.

342. Delfgaauw, 'Saint Bernard, mâitre de l'amour divin', 73, explains the problem as an inadequacy in Bernard's 'conception expérimentale de l'amour-affectus': 'L'*affectio* du corps, bien que conforme à l'ordre divin, comporte toujours, portant sur un objet sensible, un autre 'sapor' que l'amour spirituel de Dieu'. But, 'l'*affectio*

du corps' is a poor formulation for Bernard's *affectio*: it begs the question regarding the role of the body in a human being's love for God; it seems to assume what Bernard disputes—i.e., that bodiliness is not according to the 'divine order', that it is inconsistent with 'the spiritual love of God'. Bertola, *Introduzione* 261, rightly points out that Bernard's 'technical' formulation for the consummation of love is *sic affici, deificari est.* Love in the end is still *affectus*, it is still 'expérimentale', a notion which Delfgaauw seems to tie in too limited a manner to *sensibilis*.

343. The relationship of christian spirituality to a theology overwhelmed by the necessity for exhaustive metaphysical exposition has always been a troubled one. The theology of the patristic tradition, Saint Bernard's heritage, was closer to spirituality because it had not yet suffered this handicap. Bertola's comment on what he takes to be a metaphysical 'flaw' in Bernard's view of the general resurrection would—contrary to Bertola's own appreciation for our treatise—spell disaster for Bernard's concept of love. He writes (*Introduzione* 260) that metaphysics is the 'true basis of Christian theology'. But, he excuses what he understands as Bernard's inadequacy, 'because the Western world had no true knowledge of metaphysics [perchè una vera conoscenza della metafisica il mondo occidentale non la ebbe] until near the middle of the twelfth century'. Combining the two assertions, one would not be able to salvage much that was of theological merit from the patristic and monastic traditions.

344. *At non ita affectualis; nam a primis ipsa ducit ordinem. Est enim sapientia, per quam utique quaeque res sapiunt prout sunt.* SC 50.6 (SBOp 2:81,22–23).

345. 'une imperfection du concept bernardin de l'amour', 'La nature', 251.

346. This contrast, in the abstract, is outlined in Karl Rahner and Herbert Vorgrimler, *Theological Dictionary*, ed. Cornelius Ernst, trans. Richard Strachan (New York: Herder and Herder, 1965), s.v. 'Eschatology'.

347. Karl Rahner, 'The Resurrection of the Body', *Theological Investigations* (Baltimore: Helicon, 1963) 2:206.

348. Bertola, *Introduzione*, 233–235, 250–251.

349. OS 2,3 and 4 (SBOp 5:342–360) all treat the theme *De statu sanctorum ante resurrectionem.* See OS 4.2 (SBOp 5:356,3–4): *Porro altare ipsum, de quo nobis habendus est sermo, ego pro meo sapere nihil aliud arbitror esse quam corpus ipsum Domini Salvatoris.* Cited in DeVrégille, 239. On Ambrose as source, see Bertola, *Introduzione*, 250–251.

350. Rahner, 'The Resurrection of the Body', *Theological Investigations*, 2:207, complained: 'Even for the theologian, the [general] "resurrection" . . . is very much a supplementary matter'.

351. Karl Rahner, 'The Hermeneutics of Eschatological Assertions', *Theological Investigations*, 4:331: 'The prognosis [of eschatology] must be concerned with the whole man'. Rahner and Vorgrimler, under 'Judgment, Last': 'Even as a spirit he [the human being] is only consummated in the full sense in that event [the resurrection of the body]'.

352. Regarding Benedict XII's text of condemnation (see Denziger-Schönmetzer, eds. *Enchiridion Symbolorum*, 1000–1001), expressions such as *etiam ante resumptionem suorum corporum* cannot be read as the canonizing of a particular philosophical anthropology.

353. In Csi 5,23 (SBOp 3:485,23), after speculating briefly upon whether the body of Christ was of Mary's body or of newly created matter, Bernard dismisses the question, asking, 'But what is this to our salvation?' *Quid hoc ad nostram salutem?*

354. *Bonus plane fidusque comes caro spiritui bono.* Dil 31 (SBOp 3:145,17).

355. *Comedite, inquit, amici, et bibite, et inebriamini carissimi.* Dil 31 (SBOp 3:145,21). Notice, especially, allusions to Mt 6:10, Rom 7:24, Mk 12:30, 1 Cor 15:28, Is 38:14. For the use of Song 5.1, see Div 41.12 (SBOp 6/1:253,21–24) and Div 87.4 (SBOP 6/1:331,21–332,8).

356. Bertola, *Introduzione*, 226. For Augustine's treatment of the milk-and-solid food metaphor, see McGinn, *The Foundations of Mysticism*, 256.

357. Déchanet, 'Aux sources de la pensée philosophique de s. Bernard', 67–68, finds Bernard's conception of the body-soul relationship preeminently in *On Loving God.*

358. Rousselot, 53, n.1.

359. *In secundo quoque [statu] non sine aliqua proprietate desiderii expectetur.* Dil 31 (SBOp 3:146,4–5). For selected texts on the body, see John R. Sommerfeldt, *The Spiritual Teachings of Bernard of Clairvaux: An Intellectual History of the Early Cistercian Order*, CS 125 (Kalamazoo: Cistercian Publications, 1991) 13–17. I have profited, with generous permission, from the abundant documentation of Sommerfeldt's expanded treatment, 'The Body in Bernard's Anthropology', as yet unpublished.

360. E.g., Div 86.1 (SBOp 6/1:328,11–14); QH 1.4 (SBOp 4:389, 1–8); Div 106.2 (SBOp 6/1:378,15–17).

361. Johannes Meyer, 'Welt, Leib, Frau, Ehe—Beobachtungen zur polaren Konzeption der Wirklichkeit bei Bernhard von Clairvaux', *Archiv für Religionspsychologie* 17 (1985) 111, writes of an anthropological dualism in Bernard, proper of the philosophical culture of the era, but finds in Bernard's antithetical manner of speaking symbolic meanings rather than the simplistic body-soul antagonism frequently read into it. Wilhelm Hiss, *Die Anthropologie Bernhards von Clairvaux*, Quellen und Studien zur Geschichte der Philosophie 7 (Berlin: Walter de Gruyter, 1964) 55, 58, asks whether Bernard saw the soul as the form of the body. In finding, predictably, that this is not the case, the author fails to advance the enquiry with a discovery of the extent of Bernard's body-soul unity. See Delfgaauw, 'La lumière de la charité' 52, n.54, for a comparison of Bernard's treatment of the body to that of Augustine and of Aquinas. Regarding Platonic dualism, see A. Hilary Armstrong, 'Neoplatonic Valuations of Nature, Body and Intellect', *Augustinian Studies* 3 (1972) 35–59; also Armstrong's 'Man in the Cosmos: A Study of Some Differences between Pagan Neoplatonism and Christianity', in *Romanitas et Christianitas* (Amsterdam: North-Holland Publ. Co., 1973) 5–14.

362. Emero Stiegman, 'The Language of Asceticism in Saint Bernard of Clairvaux's *Sermones super Cantica Canticorum*', diss., Fordham University, 1973 (Ann Arbor, Michigan.: University Microfilms) 313: This language can be clarified only in a large context but is demonstrably not negativistic.

363. *per legem naturalem ex perceptis bonis corporis animaeque moneri.* Dil 6 (SBOp 3:123,18–19).

364. *recepta iam secundo stola, in corporibus utique cum gloria resumptis . . .* Dil 31 (SBOp 3:145,29–146,1).

365. *Bonus plane fidusque comes caro spiritui bono.* Dil 31 (SBOp 3:145,17). The term *caro* can never be presumed to mean *body*; that it has this meaning, however, in this text is evident from its position in a topic sentence developed through the three stages of the body—*laborantes in corpore . . . iam posito corpore . . . resumentes corpora.*

366. *In carne quippe manens adhuc ambulat per fidem, quam sane operari per dilectionem necesse est.* Dil 32 (SBOp 3:146,7–8).

367. *Dehinc, carne exuta, iam pane doloris non cibatur, sed vinum amoris, tamquam post cibum, plenius haurire permittitur, non purum tamen, sed quomodo sub sponsae nomine ipsa dicit in Canticis: Bibi vinum meum cum lacte meo.* Dil 32 (SBOp 3:146,10–13).

368. *Ebrietas denique solet evertere mentes, atque omnino reddere immemores sui.* Dil 32 (SBOp 3:146,17–18). For Augustine's development of 'spiritual drunkenness', see especially *Enar. in Ps,* 35:14; PL 36:351–352.

369. *. . . quid iam impedit . . . penitus sibi dissimillimam fieri, quo Deo simillimam effici donatur?* Dil 32 (SBOp 3:146,20–21).

370. Bernard's *self* is a positive reality—e.g., *Utrumque ergo scias necesse est, et quid sis, et quod a teipso non sis.* Dil 4 (SBOp 3:122,8).

371. *. . . cum te senseris nil habere prorsus unde te ames, nisi in quantum Dei es.* SC 50.6 (SBOp 2:82,4–5).

372. *nulla mordente cura de proprio.* Dil 32 (SBOp 3:146,24).

373. Bernard's eulogy for Gerard is, in large part, a testimonial of his brother's care for the brethren and a reflection upon *cura: Nec quando Deum induisti, nostri cura te exuisti: et ipsi enim cura est de nobis.* SC 26.5 (SBOp 2:173,20–21). Care for the necessities of oneself and of others is distinguished from vain preoccupations.

374. *Nam actualis inferiora praefert, affectualis superiora.* SC 50.5 (SBOp 2:80,29–81,1).

375. *Hoc vero convivium triplex celebrat Sapientia, et ex una complet caritate, ipsa cibans, ipsa potans quiescentes, ipsa regnantes inebrians.* Dil 33 (SBOp 3:146,26–147,2).

376. *Merito inebriati, qui ad nuptias Agni introduci merentur, edentes et bibentes super mensam illius in regno suo, quando sibi iam exhibet gloriosam Ecclesiam, non habentem maculam neque rugam aut aliquid huiusmodi.* Dil 33 (SBOp 3:147,11–13).

377. Delfgaauw, 'La nature' 242–243. Casey, 'In Pursuit of Ecstasy', 149–151.

378. Twenty times Bernard cites the Septuagint version of Lamentations 4:20 *Spiritus ante faciem nostram Christus Dominus* (e.g., in SC 3.5; SBOp 1:17, 11 and SC 20.3; SBOp 1:115,22). See J. M. Déchanet, 'La Christologie de S. Bernard', in *Saint Bernard théologien* 87, n.2.

379. See SC 18.5 (SBOp 1:107,4); SC 26.14 (SBOp 1:181,2); SC 71.13 (SBOp 2:223,5); SC 72.2 (SBOp 2:226,16); our own instance, Dil 32 (SBOp 3:146,9); Palm 3.4 (SBOp 5:54,5); pP6, 2S2 (SBOp 5:208.21); Assp 5.5 (SBOp 5:253.20); OS 1.3 (SBOp 5:329.14); Ded 3.2 (SBOp 5:380.17); Div 2, 4 (SBOp 6/1:82.6); Sent 3,70 (SBOp 6/2:103.24).

380. Gary Macy, *The Theologies of the Eucharist in the Early Scholastic Period: A Study of the Salvific Function of the Sacrament according to the Theologians c. 1080-c. 1220* (Oxford: Clarendon Press, 1984) 73–105, studies a mystical approach to the Eucharist among many in Bernard's generation. William of Saint Thierry's

*De corpore et sanguine domini* (PL 180:343 ff), written around 1120, before any of Bernard's works, is an important contribution to eucharistic theology; it embodies much of Macy's 'mystical approach'. Bernard, to whom it was dedicated, had a very similar sense of the sacrament. The same may be said of the later work by the Cistercians Isaac of Stella, *Epistola ad Joannem Episcopum Pictaviensum de officio Missae* (ca. 1165); PL 194:1889–1896, and Baldwin of Ford, *De sacramento altaris* (J. Morson, ed. *Baudouin de Ford. Le sacrement de l'autel*, SC 93–94, Paris, 1963).

381. Mary M. Schaefer, 'Twelfth-Century Latin Commentaries on the Mass: The Relationship of the Priest to Christ and to the People', *Studia Liturgica*, 15 (1982/1983), 78, charts the division of the period. The same author's 'Twelfth-Century Latin Commentaries on the Mass: Christological and Ecclesiological Dimensions', diss., University of Notre Dame, 1983, 207–396, compares monastic and scholastic commentaries.

382. SC 1.5 (SBOp 1:5,3–4) opens the commentary on the text of the Song of Songs, 'Let him kiss me with the kiss of his mouth'. In SC 4, which expands upon the initial kiss, to the feet of the Bridebroom, the author explains that it is 'the sign of a genuine conversion of life': *In primo quidem sane primordia dedicantur nostrae conversionis* (SC 4.1; SBOp 1:18,9–10). He includes two preliminary kisses because 'the very nature of the discourse clearly suggests that they be included'—*Puto enim facies ipsa eloquii facile admonet et ista requirere'* (SC 4.1; SBOp 1:18,14).

383. *quando sibi iam exhibet gloriosam Ecclesiam, non habentem maculam neque rugam aut aliquid huiusmodi.* Dil 33 (SBOp 3:147,12–13). Cf Eph 5:27.

384. Helmut Riedlinger, *Die Makellosigkeit der Kirche in den lateinischen Hohenliedkommentaren des Mittelalters*, Beiträge zur Geschichte der Philosophie und Theologie des Mittelalters 38, 3 (Münster i.W., 1958) 163.

385. Yves Congar, OP, 'L'ecclésiologie de s. Bernard', in *Saint Bernard théologien* 136–190; trans. as 'The Ecclesiology of Saint Bernard', *Cistercian Studies* 1 (May, 1961) 86. This spirituality of the Church did not compromise Bernard's conviction of its earthly visibility.

386. . . . *hinc aeternum illud atque inexplebile desiderium, nesciens egestatem.* Dil 33 (SBOp 3:147,20).

387. *Ex hoc iam quartus ille amoris gradus perpetuo possidetur, cum summe et solus diligitur Deus, quia nec nosipsos iam nisi propter ipsum diligimus, ut sit ipse praemium amantium se, praemium aeternum amantium in aeternum.* Dil 33 (SBOp 3:147,24–25).

388. Ep 11.3–9 (SBOp 7:54,18–60,10). See James, *The Letters of St. Bernard of Clairvaux*, 41–48, letter 12. The seven paragraphs (3–9) from the letter correspond to Dil 34–40 (SBOp 3:148,1–154,18), with minor discrepancies in the editorial numbering. The opening and closing of the letter are expressions of personal friendship from Bernard, who is writing the Carthusian prior Guy for the first time, after having received more than one letter from him. The prior's charitry toward him inspires the author to write about charity. These paragraphs are appropriately omitted from the treatise.

389. *Forte autem alia ibi, etsi non aliena, de caritate locutus sum.* Dil 34 (SBOp 3:148,3–4).

390. Leclercq, *Recueil d'études* 3:111.

391. Bernard's subject in the letter is *caritas*, with only two unimportant substitutions of *amor* in paragraph 3 (SBOP 7:55,5–6); but, in the two paragraphs which serve as recapitulation for *De diligendo Deo* (8–9, or 39–40 in Dil), which has spoken of *amor*, we find *amor* consistently.

392. Leclercq, *Recueil d'études* 3:112. Both works are found only in the integrity in which they are now printed.

393. See n.18, above.

394. Bertola 'Introduzione' 244.

395. *Idem.*

396. *Sola quae in filio est caritas, non quaerit quae sua sunt.* Dil 34 (SBOp 3:148,20–21).

397. *Est qui confitetur Domino quoniam potens est, et est qui confitetur quoniam sibi bonus est, et item qui confitetur quoniam simpliciter bonus est.* Dil 34 (SBOp 3:148,17–18)).

398. *Caritas vero convertit animas, quas facit et voluntarias.* Dil 34 (SBOp 4273:149,11–12).

399. *Vacua namque vera caritas esse non potest, nec tamen mercenaria est: quippe non quaerit quae sua sunt. . . . Verus amor seipso contentus est.* Dil 17 (SBOp 3:133,22–134,2).

400. Z. Alszeghy, *Grundformen der Liebe* 218. Let us note that even in the opening paragraph of this Ep 11 (the omitted introduction) Bernard refers to spousal love: *Egone tam temerarius essem, ut inter sponsi brachia suaviter quiescentem auderem suscitare dilectam, quousque vellet ipsa?* (SBOp 7:53,12–14).

401. *Si filius, honorat patrem: quae vero osculum postulat, amat. . . . sponsus et sponsa: quippe quibus omnia sunt communia, nil proprium, nil a se divisum habentibus.* SC 7.2 (SBOp 1:31,20–32,1). Regarding ambiguities in the mentality of sons: *Magna res amor; sed sunt in eo gradus. Sponsa in summo stat. Amant enim et filii, sed de hereditate cogitant.* SC 83.5 (SBOp 2:301,12–13).

402. Delfgaauw, 'Saint Bernard, maître de l'amour divin' 76–77.

403. *Lex autem Domini dicitur, sive quod ipse ex ea vivat, sive quod eam nullus, nisi eius dono, possideat.* Dil 35 (SBOp 3:149,17–18).

404. *Lex est ergo, et lex Domini, caritas, quae Trinitatem in unitate quodammodo cohibet et colligat in vinculo pacis.* Dil 35 (SBOp 3:149, 21–22).

405. *Nemo tamen me aestimet caritatem hic accipere qualitatem vel aliquod accidens, . . . sed substantiam illam divinam, . . . dicente Ioanne: Deus caritas est.* Dil 35 (SBOp 3:149,22–26).

406. *Itaque caritas dat caritatem, substantiva accidentalem. . . . Siquidem in pondere, et mensura, et numero per eam facta sunt universa.* Dil 35 (SBOp 3:149,27–150,1).

407. *Haec est lex aeterna, creatix et gubernatrix universitatis.* Dil 35 (SBOp 3:149,28–29).

408. *Nemo tamen me aestiment caritatem hic accipere qualitatem vel aliquod accidens. . . .* Dil 35 (SBOp 3:149,22–23).

409. *The Glory of the Lord* 4:356–357. For the links between classical and Christian, Von Balthasar refers to Ender von Ivankà, *Plato Christianus: Platonismus durch die Väter.*

410. Von Balthasar, *The Glory of the Lord,* 4:361. 'This vision of unity,' he adds, 'is the signature of the age and embraces such contrary spirits as Bernard and Suger of Saint Denys.' See also DeBruyne 2:111.

411. *Ceterum servus et mercenarius habent legem non a Domino. . . . illi tamen, quae Domini est subiectam.* Dil 36 (SBOp 3:150,4–7).

412. [*Quare non aufers iniquitatem meam, ut*] . . . *nec iam servili timore coercear, nec mercenaria cupiditate illiciar?* Dil 36 (SBOp 3:151, 2–4).

413. *Idem.*

414. *Grave utique et importabile iugum super omnes filios Adam, heu!* Dil 36 (SBOp 3:150,12–13).

415. *Infelix ego homo, quis me liberabit de corpore mortis huis . . .!* (Rom 7:24) Dil 36 (SBOp 3:150,14–15).

416. *Ergo his omnibus humilitatis gradibus ascensis, monachus mox ad caritatem Dei perueniet illam quae perfecta foras mittit timorem.* (*The Rule of Saint Benedict,* 7.67; p. 32,23–25).

417. *Et quidem suam sibi quisque legem facere potuerunt; non tamen eam incommutabili aeternae legis ordini subducere potuerunt.* Dil 36 (SBOp 3:150,7–8).

418. *Posuisti me contrarium tibi* [Job 7:20], *Dei se tamen non effugisse legem indicavit.* Dil 36 (SBOp 3:150,20–21).

419. *Eadem mihi lex fuerit quae et tibi.* Dil 36 (SBOp 3:151,6).

420. *Quisque sponte iugum suave et onus leve caritatis abiecit, propriae voluntatis onus importabile sustineret invitus.* Dil 36 (SBOp 3:150,23–24).

421. 'Conference Notes', 38. Merton suggests a near-parallel in Guy's *Meditationes.*

422. *Inest omni utenti ratione naturaliter pro sua semper aestimatione atque intentione appetere potiora. . . . citra summum vel optimum quiescere non potest.* Dil 18 (SBOp 3:134,16–29).

423. 'Conference Notes', 39.

424. *Iustis non est lex posita.* Dil 37 (SBOp 3:151,11).

425. [*Lex caritatis*] *leviter suaviterque portatur.* Dil 38 (SBOp 3:152, 1–2).

426. C. Bodard, OCSO, 'La Bible, expression d'une expérience religieuse chez S. Bernard', *Saint Bernard théologien,* 26.

427. . . . *non destruit, sed facit ut impleantur. . . . Illam temperat, istam ordinat, utramque levigat.* Dil 38 (SBOp 3:152,3–5).

428. *Nam quod legitur: Perfecta caritas foras mittit timorem, poena intelligenda est, quae servili, ut diximus, numquam deest timori, illo scilicet genere locutionis, quo saepe causa ponitur pro effectu.* Dil 38 (SBOp 3:152,10–12).

429. *Deinde cupiditas tunc recte a superveniente caritate ordinatur, cum mala quidem penitus respuuntur, bonis vero meliora praeferuntur. . . .* Dil 38 (SBOp 3:152,12–14).

430. *Longum quidem adhuc texere sermonem insatiabili colloquendi ad vos desiderio pulsor . . . sed . . . domesticis urgeor curis.* Ep 11.10 (SBOp 7:60,11–14).

431. *Verumtamen, quia carnales sumus et de carnis concupiscentia nascimur, necesse est cupiditas vel amor noster a carne incipiat, quae si recto ordine dirigitur, quibusdam suis gradibus duce gratia proficiens, spiritu tandem consummabitur, quia non prius quod spirituale, sed quod animale, deinde quod spirituale.* Dil 39 (SBOp 3:152,18–22).

432. See 'Discussion: The Question of Faith and Conversion', above.

433. *Tunc autem dixerim quemque sibi fecisse suam legem, quando communi et aeternae legi propriam praetulit voluntatem, perverse utique volens suum imitari Creatorem, ut sicut ipse sibi lex suique iuris est, ita is quoque seimpsum regeret, et legem sibi suam faceret voluntatem.* Dil 36 (SBOp 3:150,8–12).

434. *spiritu tandem consummabitur.* Dil 39 (SBOp 3:152.20–21)—a reminiscence of Gal 3:3: *cum spiritu coeperitis, nunc carne consummemini.*

435. Pannenberg, 87–88, n.14, documents the view in Augustine according to which one meaning of concupiscence, under the rubric of *cupiditas,* is identical with the *perversa voluntas,* citing *Ennar. in Ps.* 9.15: *cupiditas* or *libido* when depraved is contrasted to *dilectio* or *caritas* when virtuous. Also Conf 8.5.10. And *De diversis questionibus* 83 (396): 'That [love] is base with which the soul pursues what is less than itself; it is more correctly called *cupiditas,* which is the root of all evil' (q. 35,1; PL 40: 23ff). Also De libero arbitrio 1.3.8; PL 32:1225: 'It is naught but lust (*libido*) that reigns in every kind of evil doing'. Gilson, *The Mystical Theology,* 220, n.24, remarks, acknowledging great surprise, that, while borrowing much from Augustine on the doctrine of love, Saint Bernard differed considerably from him: 'His doctrine is not the same in fibre as that of Augustine'.

436. *Moralia* in Job 22.19; PL 76:240CD. For an overview of the tradition of gradual ascent, see Emile Bertaud and Andre Rayez, 'Echelle spirituelle' *Dictionnaire de Spiritualite* 4 (1961) 62–86. A. Forest, 292, studies Bernard's use of Ps 83:6, *Ascensiones in corde suo disposuit,* and catalogs his several ascent schemata.

437. *Nemo repente fit summus, sed gradatim quisque ascendit.* Hum 26 (SBOp 3:36,25).

438. *In primis ergo diligit seipsum homo propter se: caro quippe est, et nihil sapere valet praeter se.* Dil 39 (SBOp 3:152,23–24).

439. *Cumque se videt per se non posse subsistere, Deum quasi sibi necessarium incipit per fidem inquirere et diligere.* Dil 39 (SBOp 3:152, 23–25).

440. *Gustato quam suavis est Dominus, transit ad tertium gradum, ut diligat Deum, non iam propter se, sed propter ipsum.* Dil 39 (SBOp 3:153,2–3).

441. *Nescio si a quoquam hominum quartus in hac vita perfecte apprehenditur, ut se scilicet homo diligat tantum propter Deum.* Dil 39 (SBOp 3:153,4–5). The Walton translation omits Bernard's 'perfectly' (*perfecte*)—a crucial qualifier.

442. *Asserant hoc si qui experti sunt.* Dil 39 (SBOp 3:153,5).

443. *Totus perget in Deum.* Dil 39 (SBOp 3:153,9).

444. *Totus is spiritu memoraretur iustitiae Dei solius.* Dil 39 (SBOp 3:153,14).

445. *Nemo ibi se cognoscet secundum carnem.* Dil 39 (SBOp 3:153, 17).

446. *quod carnalis omnis necessitudo sit defutura.* Dil 39 (SBOp 3:153,19).

447. *et infirmae quae nunc sunt, humanae affectiones in divinas quasdam habeant commutari.* Dil 39 (SBOp 3:153,20–21).

448. *Tunc sagena caritatis, quae nunc tracta per hoc mare magnum et spatiosum ex omni genere piscium congregare non desinit, cum perducta ad littus fuerit, malos foras mittens, bonos solummodo retinebit.* Dil 40 (SBOp 3:153,21–24).

449. *Proinde ubi iam non erit miseriae locus aut misericordiae tempus, nullus profecto esse poterit miserationis affectus.* Dil 40 (SBOp 3:154, 16–18).

# ABBREVIATIONS FOR THE
# WORKS OF SAINT BERNARD

(Latin Titles Referred to in the Commentary)
SBOp Sancti Bernardi Opera

| | |
|---|---|
| AdvA | *Sermo [S] in adventu Domini* |
| Apo | *Apologia ad Guillelmum abbatem* |
| Assp | *S. in assumptione beatae Mariae Virginis* |
| Conv | *S. de conversione ad clericos* |
| Csi | *De consideratione libri V* |
| Ded | *S. in dedicatione ecclesiae* |
| Dil | *Liber de diligendo Deo* |
| Div | *S. de diversis* |
| Ep | *Epistolae* [except for three epistolary tracts] |
| Gra | *Liber de Gratia et de libero arbitrio* |
| Hum | *Liber de gradibus humilitatis et superbiae* |
| Mart | *S. in festo s. Martini* |
| Miss | *Homiliae super Missus est (In laudibus virginis matris)* |
| OS | *S. in festivitate omnium sanctorum* |
| Palm | *S. in ramis palmarum* |
| Pre | *Liber de praecepto et dispensatione* |
| QH | *S. super psalmum "Qui habitat"* |
| Sept | *S. in septuagesima* |
| SC | *S. super Cantica Canticorum* |

# BIBLIOGRAPHY

The bibliography related to Saint Bernard is vast. Following is a list of successive publications that treat of it: First, covering works to the year 1890 is Leopoldus Janauschek, *Bibliographia Bernardina* (*Xenia Bernardina*) (Vienna 1891), reprinted at Hildesheim, 1959. This is succeeded by Jean De la Croix Bouton, *Bibliographie bernardine (1891–1957)*, Commission d'histoire de l'Ordre de Cîteaux 5 (Paris: Lethielleux, 1958); and E. Manning, *Bibliographie bernardine (1957–1970)* (5430 Rochefort, Belgium: Abbaye Nôtre-Dame de Saint-Remy, Belgium: 1972). Two annotated bibliographies by Jean Leclercq are 'Les études bernardines en 1963 [1953–1963]', *Bulletin de la Société internationale pour l'étude de la philosophie médiévale*, 5 (1963) 121–28; and 'S. Bernard parmi nous: dix années d'études bernardines [1963–1973]', *Collectanea cisterciensia*, 36 (1974), 3–23. Periodic bibliographical supplements are published by *Cîteaux: commentarii cistercienses*—e.g., No. 1, Supplément au tome 38 (1987); and Nos. 2–3, Suppléments aux tomes 39 (1988) et 40 (1989). Among selected bibliographies is P. Zerbi, 'Bernardo di Chiaravalle', *Bibliotheca Sanctorum*, 3 (Rome 1963), coll 31–37. A practical orientation to Bernard's works and to some basic studies is Jean Leclercq, 'Comment aborder S. Bernard', *Collectanea OCR*, 19 (1957) 18–21; and Leclercq's expanded version, 'Un guide de lecture pour S. Bernard', *La Vie Spirituelle*, 102 (1960) 440–47.

TEXTS AND TRANSLATIONS OF *ON LOVING GOD*

Bégin, Albert. *Traité de l'amour de Dieu* in *Œuvres mystiques*. Paris: Seuil, 1953. 27–82.

Charpentier, R. *Traité de l'amour de Dieu* in *Œuvres complètes*, vol. 2. Paris: vives, 1866. Intro., pp. 457–459. Trans., pp. 460–492.

Connolly, Terence L. *On the Love of God.* New York: Spiritual Book Associates, 1937. Techny, Illinois: Mission Press, 1943.

Gardner, Edmund Garrot, *The Book of Saint Bernard on the Love of God.* New York: Dutton, 1916.

[Lawson,] Penelope, CSMV. *On the Love of God.* London: Mowbrays, 1950.

Leclercq, Jean and Rochais, Henri. *Liber de diligendo Deo* in *S. Bernardi opera*, vol. 3. Rome: Editiones Cistercienses, 1963. Intro., pp. 111–117. Text, pp. 119–154.

Mabillon, Joannes. *De diligendo Deo liber seu tractatus ad Haimericum S.R.E. Cardinalem et Cancellarium* in *S. Bernardi, Clarae-Vallensis abbatis primi, opera omnia*, vol. 1, PL 182. Intro., 971–974. Text, 973–1000.

Martin, H. ed. *On Loving God and Selections from Sermons.* London: SCM Press, 1959. trans. by W. H. van Allen. 15–64.

Patmore, Marianne Caroline and Coventry. *Saint Bernard on the Love of God.* London: Kegan Paul, 1881. London: Burns and Oates, 1884.

Ramos, G. Diez. *Del Amor de Dios* in *Obras Completas de San Bernardo*, vol. 2, Biblioteca de Autores Cristianos, 130. Madrid: Editorial Católica, 1955. Trans., pp. 742–776.

Solms, E. *Traité de l'amour de Dieu in Saint Bernard..* Namur: Soleil Levant, 1958. Intro. by Jean Leclercq, pp. 88–93. Trans., pp. 94–148.

Van Allen, W. H. *On Loving God*, Caldey Books, 1. Tenby: Caldey Abbey, 1909.

Williams, Watkin W. S. *Bernardi liber de diligendo Deo.* In *Select Treatises of S. Bernard of Clairvaux.* Cambridge Patristic Texts. Cambridge: University Press, 1926. Intro., 1–7; text and notes, 8–69.

STUDIES DIRECTLY PERTAINING TO *ON LOVING GOD*

Bertola, Ermenegildo. 'Introduzione' to *Liber de diligendo Deo* (Sul Dovere di Amare Dio), in *Opere di San Bernardo IV: Trattati.* ed. Ferruccio Gastaldelli. Milan, 1987. 221–69.

———. *San Bernardo e la teologia speculativa.* Padua: CEDAM, 1959.

Blanpain, J. 'Langage mystique, expression du désir, dans les Sermons sur le Cantique de Bernard de Clairvaux'. *Collectanea cisterciensia* 36 (1974). 45–68, 226–77.

Butler, Cuthbert. *Western Mysticism: The Teachings of SS. Augustine, Gregory and Bernard on Contemplation and the Contemplative Life.* London: Constable, 1922. Reprinted New York: Harper & Row, 1966.

Casey, Michael, OCSO. 'In Pursuit of Ecstasy: Reflections on Bernard of Clairvaux's *De diligendo Deo*'. *Monastic Studies* 16 (Christmas 1985). 139–56.

———. *Athirst for God: Spiritual Desire in Bernard of Clairvaux's Sermons on the Song of Songs.* CS 77. Kalamazoo: Cistercian Publications, 1988.

Connolly, T.L., trans. *Saint Bernard on the Love of God.* Westminster, Md.: Newman Press, 1951.

Delfgaauw, Pacifique, OCSO. 'Saint Bernard maître de l'amour divin', diss. [unpublished], Rome, 1952.

———. 'La nature et les degrès de l'amour selon saint Bernard'. *Saint Bernard théologien* (q.v.), 235–51.

———. 'La lumière de la charité chez saint Bernard'. *Collectanea OCR* 18 (1956). 42–67, 302–20.

Delsart, H. M. *Traité de l'amour de Dieu par saint Bernard,* traduction nouvelle. Paris: Desclée et Lethielleux, 1929. 'Introduction', 1–11.

Depiney, M. A. *L'âme embrasée de saint Bernard.* Paris: 1950.

Diez Ramos, Gregorio. *Del Amor de Dios.* In *Obras Completas de San Bernardo.* 2 Vols. Biblioteca de Autores Cristianos, 110 and 130. Madrid: Editorial Católica, 1953–1955. 'Introduccion General a la Doctrina de San Bernardo' 1: esp. 92–113. Trans. at 2: 742–76.

Dotto, Gianni. 'La "caritas" come principio di vita e di dottrina in S. Bernardo.' *Studi su S. Bernardo di Chiravalle* (q.v.), 349–58.

Gilson, Etienne. *La théologie mystique de saint Bernard.* Paris: Vrin, 1934. Translated as *The Mystical Theology of Saint Bernard.* trans. A. H. C. Downes. London: Sheed and Ward, 1940. Reprinted Kalamazoo: Cistercian Publications, 1990.

———. *Un itinéraire de retour à Dieu.* Paris: Vrin, 1953. This includes a translation of *De diligendo Deo* by Dom de Saint-Gabriel.

Grill, Leopold. 'Epistola de charitate: der älteste St.-Bernhards Brief', *Cîteaux* 15 (1964). 26–51, 386–88.

Hourlier, Jacques, OSB. 'S. Bernard et Guillaume de Saint-Thierry dans le "Liber de Amore Dei"' in *Saint Bernard theologien* (q.v.), 223–33.

Leclercq, Jean, OSB. 'Introduzione Generale', in Ferruccio Gastaldelli, ed. *Opere di San Bernardo, Vol. IV: Trattati.* Milan, 1987, XI–LXIV.

––––––. 'L'art de la composition dans les traités de s. Bernard'. In *Recueil d'études sur saint Bernard et ses écrits.* 3 Vols. Rome: Storia e Letteratura, 1969. 3: 105–62.

––––––. 'Le premier traité authentique de saint Bernard'? In *Recueil d'études sur saint Bernard et ses écrits.* 3 Vols. Rome: Storia e Letteratura, 1966. 2: 51–68.

––––––. 'Pour l'histoire des traités de s. Bernard'. In *Recueil d'études sur saint Bernard et ses écrits.* 3 Vols. Rome: Storia e Letteratura, 1966. 2: 101–30.

––––––. *Saint Bernard mystique.* Bruges et Paris: Desclée de Brouwer, 1948.

––––––. 'The Imitation of Christ and the Sacraments in the Teaching of Saint Bernard', *Cistercian Studies,* vol. 9 (1974), 36–54; originally published as 'Christusnachfolge und Sakrament in der Theologie des heiligen Bernhard', *Archiv für Liturgiewissenschaft* 8/1 (1963), 58–72.

Levasti, A. *Profilo di san Bernardo mistico.* In *Città di Vita* 1 (1946). 275–84.

Mahamé, Chrysologue. 'Les auteurs spirituels dans l'élaboration de la philosophie blondelienne (1883–1893)'. *Recherches de science religeuse* 56 No. 2 (1968). 232–37.

Maynard, Theodore. 'Saint Bernard of Clairvaux, Doctor and Mystic'. In *American Benedictine Review* 4 (1953). 230–49.

Mellet, P. *Notes sur le désir de Dieu chez saint Bernard.* Valais: N.-D. de Gérande, 1966.

Merton, Thomas. 'Conference Notes by Thomas Merton: The Cistercian Fathers and Their Monastic Theology' Part One: Saint Bernard, *De diligendo Deo,* ed. Chrysogonus Wadell, OCSO, in *Liturgy, Cistercians of the Strict Observance,* Vol. 27, No. 1 (1993), 15–53.

Patmore, Marianne Caroline and Coventry. *Saint Bernard on the Love of God.* London: Kegan Paul, 1881. London: Burns and Oates, 1884.

Piazzoni, Ambrogio M., Introduzione e note, *San Bernardo di Chiaravalle, Il dovere di amare Dio,* Traduzione di Ettore Paratore. Torino: Edizioni Paoline, 1990.

Rousselot, Pierre. *Pour l'histoire du problème de l'amour au moyen âge.* Baeumker, ed. Beiträge zur Geschichte der Philosophie des Mittelalters, Texte und Untersuchungen. Bd 6, 6 Münster, i/W.: 1908.

Standaert, Maur, OCSO. 'La doctrine de l'image chez saint Bernard', *Ephemerides Theologicae Lovaniensis* 23 (1947) 70–129.

———. 'Le principe de l'ordination dans la théologie spirituelle de saint Bernard', *Collectanea OCR* 8 (1946). 178–216.

Stoeckle, B. 'Amor carnis—abusus amoris. Das Verständnis von der Konkupiszenz bei Bernhard von Clairvaux und Aelred von Rieval'. In *Analecta monastica* 7, Studia Anselmiana 54. Rome: Herder, 1965. 147–76.

Van den Eynde, Damien, OFM. 'Les premiers écrits de S. Bernard', *Antonianum* 41 (1966) 189–259.

DeVrégille, Bernard, SJ. 'L'attente des saints d'après saint Bernard'. *Nouvelle revue théologique* No. 3 (March 1948). 225–44.

Walton, Robert, OSB. 'Introduction' and translation [to *On Loving God*] in *Bernard of Clairvaux, Treatises II: The Steps of Humility and Pride* and *On Loving God.* CF 13. Kalamazoo: Cistercian Publications, 1980. 85–135.

Wellens, P. W., OCSO. 'Saint Bernard mystique et docteur de la mystique'. In *San Bernardo: Pubblicazione commemorativa nell'ottavo centenario della sua morte.* Milano: 1954. 66–91.

OTHER WORKS CITED

Alfaro, Juan. 'Nature: (B) The Theological Concept', in Karl Rahner, SJ, *et al.* edd. *Sacramentum Mundi* (q.v.) 4:172–175.

Alszeghy, Zoltan. *Grundformen der Liebe. Die Theorie der Gottesliebe bei dem heiligen Bonaventure.* Rome: Gregorian Univeristy, 1946.

Anderson, Luke, O.Cist. 'The Appeal to Reason in Saint Bernard's *De diligendo Deo*', in E. Rozanne Elder and John R. Sommerfeldt, edd., *The Chimaera of His Age: Studies on Bernard of Clairvaux,* Studies in Medieval Cistercian History 5, CS 63. Kalamazoo: Cistercian Publications, 1980, 132–39.

Armstrong, A. Hilary. 'Man in the Cosmos: A Study of Some Differences between Pagan Neoplatonism and Christianity', *Romanitas et Christianitas.* Amsterdam: North-Holland Publ. Co., 1973, 5–14.

———. 'Neoplatonic Valuations of Nature, Body and Intellect', *Augustinian Studies* Vol. 3 (1975), 35–59.

Auberger, Jean-Baptiste, OFM. *L'Unanimité cistercienne primitive: mythe ou réalité?* Achel: Administration de *Cîteaux,* 1986.

Balthasar, Hans Urs von. *Herrlichkeit: Eine Theologische Ästhetik,* 3 vols. Freiburg im Breisgau, 1961–69), translated in part in Hans Urs von Balthasar, *The Glory of the Lord: A Theological Aesthetics* New York: Crossroad; San Francisco: Ignatius Press, 1982, 1984, 1986, 1989.

Baum, Gregory. *Man Becoming: God in Secular Experience.* New York: Herder and Herder, 1970.

Beck, Hans Georg, *et al. From the High Middle Ages to the Eve of the Reformation,* trans. Anselm Biggs. vol. 4 of Hubert Jedin and John Dolan, edd. *History of the Church.* London: Burns & Oates, 1980.

Bell, David N. *Image and Likeness: The Augustinian Spirituality of William of Saint Thierry,* Cistercian Studies Series, 77. Kalamazoo: Cistercian Publications, 1984.

Blanpain, J. 'Langage mystique, expression du désir', *Collectanea cisterciensia* 36 (1974), 45–68 and 226–277.

Blondel, Maurice. *L'Action: Essai d'une critique de la vie et d'une science de la pratique,* 2 vol. Paris, 1893.

Bodard, Claude, OCSO. 'La bible, expression d'une expérience religieuse chez S. Bernard', *Saint Bernard théologien* (q.v.), 24–45.

Bougerol, Jacques Guy. 'Saint Bonaventure et Saint Bernard', *Antonianum* 46 (Rome, 1971), 3–79; repr. in *Saint Bonaventure: Études sur les sources de sa pensée.* Northampton: Variorum, 1989.

Bouillard, Henri. *Blondel and Christianity,* trans. James M. Somerville. Washington, D.C.: Corpus Books, 1969.

Braun, F.-M. 'L'accueil de la foi selon S. Jean', *La Vie Spirituelle* 92 (1955), 344–63.

Ceglar, Stanislaus. *William of Saint Thierry: The Chronology of his Life with a Study of his Treatise* On the Nature of Love, *His authorship of the* Brevis Commentatio,*the* In Lacu, *and the* Reply to Cardinal Matthew. Ann Arbor, Mich.: University Microfilms, 1971.

Chatillon, J. 'Influence de S. Bernard sur la scholastique', *Saint Bernard théologien* (q.v.), 278–89.

Congar, Yves, OP. 'L'écclésiologie de s. Bernard', *Saint Bernard théologien* (q.v.), 136–190.

D'Arcy, M.C., SJ. *The Mind and Heart of Love: Lion and Unicorn. A Study in Eros and Agape.* New York: 1947, 1956.

Daly, Mary. 'Faith, Hope, and Charity', in Philip P. Wiener, ed. *Dictionary of the History of Ideas: Studies of Selected Pivotal Ideas,* 5 vols. New York: Charles Scribner's, 1973. 2:209–216.

De Bruyne, Edgar. *Études D'Esthétique Médiévale,* 3 vols. Bruges: De Tempel, 1946.

Déchanet, Jean-Marie, OSB. 'Aux sources de la pensee philosophique de saint Bernard', *Saint Bernard théologien* (q.v.), 56–77.

———. 'La Christologie de S. Bernard', in *Saint Bernard théologien* (q.v.), 78–91.

———. *William of St-Thierry: The Man and His Work,* CS 10. Spencer, Mass.: Cistercian Publications, 1972.

Delhaye, Philippe. 'La conscience morale dans la doctrine de S. Bernard', *Saint Bernard théologien* (q.v.), 219–21.

DeLubac, Henri. *Exegèse médiévale: Les Quatre sens de l'Ecriture,* 4 vols. Paris, 1959–64.

Denziger-Schönmetzer, edd. *Enchiridion Symbolorum.* Freiburg im Breisgau: Herder, 1967.

Doran, Robert M. *The Theology and Dialectics of History.* Toronto: University of Toronto Press, 1990.

Dresser, Robert M. 'Gradation: Rhetoric and Substance in Saint Bernard', in E. Rozanne Elder, ed., *Goad and Nail,* CS 84. Kalamazoo: Cistercian Publications, 1985, 71–85.

Drewery, Ben. 'Deification', in Peter Brooks, ed. *Christian Spirituality: Essays in Honour of Gordon Rupp.* London: SCM Press, 1975.

Elder, E. Rozanne. 'William of Saint Thierry: Rational and Affective Spirituality', in *The Spirituality of Western Christendom*, ed. E. Rozanne Elder, CS 30. Kalamazoo: Cistercian Publications, 1976, 85–105.

Evans, G. R. *The Thought of Gregory the Great*. Cambridge: Cambridge University Press, 1986.

Farkasfalvy, Denis, O.Cist. 'L'ispiration de l'Ecriture Sainte dans la théologie de S. Bernard', *Studia Anselmiana* 53. Rome, 1964, 7–146.

————. 'La conoscenza di Dio nel pensiero di san Bernardo', *Studi su S. Bernardo di Chiaravalle* (q.v.), 201–214.

Forest, Aimé. 'S. Bernard et Nôtre Temps', *Saint Bernard théologien* (q.v.), 289–299.

Francis de Sales, Saint. *Treatise on the Love of God*, trans. Henry Benedict Mackey, OSB, With Introduction by the Translator. Westport, Connecticut: Greenwood Press, 1971; 1942.

Fromm, Eric. *The Art of Loving*. New York: Harper & Row, 1956; 1962.

Gay, Volney P. 'Kohut on Narcissism: Psychoanalytic Revolution from Within', *Religious Studies Review*, 7.3 (July 1981), 199–203.

Gilson, Étienne. *The Christian Philosophy of Saint Augustine*. New York, 1960.

————. *The Spirit of Mediaeval Philosophy*. New York: Scribner's, 1948.

Grundmann, W. 'Verständnis und Bewegung des Glaubens im Johannesevangelium', *Kerygma und Dogma* 6(1960), 131–54.

Guy the Carthusian. *Le Recueil des pensées du B. Guigue*, ed. Dom Wilmart. Paris: J. Vrin, 1936.

————. *Meditations of Guigo, Prior of the Charterhouse*. ed. John J. Jolin. Milwaukee: Marquette University Press, 1951.

————. *Meditations of Guigo I, Prior of the Charterhouse*. Trans. A. Gordon Mursell. Kalamazoo: Cistercian Publications, 1994.

Hesbert, René-Jean. 'Saint Bernard et L'Eucharistie', in *Mélanges Saint Bernard*. Dijon, 1953, 156–176.

Hiss, Wilhelm. *Die Anthropologie Bernhards von Clairvaux*, Quellen und Studien zur Geschichte der Philosophie 7. Berlin: Walter de Gruyter, 1964.

Homans, Peter. 'Introducing the Psychology of the Self and Narcissism into the Study of Religion', *Religious Studies Review,* 7.3 (July 1981), 1993–99.

James, Bruno Scott, trans., *The Letters of Saint Bernard of Clairvaux.* London: Burns & Oats; Notre Dame, Indiana: University of Notre Dame Press, 1953.

Javelet, R. *Image et ressemblance au douzieme siècle: De saint Anselme à Alain de Lille,* 2 vols. Paris: 1967.

Le Bachelet, X. 'Benôit XII', in *Dictionnaire de théologie catholique,* 2:659–961.

Lonergan, Bernard J. F., SJ. *Method in Theology.* New York: Herder and Herder, 1972.

Lottin, O. *Psychologie et morale au XIIe et XIIIe siècles.* Louvain, 1942

Louth, Andrew. 'Bernard and Affective Mysticism', in Sister Benedicta Ward, SLG, ed. *The Influence of Saint Bernard: Anglican Essays.* Oxford: Fairacres, 1976, 1–10.

Macy, Gary. *The Theologies of the Eucharist in the Early Scholastic Period: A Study of the Salvific Function of the Sacrament according to the Theologians c. 1080-c.1220.* Oxford: Clarendon Press, 1984.

Maréchal, Joseph, SJ. *Studies in the Psychology of the Mystics,* trans. with an Introduction and Foreword by Algar Thorold. Albany, N.Y.: Maji Books, 1964.

McGinn, Bernard. 'Introduction', *The Works of Bernard of Clairvaux, Vol. 7: Treatises 3, On Grace and Free Choice* and *In Praise of the New Knighthood,* CF 19. Kalamazoo: Cistercian Publications, 1977, 3–50.

———. and John Meyendorff, edd., in collaboration with Jean Leclercq. *Christian Spirituality: Origins to the Twelfth Century,* Vol. 16 of *World Spirituality: An Encyclopedic History of the Religious Quest,* New York: Crossroad, 1987.

———. 'Saint Bernard and Eschatology', in *Bernard of Clairvaux: Studies Presented to Dom Jean Leclercq,* CS 23. Wahington, D.C.: Cistercian Publications, 1973, 161–185.

———. 'Saint Bernard and Meister Eckhart', *Cîteaux, commentarii cistercienses,* 31 (1980), 370–392.

———. *The Presence of God: A History of Western Christian Mysticism;* Vol.1:*The Foundations of Mysticism.* New York: Crossroad, 1991.

Meyer, Johannes. 'Welt, Leib, Frau, Ehe: Beobachtungen zur polaren Konzeption der Wirklichkeit bei Bernhard von Clairvaux', *Archiv für Religionspsychologie* 17 (1985), 111–123.

Moore, Sebastian. *The Fire and the Rose Are One.* New York: The Seabury Press, 1980.

Nygren, Anders. *Agape and Eros,* trans. Philip S. Wetson. Philadephia: Westminster, 1953.

Otto, S. *Die Funktion des Bildbegriffes in der Theologie der 12. Jahrhunderts. Beiträge zur Geschichte der Philosophie und Theologie des Mittelalters* 40.1. Münster, 1963.

Pannenberg, Wolfhart. *Anthropology in Theological Perspective,* trans. Matthew J. O'Connell. Philadelphia: Westmister Press, 1985.

Penelhum, Terrence. ed. *Faith.* New York: Macmillan, 1989.

Pennington, M. Basil, OCSO. 'Two Treatises on Love', in *Saint Bernard of Clairvaux: Studies Commenmorating the Eighth Centennary of his Canonization,* ed. the author. Kalamazoo: Cistercian Publications, 1977, 137–54.

Rahner, Karl, SJ. *Theological Investigations.* Baltimore: Helicon, 1961- Vols. 1, 2, and 4.

———. and Herbert Vorgrimler. *Theological Dictionary,* ed. Cornelius Ernst, trans. Richard Strachan. New York: Herder and Herder, 1965.

Riedlinger, Helmut. *Die Makellosigkeit der Kirche in den lateinishcen Hohenliedkommentaren des Mittelalters,* Beiträge zur Geschichte der Philosophie und Theologie des Mittelalters 38, 3. Münster i/W, 1958.

Rousselot, Pierre. *Pour l'histoire du problème de l'amour au moyen ge,* Beiträge zur Geschichte de Philosophie des Mittelalters, Texte und Untersuchungen, 4/6. Münster i/Westfalen, 1908.

*Sacramentum Mundi,* 6 vols., edd. Karl Rahner, SJ, *et al.* New York: Herder and Herder, 1968–1970.

*Saint Bernard théologien,* Actes du congrès de Dijon 15–19 septembre, *Analecta SOC* 9. Rome: Curia generalis S.O.C., 1953.

Schaefer, Mary M. 'Twelfth-Century Latin Commentaries on the Mass: The Relationship of the Priest to Christ and to the People', *Studia liturgica* 15 (1982/1983), 76–86.

Schuck, J. *Das religiöse Erlebnis beim hl. Bernhard von Clairvaux.* Würzburg, 1922.

Singer, Irving. *The Nature of Love,* 3 vols. Chicago: University of Chicago Press, 1966–1984.

Smith, Wilfred Cantwell. *Faith and Belief.* Princeton: Princeton University Press, 1979.

Sommerfeldt, John R. *The Spiritual Teachings of Bernard of Clairvaux: An Intellectual History of the Cistercian Order,* CS 125. Kalamazoo: Cistercian Publications, 1991.

Stiegman, Emero. 'Action and Contemplation in Saint Bernard's Sermons on the Song of Songs', Introduction to *Bernard of Clairvaux* On the Song of Songs *III,* trans. Kilian Walsh, ocso, and Irene M. Edmonds, CF 31. Kalamazoo, Cistercian Publications, 1979, xiii-xviii.

————. 'Metaphysics in the Prayer of Saint Augustine', *Atti del Congresso internazionale su s. Agostino nel XVI centenario della conversione; Roma, 15–20 settembre 1986,* Vol. 2. *Studia Ephemeridis 'Augustinianum'* 25 (Rome, 1987), 59–77.

————. *The Language of Aceticism in Saint Bernard of Clairvaux's Sermones super Cantica Canticorum,* diss. Fordham University, 1973. Ann Arbor, Mich.: University Microfilms.

*Studi su S. Bernardo di Chiaravalle nell'ottavo centenario della canonizzazione,* Convegno internazionale Certosa di Firenze: 6–9 Novembre 1974. Rome: Editiones cistercienses, 1975.

Taylor, Charles. *Hegel and Modern Society.* Cambridge: Cambridge University Press, 1979.

*The Rule of Saint Benedict: The Abingdon Copy,* ed. from Cambridge, Corpus Christi College Ms 57 by John Chamberlin. Toronto: Pontifical Institute of Mediaeval Studies, 1982.

Tracy, David. *Blessed Rage for Order: The New Pluralism in Theology.* New York: Crossroad, 1975.

Vacandard, Elphege. *Vie de Saint Bernard, abbé de Clairvaux,* 2 vols. Paris, 1927.

Vanni Rovighi, S. 'S. Bernardo e la filosofia', *Revista di filosofia neo-scholastica,* 46 (1954), 32–44.

Venuta, G. *Libero Arbitrio e Libertà della Grazia nel Pensiero di San Bernardo* (Rome, 1953).

Von Ivanka, E. 'La structure de l'âme selon S. Bernard', *Saint Bernard théologien* (q.v.), 202–209.

————. *Plato Christianus: Übernahme und Umgestaltung des Platonismus durch die Väter*. Munich: Johannesverlag, 1964.

Williams, Daniel Day. *The Spirit and the Forms of Love*. New York: Harper and Row, 1968.

Williams, Rowan. *Christian Spirituality: A Theological History from the New Testament to Luther and Saint John of the Cross*. Atlanta: John Knox Press, 1979.

Williams, Watkin. *Saint Bernard of Clairvaux*. Manchester: Manchester University Press, 1935.

Wilmart, A. 'La série et la date des ouvrages de Guillaume de Saint-Thierry', *Revue Mabillon* 14 (1924), 156–67.

# ANALYTIC INDEX
## TO
### *ON LOVING GOD*

Numbers refer to paragraphs numbered in Arabic numerals in the text.

211

# ANALYTIC COMMENTARY
# SUBJECT INDEX

# CISTERCIAN PUBLICATIONS
## Texts and Studies in the Monastic Tradition

## TEXTS IN ENGLISH TRANSLATION

### THE CISTERCIAN MONASTIC TRADITION

#### Aelred of Rievaulx

- Dialogue on the Soul
- The Historical Works
- Liturgical Sermons, I
- The Lives of the Northern Saints
- Spiritual Friendship
- Treatises I: Jesus at the Age of Twelve; Rule for a Recluse; Pastoral Prayer
- Walter Daniel: The Life of Aelred of Rievaulx

#### Bernard of Clairvaux

- Apologia to Abbot William (Cistercians and Cluniacs)
- Five Books on Consideration: Advice to a Pope
- Homilies in Praise of the Blessed Virgin Mary
- In Praise of the New Knighthood
- Letters
- Life and Death of Saint Malachy the Irishman
- On Baptism and the Office of Bishops
- On Grace and Free Choice
- On Loving God
- Parables and Sentences
- Sermons for the Summer Season
- Sermons on Conversion
- Sermons on the Song of Songs, I-IV
- The Steps of Humility and Pride

#### Gertude the Great of Helfta

- Spiritual Exercises
- The Herald of God's Loving-Kindness, Books 1 and 2
- The Herald of God's Loving-Kindness, Book 3

#### William of Saint Thierry

- The Enigma of Faith
- Exposition on the Epistle to the Romans
- Exposition on the Song of Songs
- The Golden Epistle
- The Mirror of Faith
- The Nature and Dignity of Love
- On Contemplating God, Prayer, Meditations

#### Gilbert of Hoyland

- Sermons on the Song of Songs, I-III
- Treatises, Sermons, and Epistles

### John of Ford

- Sermons on the Final Verses of the Song of Songs, I-VII

### Other Cistercian Writers

- Adam of Perseigne, Letters, I
- Alan of Lille: The Art of Preaching
- Amadeus of Lausanne: Homilies in Praise of Blessed Mary
- Baldwin of Ford: Commendation of Faith
- Geoffrey of Auxerre: On the Apocalypse
- Guerric of Igny: Liturgical Sermones, I-II
- Helinand of Froidmont: Verses on Death
- Idung of Prüfening: Cistercians and Cluniacs. The Case of Cîteaux
- In The School of Love. An Anthology of Early Cistercian Texts
- Isaac of Stella: Sermons on the Christian Year, I-[II]
- The Letters of Armand-Jean de Rancé, Abbot of la Trappe
- The Life of Beatrice of Nazareth
- Mary Most Holy: Meditating with the Early Cistercians
- Ogier of Locedio: Homilies [on Mary and the Last Supper]
- Serlo of Wilton & Serlo of Savigny: Seven Unpublished Works (Latin-English)
- Sky-blue the Sapphire, Crimson the Rose: The Spirituality of John of Ford
- Stephen of Lexington: Letters from Ireland
- Stephen of Sawley: Treatises
- Three Treatises on Man: A Cistercian Anthropology / Bernard McGinn

### EARLY AND EASTERN MONASTICISM

- Besa: The Life of Shenoute of Atripe
- Cyril of Scythopolis: The Lives of the Monks of Palestine
- Dorotheos of Gaza: Discourses and Sayings
- Evagrius Ponticus: Praktikos and Chapters on Prayer
- Handmaids of the Lord: Lives of Holy Women in Late Antiquity and the Early Middle Ages / Joan Petersen
- Harlots of the Desert. A Study of Repentance / Benedicta Ward
- Isaiah of Scete: Ascetic Discourses

# CISTERCIAN PUBLICATIONS Titles Listing

- John Moschos: The Spiritual Meadow
- The Life of Antony (translated from Coptic and Greek)
- The Lives of the Desert Fathers. The *Historia monachorum in Aegypto*
- The Spiritually Beneficial Tales of Paul, Bishop of Monembasia
- Symeon the New Theologian: The Practical and Theological Chapters, and The Three Theological Discourses
- Theodoret of Cyrrhus: A History of the Monks of Syria
- Stewards of the Poor. [Three biographies from fifth-century Edessa]
- The Syriac Book of Steps *[Liber graduum]*
- The Syriac Fathers on Prayer and the Spiritual Life / Sebastian Brock

## LATIN MONASTICISM

- Achard of Saint Victor: Works
- Anselm of Canterbury: Letters, I–III
- Bede the Venerable: Commentary on the Acts of the Apostles
- Bede the Venerable: Commentary on the Seven Catholic Epistles
- Bede the Venerable: Homilies on the Gospels, I–II
- Bede the Venerable: Excerpts from the Works of Saint Augustine on the Letters of the Blessed Apostle Paul
- The Celtic Monk [An Anthology]
- Gregory the Great: Forty Gospel Homilies
- Guigo II: The Ladder of Monks and Twelve Meditations / Colledge, Walsh edd.
- Halfway to Heaven
- The Life of the Jura Fathers
- The Maxims of Stephen of Muret
- Peter of Celle: Selected Works
- The Letters of Armand-Jean de Rancé, I–II
- The Rule of the Master
- The Rule of Saint Augustine
- Saint Mary of Egypt. Three Medieval Lives in Verse

# STUDIES IN MONASTICISM / CISTERCIAN STUDIES

## Cistercian Studies and Reflections

- Aelred of Rievaulx. A Study / Aelred Squire
- Athirst for God. Spiritual Desire in Bernard of Clairvaux's Sermons on the Song of Songs / Michael Casey
- Beatrice of Nazareth in her Context, I–II: Towards Unification with God / Roger DeGanck
- Bernard of Clairvaux. Man. Monk. Mystic / Michael Casey
- The Cistercian Way / André Louf
- Dom Gabriel Sortais. An Amazing Abbot in Turbulent Times / Guy Oury
- The Finances of the Cistercian Order in the Fourteenth Century / Peter King
- Fountains Abbey and Its Benefactors / Joan Wardrop
- A Gathering of Friends. Learning and Spirituality in John of Ford
- Hidden Springs: Cistercian Monastic Women, 2 volumes
- Image of Likeness. The Augustinian Spirituality of William of St Thierry / D. N. Bell
- Index of Authors and Works in Cistercian Libraries in Great Britain / D. N. Bell
- Index of Cistercian Authors and Works in Medieval Library catalogues in Great Britain / D. N. Bell
- The Mystical Theology of Saint Bernard / Etienne Gilson
- The New Monastery. Texts and Studies on the Earliest Cistercians
- Monastic Odyssey [Cistercian Nuns & the French Revolution]
- Nicolas Cotheret's Annals of Cîteaux / Louis J. Lekai
- Pater Bernhardus. Martin Luther and Bernard of Clairvaux / Franz Posset
- Rancé and the Trappist Legacy / A. J. Krailsheimer
- A Second Look at Saint Bernard / Jean Leclercq
- The Spiritual Teachings of St Bernard of Clairvaux / John R. Sommerfeldt
- Studies in Medieval Cistercian History
- Three Founders of Cîteaux / Jean-Baptiste Van Damme
- Understanding Rancé. Spirituality of the Abbot of La Trappe in Context / D. N. Bell
- William, Abbot of Saint Thierry
- Women and Saint Bernard of Clairvaux / Jean Leclercq

## Cistercian Art, Architecture, and Music

- Cistercian Abbeys of Britain [illustrated]
- Cistercian Europe / Terryl N. Kinder
- Cistercians in Medieval Art / James France
- SS. Vincenzo e Anastasio at Tre Fontane Near Rome / J. Barclay Lloyd
- Studies in Medieval Art and Architecture, II–VI / Meredith P. Lillich, ed.
- Treasures Old and New. Nine Centuries on Cistercian Music [CD, cassette]
- Cistercian Chants for the Feast of the Visitation [CD]

## Monastic Heritage

- Community and Abbot in the Rule of St Benedict, I–II / Adalbert de Vogüé
- Distant Echoes: Medieval Religious Women, I / Shank, Nichols, edd.
- The Freedom of Obedience / A Carthusian
- Halfway to Heaven [The Carthusian Tradition] / Robin Lockhart
- The Hermit Monks of Grandmont / Carole A. Hutchison
- A Life Pleasing to God: Saint Basil's Monastic Rules / Augustine Holmes
- Manjava Skete [Ruthenian tradition] / Sophia Seynk
- Monastic Practices / Charles Cummings
- Peace Weavers. Medieval Religious Women, II / Shank, Nichols, edd.
- Reading Saint Benedict / Adalbert de Vogüé
- The Rule of St Benedict. A Doctrinal and Spiritual Commentary / Adalbert de Vogüé
- Stones Laid Before the Lord [Monastic Architecture] / Anselme Dimier
- What Nuns Read [Libraries of Medieval English Nunneries] / D. N. Bell

## Monastic Liturgy

- From Advent to Pentecost / A Carthusian
- The Hymn Collection from the Abbey of the Paraclete, 2 volumes
- The Molesme Summer Season Breviary, 4 volumes
- The Old French Ordinary and Breviary of the Abbey of the Paraclete, 5 volumes
- The Paraclete Statutes: *Institutiones nostrae*
- The Twelfth Century Cistercian Hymnal, 2 volumes
- The Twelfth Century Cistercian Psalter [NYP]
- Two Early Cistercian *Libelli Missarum*

## MODERN MONASTICISM

### Thomas Merton

- Cassian and the Fathers: Initiation into the Monastic Tradition
- The Climate of Monastic Prayer
- The Legacy of Thomas Merton
- The Message of Thomas Merton
- The Monastic Journey of Thomas Merton
- Thomas Merton Monk
- Thomas Merton on Saint Bernard
- Thomas Merton: Prophet of Renewal / John Eudes Bamberger
- Toward An Integrated Humanity [Essays on Thomas Merton]

### Contemporary Monastics

- Centered on Christ. A Guide to Monastic Profession / Augustine Roberts
- Inside the Psalms. Reflections for Novices / Maureen McCabe
- Passing from Self to God. A Cistercian Retreat / Robert Thomas
- Pathway of Peace. Cistercian Wisdom according to Saint Bernard / Charles Dumont
- Poor Therefore Rich / A Carthusian
- The Way of Silent Love / A Carthusian

# CHRISTIAN SPIRITUALITY PAST AND PRESENT

## Past

- A Cloud of Witnesses. The Development of Christian Doctrine [to 500] / D. N. Bell
- Eros and Allegory: Medieval Exegesis of the Song of Songs / Denys Turner
- High King of Heaven. Aspects of Early English Spirituality / Benedicta Ward
- In the Unity of the Holy Spirit. Conference on the Rule of Benedict
- The Life of St Mary Magdalene and of Her Sister St Martha [Magdalene legend]
- The Luminous Eye. The Spiritual World Vision of St Ephrem / Sebastian Brock
- Many Mansions. Medieval Theological Development East and West / D. N. Bell
- The Name of Jesus / Irénée Hausherr
- Penthos. The Doctrine of Compunction in the Christian East / Irénée Hausherr

# CISTERCIAN PUBLICATIONS Titles Listing

## EDITORIAL OFFICES

Cistercian Publications • WMU Station
1903 West Michigan Avenue
Kalamazoo, MI 49008-5415   USA
tel 269 387 8920   fax 269 387 8390
e-mail cistpub@wmich.edu

## CUSTOMER SERVICE—NORTH AMERICA: USA AND CANADA

Cistercian Publications at Liturgical Press
Saint John's Abbey
Collegeville, MN 56321-7500 USA
tel 800 436 8431   fax 320 363 3299
e-mail sales@litpress.org

## CUSTOMER SERVICE—EUROPE: UK, IRELAND, AND EUROPE

Cistercian Publications at Columba Book Service
55A Spruce Avenue
Stillorgan Industrial Park
Blackrock, Co. Dublin, Ireland
tel 353 1 294 2560    fax 353 1 294 2564
e-mail sales@columba.ie

## WEBSITE

**www.cistercianpublications.org**

*Cistercian Publications is a non-profit corporation.*